THE VINE *and* THE BRANCHES

A HISTORY *of the* INTERNATIONAL CHURCH *of the* FOURSQUARE GOSPEL

THE VINE *and* THE BRANCHES

A HISTORY *of the* INTERNATIONAL CHURCH *of the* FOURSQUARE GOSPEL

NATHANIEL M. VAN CLEAVE

Foursquare Media

THE VINE AND THE BRANCHES by Nathaniel M. Van Cleave
Published by Foursquare Media
1910 W. Sunset Blvd., Suite 200
Los Angeles, California 90026

This book is produced and distributed by Creation House, a part of Charisma Media, www.charismamedia.com.

Design Director: Bill Johnson, Charisma Media
Cover design by Terry Clifton

Visit Foursquare's website: www.foursquare.org

Library of Congress Cataloging-in-Publication Data: 2013948554
International Standard Book Number: 978-1-62136-663-8
E-book International Standard Book Number: 978-1-62136-664-5

Previously published by the International Church of the Foursquare Gospel, copyright © 1992, ISBN 0-9635581-0-2

14 15 16 17 18 — 987654321

Printed in Canada

DEDICATION

Dedicated to Dr. Rolf K. McPherson, who, with integrity, strength, and dedication, served as president and chairman of the board of directors, International Church of the Foursquare Gospel, for forty-four years, and under whose outstanding leadership the Foursquare Church grew from 410 churches to more than 23,000 congregations around the world with more than 1.5 million members; and to the thousands of men and women who served with him over many years in providing a heritage that will benefit the Foursquare Church for generations to come.

CONTENTS

FOREWORD

WHERE SHOULD A history book for the International Church of the Foursquare Gospel actually start? Does it begin with the outpouring of the Holy Spirit in Topeka, Kansas; Azusa Street in Los Angeles, California; or one of the many historic church awakenings prior to that time? Or should we go all the way back to Pentecost and the birth of the church?

The idea of a book to recount, in a factual way, the history of the Foursquare Movement came from a committee for transition formed in the fall of 1987. This was after Dr. Rolf K. McPherson had announced retirement from the presidency of our denomination and after I had been selected as the president-elect of the International Church of the Foursquare Gospel. The committee was considering ways to honor the McPherson family for their contribution to the ministry of our movement in particular and the church of our Lord Jesus Christ in general. The desire was to have the book published by the 1989 International Foursquare Convention, when we would honor Dr. McPherson for his devotion and diligence.

Little did we realize the enormous effort being undertaken or how long it would take. We did recognize, however, this special moment in time and understood the unique value of a written account of our church to preserving as much of God's grace and our experience as humanly possible.

History is not a publicity piece. No one can stand in the spotlight of the world without casting a shadow or exposing a human blemish. Yet in this work we desired to glorify the Lord as the faithful, loving Father of us all.

Dr. Nathaniel M. Van Cleave, coauthor of *Foundations of Pentecostal Theology*, accepted the invitation to be the author. We knew him to be a man of personal integrity, vast experience, brilliance of mind, and exemplary scholarship. We were on our way to realizing our vision—a history book that was factual even when we did not look good and accurate when we might have boasted.

After the initial point of reference had been established, the real work began. There was the laborious research, mind-wearying reading, evaluation of material, and taking notes on important things, people, and places. Then came the grouping, indexing, and classifying of the facts.

The Vine and the Branches relates the grace of God in the life of an entire movement. It describes a body of people who, born in the fervor of a great revival, have now expanded into a mighty force of evangelism and church growth in the world today.

The message germinated in the heart of a young woman named Aimee who traveled to China with her missionary husband, Robert Semple, in the year 1910. Shortly thereafter Robert succumbed to malaria in the colony of Hong Kong near the place of his calling. Early moments of her ministry that followed were in the sawdust aisles of tent meetings and the dusty challenge of the streets, where she sang and shared her message. It then spread to small towns and on to metropolitan centers, in time finding a home in Los Angeles, the "City of the Angels." Here a worldwide movement would be born.

Angelus Temple was to become a center of ministry known

all over the world. More than twenty thousand people would attend the Sunday services, and during the Great Depression over a million needy souls would be fed and clothed. The words "DEDICATED UNTO THE CAUSE OF INTERDENOMINATIONAL AND WORLDWIDE EVANGELISM" were carved into the cornerstone, here at the very heart of the movement.

Unfortunately, I never met this remarkable lady. I became a Christian after her death in one of the churches that sprang from the white heat of her vision. I have been the pastor of Angelus Temple, the church she founded, and I now occupy the president's chair where she sat. What I have learned in this passage of my life is voluminous, and at this point, I want to relate one important part of our heritage.

In a vision "Sister," as her generation called her, saw herself being given a scythe for harvesting the golden grain. The Lord told her she had been given this great tool for reaping the harvest, but she was never to use it as a weapon against a brother or sister. As a result, we in the Foursquare Church are family. From the largest to the smallest of our congregations, we have a gentle spirit. We do not contend. Our weapons are for the harvest, not for hostility. In the pages of this composition I trust you will find the footprints of our "family" history.

One day in Oakland, California, in a moment of inspiration, that vision was verbalized when Sister McPherson exclaimed, "Why, that's the Foursquare Gospel!" A movement had grown from a message emphasizing the four distinct facets of Jesus' ministry. Now it has grown far beyond what anyone envisioned, at this writing ministering in over seventy-four countries of the world with more than twenty-three thousand congregations. But I am getting ahead of myself.

When Aimee Semple McPherson's life was concluded (in the very city in which she had received the name for her already flourishing ministry), the leadership of the movement was entrusted to her only son, Rolf K. McPherson. Subsequently he would serve as the president and chairman of the board of directors for forty-four years. It would be a long and peaceful tenure of leadership. When the desire to publish a chronicle of the victories won, the burdens borne, and the tasks completed was expressed, Dr. McPherson's appeal was, "Please give credit to the thousands upon thousands who have worked to make this movement a reality."

This process has been a happy, joyous, and blessed pathway leading through old newspapers, magazines, sermons, archives, statistics, and reference materials. Enormous time was given to interviewing, consolidating, writing, and rewriting of the text. Then the manuscript was passed to the editor for review, to the editorial committee for evaluation, and again, back to the author. So the days worked themselves into months and the months into years.

The book is now completed, and we offer it to you. This has not been a casual or hurried work; thus, we can release it with a deep and abiding conviction. This volume has integrity. It is conservative and reflects the truth regarding the beginning and development of the International Church of the Foursquare Gospel.

May the Lord of the harvest bless the message the book carries and use it to inspire other pilgrims to persevere. Where there is personal loss and tragedy, may the people the world around come to know "Jesus Christ, the same yesterday and today and forever." What our Savior, Jesus Christ, has accomplished in the Foursquare Movement is offered to every sincere believer—a vital and personal relationship with God through His Son, Jesus Christ, and the power of the Holy Spirit to live victoriously in a world of extraordinary challenge.

On the pulpit of Angelus Temple are carved the words of the Greeks who were searching for the miracle worker: "We would see Jesus." This too is our goal, our passion, our history...and my prayer for our future.

—John R. Holland, D.D.
Former President
International Church of the Foursquare Gospel

FROM THE AUTHOR

To be invited to write a history of the Foursquare Church presented both a privilege and a challenge. The Foursquare family already had the matchless autobiography *This Is That* and other books by its founder, Aimee Semple McPherson. There was an excellent book about Mrs. McPherson and the Foursquare Gospel, authored by Dr. Raymond Cox. Now the need existed for a history of our church, beginning with the unparalleled revival of the 1920s and continuing to grow through the 1980s. The thought was almost overwhelming. I would once again live through the seven decades of one of the most dynamic Pentecostal denominations of the twentieth century.

I had been an eyewitness to all but one year of the ministry that emanated from Angelus Temple and to the entire span of the fellowship, which was incorporated as a denomination in 1927. The vast majority of names mentioned within this volume were my peers and fellow ministers, and many were called into the ministry, served, and grew into fine mature leaders in areas of my responsibility. And during the months of research and writing, my spirit was filled with the warmth of memories and the faithfulness of God. It was the Lord who brought the International Church of the Foursquare Gospel into being, and

I am grateful that through His immutable grace He has allowed me to be a part of it.

The Vine and the Branches is written as a history, not one person's memory. Much effort has been dedicated to verifying dates and the accuracy of facts and names. It discusses the church's departments, activities, and development, mentioning God's servants who initiated and carried out those activities. Many were asked to submit significant details of their ministries. And because many covered more than one period of time, the format of the book is as much topical as it is chronological. Unfortunately, it was not possible to include every event or everyone who has so faithfully and fervently had a part in the expansion of the Foursquare vine. Fortunately, the entire history is recorded in divine detail in the heavenly annals.

I have been enabled throughout this project by Dr. Rolf K. McPherson and by the Heritage Department archives. Valuable assistance came from Dr. Leland Edwards and a doctorate thesis on the history of Foursquare missions, written by Dr. Y. S. Eim. The story of the Bible colleges was abetted by the college yearbooks and by Dr. Dorothy Jean Furlong, Dr. Harold Helms, and Rev. Mari Hanes. Other important details were supplied by Dr. Leita Mae Steward, Dr. and Mrs. Harold Jefferies, and Drs. Howard and Vaneda Courtney.

I also thank Lois, my faithful and lovely wife of sixty-two years, who supplied helpful encouragement.

While the names of the editorial committee will be given in another place, I give special thanks to the general editor, Dr. Ronald D. Williams, without whom the work would not have been finished.

During the 1992 International Foursquare Convention in Van Nuys, California, nearly sixty ministers were awarded gold pins in recognition of their sixty years of Foursquare ministry. With standing applause, the Foursquare family expressed to them, "Well done!" It is my prayerful hope that through the chronicling of the Foursquare Church's history, many others will also be remembered and honored with that same gratefulness.

—Nathaniel M. Van Cleave, D.D.
November 2, 1907 - December 24, 2002

ACKNOWLEDGMENTS

IT IS ALWAYS dangerous to write a history book. There's that detail that should have been included, or that person who has been inadvertently omitted. Also, there is the challenge of perspective—how one views an event or interprets a chain of experience. Very few people could have accepted and accomplished such a monumental task of writing the history of our church as Dr. Nathaniel Van Cleave has done. To him, and to his wife, Lois, who walked through the research for this history with her husband, we express our deepest appreciation. Their labor of love will greatly benefit our church for generations to come, should the Lord tarry.

Assisting Dr. Van Cleave has been an editorial committee, of which I have served as chairman. Reading through the manuscripts, giving literally hundreds of hours, have been Dr. Dorothy Jean Furlong, Dr. Jack Hayford, Dr. Harold Helms, and Rev. Mari Hanes. In addition, Dr. Leland Edwards' input regarding the missions history of our denomination was invaluable. Dr. Rolf K. McPherson, whose name appears throughout the book and under whose leadership our denomination flourished for forty-four years, has spent countless hours, untiring energy, and remarkable memory in providing background and editorial assistance. We thank Dr. John Holland, president of the International Church of the Foursquare Gospel, and the members of the international board for their continued encouragement, advice, and support in making this project possible.

Above all, we must lift grateful praise to Jesus Christ, the same yesterday, and today, and forever (Heb. 13:8), under whose lordship each of us has found eternal life and upon whom our church has been established, energized, and filled with expectant hope. One wonderful truth about the history of a church built upon the cornerstone, Jesus Christ, is that its story has only begun to be written.

—Ronald D. Williams, D.D.
General Editor

Introduction

A HISTORY OF THE INTERNATIONAL CHURCH OF THE FOURSQUARE GOSPEL

But, oh, the call of God was on my soul and I could not get away from it. For this cause I had been brought into the world. With each throb of my heart I could hear a voice saying:

"Preach the Word! Preach the Word! Will you go? Will you go?" And I would throw myself on my knees, tearfully sobbing:

"Oh, Lord, You know that I cannot go. Here are the two babies and here is the home"... but the voice still came back, clear from Heaven: "Go! DO THE WORK OF AN EVANGELIST; Preach the Word! The time is short; I am coming soon."

I became very ill in body and inside of one year two serious operations were performed. Each time, before going under the surgeon's knife, and during many other times of critical illness, when it seemed as though I were going to die, I would call the saints to pray for me that I might be delivered, but each time they prayed I could plainly hear the voice of the Lord saying: "Will you go? Will you preach the Word?" I knew that if I said, "Yes," He would heal me... With my little remaining strength, I managed to gasp: "Yes—Lord—I'll—go." And go I did![1]

—Aimee Semple McPherson

That was a history-making decision. At first she began to preach, but year after year the scope of her Spirit-anointed evangelism widened. Within a decade "Sister," as she was affectionately called, was ready to erect Angelus Temple and to launch a Holy Ghost revival, the waves of which are still undulating across the world. Aimee Semple McPherson was to plant a vine whose branches would climb over the walls of every continent.

The history of a Christian movement such as the International Church of the Foursquare Gospel cannot be a mere collection of statistics, a recital of names, dates, and events. A Pentecostal movement is a living organism like a growing plant, a vine that is planted, sprouts, grows, and bears fruit. It is a vine that responds to cultivation, enrichment of the soil, and protection from pestilence.

The Old Testament often employs with striking significance the metaphor of the vine to symbolize the chosen nation of Israel.

> Joseph is a fruitful bough, even a fruitful bough by a well; whose branches run over the wall.[2]
>
> It was planted in a good soil by great waters, that it might bring forth branches, and that it might bear fruit, that it might be a goodly vine.[3]
>
> Let us get up early to the vineyards; let us see if the vine flourish, whether the tender grape appear, and the pomegranates bud forth: there will I give thee my loves.[4]

Jesus, with great vividness, used the symbolic figure of the vine and its branches to describe His church's relationship to Himself and to reveal the priceless secrets of spiritual fruit-bearing.

> I am the vine, you are the branches. He who abides in Me, and I in him, bears much fruit; for without Me you can do nothing.[5]

Of course, Jesus declares that He Himself is the vine. All earthly vines, then, are mere shadows of the heavenly vine. Andrew Murray, the very revered Christian teacher, writes, "When Jesus says, 'I am the true Vine,' He tells us that all the vines of earth are pictures and emblems of Himself. He is the divine reality, of which they are the created expression. They all point to Him, preach Him, and reveal Him."[6]

Likening The Foursquare Church to a vine and its branches is not the creation of the present author. In 1925 Dr. Billy Black, a longtime friend of the founder and a careful observer of her dynamic ministry, wrote an article in the *Bridal Call*, the official publication of the International Church of the Foursquare Gospel, entitled "The Vine and the Branches," in which he states:

> The caption is suggested from an analogy made by the Master Himself, who took every occasion to teach by parabolic truths. *Angelus Temple* is likened to a great vine, planted some two years and four months ago. Its prolific branches are outspreading in every direction in Southern California. From dedication day to the present writing, there have been eight hundred fifty-two days of constant revival, so that it has been well named "The Church with a perpetual revival." Upon investigation at the statistic department, I find twenty-five thousand two hundred thirteen convert slips registered to date…Thirty-two official branches of the great vine have been established up to date, and it would be safe to say there have been over fifty other applications sent in to the office, offering buildings, lots and propositions for consideration.[7]

In 1930 another article appeared in the *Bridal Call* with the same caption, stating:

> Angelus Temple is likened to a great vine. Its prolific branches, numbering some 280, are outspreading in every direction.[8]

The story of what brought about such remarkable grown and multiplication in the Foursquare vineyard is what this history of the International Church of the Foursquare Gospel is all about.

Chapter 1

ROOTS IN REVIVAL

The Founder and Angelus Temple (1908–1926)

THE VITALITY AND fruitfulness of a vine and its branches depend very largely upon the nature of the soil in which the vine is planted and upon the roots that penetrate the soil.

Jesus told a parable about the gospel's seed, four kinds of soil, and three kinds of harvest. Three kinds of soil disappointingly brought no harvest at all. Yet, in one kind of soil, three qualities of harvests were described as yielding thirty, sixty, and one hundredfold.[1] The point of the impressive parable was that the most abundant harvest was produced on the richest and best prepared soil by the best informed sower.

Angelus Temple and the International Church of the Foursquare Gospel (ICFG) were rooted deeply in the soil of Holy Spirit-sent revival, one of the most remarkable moves of God in the twentieth century.

To paint a picture of that almost indescribable revival, the artist's brush is handed to a great pastor who was present in January 1923 for the opening service at Angelus Temple. Dr. Harold W. Jefferies, pastor for thirty-one years (1929-1960) of the Portland, Oregon, Foursquare Church (for many years

Foursquaredom's largest branch congregation), paints the following picture:

> We were privileged to be present for the dedication on January 1, 1923. During the years that followed, we witnessed revival unparalleled to this day. Thousands filled the auditorium seating over 5,000 people. Sitting in the choir loft, we personally saw miracle after miracle. Ambulances brought the sick and lame from hospitals and homes, laying them on cots. As Sister McPherson laid hands on those before her, God would heal them. Most of the ambulances returned to their stations empty.
>
> One side of the Temple was lined from the door entering the sanctuary to the platform with wheelchairs. As hands were laid on those with infirmities, they would immediately rise, and pushing their wheelchairs ahead of them, they would begin praising the Lord. Crutches were thrown away. The blind received their sight. The deaf heard. Steel braces were removed. The list is endless. God confirmed His Word with signs and miracles. All glory goes to Him who made it happen...The "roots of revival" brought tens of thousands into the Kingdom of God with miracles of deliverance and empowerment by the Holy Spirit. The "revival" was born out of the deep roots of the ministry of our founder.[2]

To fully understand the ministry of Aimee Semple McPherson, founder of the International Church of the Foursquare Gospel, it is vital to recognize the influences that shaped her remarkable ministry, preparing her to found an important Pentecostal denomination.

Aimee Semple McPherson was born in 1890 in Ingersoll, Ontario, Canada, to Methodist/Salvation Army parents, James and Minnie Kennedy. However, in her high school years, the young lady began drifting away from the church's influence.

In 1907 an Irish Pentecostal evangelist by the name of Robert

James Semple began holding revival services in her hometown. In spite of the opposition from her parents, she attended Robert Semple's Pentecostal revival, where she was born again and filled with the Holy Spirit.

After a storybook romance, Aimee and the evangelist were married in August 1908. In January 1909 they moved to Chicago, Illinois, and became workers in the great Pentecostal Mission of evangelist pastor William H. Durham. Pastor Durham had been filled with the Spirit in the famous Azusa Street outpouring in Los Angeles, California. Under his leadership Aimee learned great lessons in evangelism and Pentecostal doctrine.

Rising out of the Holiness tradition, Pentecostal movements held strongly to the doctrine of sanctification. However, there were two principal views of sanctification. One, the Wesleyan view, saw sanctification as a second work of grace subsequent to regeneration by which the sinful nature was eradicated by a crisis experience. This would lead to Christian perfection. To those who held this view the baptism of the Holy Spirit was a third crisis experience.

The second view looked at sanctification as beginning with regeneration and continuing throughout the Christian life as a progressive process all by virtue of the "finished work of the Cross." To the latter the baptism with the Holy Spirit was a crisis experience subsequent to regeneration. Rev. Durham was of the latter "finished work of Christ" school. This view was embraced by Aimee Semple McPherson as well as by the Assemblies of God and others.

Mrs. McPherson's doctrine was influenced by her family's Methodism, therefore Arminian. She worked with her mother in The Salvation Army, which accounts for her propensity for military terms, uniformity, and silver bands. The Salvation Army also contributed toward her strong social concerns. She was an avid reader of A. B. Simpson and A. J. Gordon, who popularized the term "Fourfold Gospel," and a great admirer of Maria Woodworth Etter, an earlier successful woman evangelist.

Therefore, the principal influences in Aimee Semple McPherson's life and ministry were (1) her husband, Robert Semple; (2) William Durham, her first Pentecostal pastor/evangelist; (3) the Methodist Church; (4) The Salvation Army; and (5) A. B. Simpson, founder of the Christian and Missionary Alliance.

But the greatest factor in Aimee Semple McPherson's success as an evangelist-pastor was her strong anointing of the Holy Spirit and her irresistible call to the ministry of soul winning. A prominent church historian, Vinson Synan, says of her: "She holds a prominent rank among all religious leaders in the twentieth century, regardless of their sex, and may well be the most important ordained woman minister in the history of Christianity."[3]

An important preparation for the founding revival in Los Angeles was the accumulated experience of the great campaigns held by Mrs. McPherson between 1915 and 1923. These campaigns extended from Maine to Florida, across America and along the Pacific Coast, as well as to a number of foreign countries. The revivals were held in tents, opera houses, and city auditoriums with overflow crowds of thousands. All the revival meetings were marked by miracles of healing and great altar calls. Many times, several altar calls were given in the same service as the Spirit directed.

Following fifteen years of revival ministry, Angelus Temple was opened. The inspiration for the name "Foursquare Gospel" came to Mrs. McPherson during a revival in Oakland, California. She was preaching from Ezekiel 1:4–10 on the four faces of the living creatures in Ezekiel's vision—those of a man, a lion, an ox, and an eagle. She describes the inspiration as follows:

> I thought upon the vision of the prophet Ezekiel; I stood still for a moment and listened, gripping the pulpit, almost shaking with wonder and joy. Then there burst from the white heat of my heart the words, "Why—why it's the Foursquare Gospel. The Foursquare Gospel!" Instantly the Spirit bore witness. Waves, billows, oceans of praises rocked the audience, which was borne aloft on the rushing winds of Holy Ghost revival.[4]

The following facts taken together indicate the extent of the Holy Ghost revival in which Angelus Temple was founded:

1. Thousands saved and baptized in water: in the first six months of 1923 at Angelus Temple there were eight thousand converts. The annual report of 1924 listed twelve thousand saved, three thousand baptized in water, three thousand new members, thirty-six hundred healings, and thousands filled with the Spirit.
2. Strong presence of the Holy Spirit.
3. Strong conviction of sin.
4. Thousands healed of bodily affliction.
5. Constant capacity crowds.
6. Believers worshipful and enthusiastic in their service.
7. Believers faithful in witness.
8. Lasting and progressively increasing results.

Mrs. McPherson, in the November 1923 edition of her famous autobiography, *This Is That*, wrote concerning the revival at Angelus Temple that had been in progress for six months:

> As this book, containing personal testimonies and writings, goes forth to the world, we are continuing the Lord's work in the great Angelus Temple at Echo Park in Los Angeles, California. During the first six months since the Temple opened, between seven and eight thousand men and women have been converted; some one thousand five hundred have been baptized in water; hundreds have been healed and filled with the Holy Spirit. And humbly, under the precious blood of Jesus Christ, our battle-cry is, "Onward Christian Soldiers."[5]

Did the revival endure? Did the crowds continue? Did the signs and wonders disappear? The following article by Mrs. McPherson appeared in the *Bridal Call* after nearly three years had passed:

> Like a perennial fountain ever flowing, ever rising, ever widening, fed from some deep underlying river, the glorious revival at Angelus Temple, Los Angeles, California, continues to grow and spread. Never, for a moment, has the flow been stayed or checked during the past nine hundred and sixty-two days. Thousands have been converted, healed, baptized with the Holy Spirit and are out now working for the Lord, counting neither time nor labor nor life itself if they may but win others to Jesus Christ. Such enthusiasm as perhaps the world has seldom known is manifest in this revival.[6]

Of course, the founder-evangelist was not alone in those days at Angelus Temple. She was assisted by outstanding preachers, teachers, and musicians: Gladwyn Nicholls (Silver Band director), Esther Fricke (organist on the Kimball organ),

Charles Walkem (pianist, music composer, teacher, radio program director), James Boersma (band assistant), Thomas Johnson (baritone singer whose talented family would bless the entire Foursquare Church Organization from the beginning to the present), Thompson Eade (artist for the illustrated sermons, teacher), Paul Rader (great Chicago pastor/evangelist), Watson Argue, Charles Schreve, Roxy Alford, B. F. Gurden, A. P. Gouthe, Alfred Garr, Hardy Mitchell, Smith Wigglesworth (renowned British evangelist), Anna Britton and Rheba Crawford (supply evangelists), Wesley Cooksey (500 Room ministry), J. W. Arthur (elder, prayer ministry, general assistance), Estelle Jones (children's evangelist), Minnie "Mother" Kennedy, and Roberta Semple and Rolf McPherson (family).

However, unless she was away in campaigns, Aimee Semple McPherson usually preached three times on Sundays, Wednesday afternoons and Saturday nights (divine healing services), and Thursday nights (weekly baptismal service). In addition, she taught in the Bible institute, edited the *Bridal Call* magazine, composed music and sacred operas, and often directed her own song services. Without a doubt, she needed considerable assistance, for there were between twenty-one and thirty services each week, including the institute classes.

The principal purpose of a vine is to bear fruit, but very much goes on between the planting time and the reaping season. Much happens that is essential to the fruit-bearing such as growth; putting forth of tendrils, leaves, and branches; drawing sugar and acidity from the soil; and much more. The purpose of evangelism is soul winning, but a successful evangelistic center must do more than preach sermons from a pulpit. Aimee Semple McPherson employed every imaginable vehicle for soul winning and the formation of a fully functioning Gospel center. Angelus Temple ministered fully to the whole person, the whole family, and to the entire community. Anyone who desires to pastor successfully in an urban setting would do well to study the full spectrum of the Temple's activity.

What were the service arms of Angelus Temple? Count them.

Dynamic Pulpit Evangelism

Aimee Semple McPherson's persistent vision was to win the benighted world for Christ. She had witnessed the results of more than ten years of charismatic evangelism. During that time literally thousands of souls had been won to Christ. In the first year after the wide doors of beautiful Angelus Temple opened, more than twelve thousand men, women, and children walked the long aisles to surrender their lives to Christ. This was repeated with God-given regularity, year after year.

Illustrated and Dramatized Sunday Night Sermons

Angelus Temple became widely known for the evangelist's illustrated and dramatized Sunday night sermons. Was this not a result to sensationalism? Some made such accusations. But Mrs. McPherson believed that the life-giving message of the gospel would be made more understandable with a more durable impact if it was rendered visible as well as audible. Her reasoning was sound, for many people still remember clearly her illustrated sermons.

Some of the sermons were rather sensational, but creating sensation only becomes sensationalism when doing so becomes an end in itself rather than a means to an end. Her object was not to create sensation but to make the message more effective. Angelus Temple was next door to Hollywood and the stars of the silver screen. A number of the Hollywood movie people were in attendance at beautiful Angelus Temple. Many would have given little heed to an ordinary spoken sermon. In other churches many pastors were giving "book reports" on Sunday nights.

Some claimed that mature Christians had no need for illustrated sermons. A few criticized the messages as being theatrical, but the children and young people loved the dramatic aspect; the elderly and the unchurched appreciated their clarity. Jesus taught with parables, many of which were recounted while the action to which He referred was happening right before their eyes. Jesus' sermons were often illustrated by real-life events. A modern feature story writer for a Canadian newspaper, commenting on the criticisms that Aimee Semple McPherson resorted to sensationalism, remarked:

> In an age of ostentation, her flamboyance was never out of place. But while others were showy for their own gratification, Aimee Semple McPherson used the avenues of show business to instill the gospel's good news into the hearts of her multitudinous following.[7]

Establishment of a Bible Institute

Within three months after the Temple was opened, a Bible institute was begun. The school was called "The Echo Park Evangelistic and Missionary Training Institute." By 1926, when the five-story school building was dedicated, the name, "L.I.F.E. Bible College" (Lighthouse of International Foursquare Evangelism), was established (presently Life Pacific College).

L.I.F.E. began with approximately fifty students in attendance; by September of 1926 the enrollment had increased dramatically to six hundred fifty. By 1929 there were approximately one thousand students who could hardly wait to get to the whitened harvest.

In earlier times, after one of her great city-wide campaigns, Mrs. McPherson would retire to her quarters, slump exhausted into a chair, or prop herself up in bed. There she would visualize what might happen if such a revival could be followed up with a group of trained workers going with the resounding message to all parts of the city. But alas, such workers were not available!

In 1918 she determined to establish a home base where she could make a home for her growing children and at the same time have a church where she could minister between campaigns. An all-important part of that home center was to be a Bible institute for training workers and evangelists.

The validity of the founder's original vision for a training institute was verified when the summer months found all sixteen of the L.I.F.E. graduates of that first class in 1925 involved in gospel meetings from which almost the same number of branch churches were pioneered.

Sending Forth and Support of Missionaries

In 1910, less than two years after Aimee had married Robert Semple, they embarked for missionary work in China. They bore with them the ecstatic hope of carrying the gospel message to distant unreached peoples. That hope was never fulfilled, for Robert succumbed to malaria in Hong Kong after only a few months of missionary service, leaving his wife expecting a child. With great disappointment she had to return home.

However, Aimee Semple McPherson did not lose the missionary burden. As soon as she established a home base at Angelus Temple, she determined to make missionary outreach a priority item on her ever-expanding agenda. Her motto became, "Around the World With the Foursquare Gospel." It is equally understandable, then, that the workers and subsequent leaders who went forth from the Missionary Training Institute (later incorporated as L.I.F.E Bible College) shared the founder's outlook: "The field is the world."

In April 1924 two graduates of a special one-year course in the Bible institute, Alfred Kleinschmidt and Carl Linden, were sent as missionaries to India. In 1931 the budget for foreign missions was $41,523; in the same year the money spent for home extension was $10,321.

The Ministry of Children's Evangelism

Children were attracted to the Angelus Temple services because of the happy, upbeat atmosphere. A picture taken in August of 1923, eight months after the grand opening, shows a crowd of about five thousand people gathered in front of the Temple following the afternoon service. The photo reveals a tremendous number of children.

Angelus Temple opened with a Sunday school of more than one hundred classes. An entire issue of the *Bridal Call* magazine (July 1924) was dedicated to children. In addition to Sunday school, Angelus Temple operated a Saturday children's church in which, under the direction of trained workers, the entire service was directed by the more mature children.

Best known of the children's workers in early Foursquare history was Miss Estelle Jones. From her children's church came pastors, pastors' wives, and missionaries. A branch church in Lankersheim (now called North Hollywood, California) was started from a children's church that Rev. Gwendolyn Pittinger conducted in a rented theater building. Consistent child evangelism and Bible teaching guarantee the permanence of gospel work.

The Foursquare Crusaders

The youth movement, called "Foursquare Crusaders," was a vehicle of effective evangelism. The Crusader meetings were conducted on Friday nights by a president assisted by other youth officers. Attendance at the exciting Friday night services ranged from one thousand upward. The lively gatherings featured joyful singing, special music, and vibrant testimonies.

Most cherished were the candlelight ceremonies in which the Crusader Covenant was signed, pledging a surrendered life free from unwholesome worldly amusements. The signing of the Crusader Covenant meant dedication to witness for Christ. A favorite activity of the Crusaders was that of participation in street meetings where many souls were won. A number of the Crusader officers later became denominational leaders, as, for example, Bert Teaford, Clarence Hall, Harold Chalfant, etc.

Radio KFSG

Radio KFSG went on the air in February 1924, just one year after the Temple's opening. Often called "The Church Without Walls," Radio KFSG (Kall FourSquare Gospel) reached millions with the Foursquare Gospel. In those days there was little wave length interference, and the station could be tuned in, not only throughout Southern California but in most areas of the nation. Multitudes did tune in to the broadcast of the Angelus Temple services; thousands were converted as a result of hearing the gospel while seated in front of their huge Atwater Kent radio sets.

The Ministry of Music

The Foursquare revival was marked by great crowds that kept coming year after year. This can be explained in part by the spiritual hunger of the people of Los Angeles, but it is best accounted for by the large number of appeals that were a part of Angelus Temple's program. Spontaneous revivals are usually short lived; the Azusa Street revival lasted scarcely more than three years. Charles Parham's revival in Topeka was of even shorter duration. The Angelus Temple revival went on for more than a decade unabated. Souls continued to be saved, sick bodies healed, believers filled with the Spirit; hundreds of trained, Spirit-filled workers kept carrying the message of the gospel to the nation and to the world.

What kept it going? The many-featured appeal and the sparkle in the great music of Angelus Temple.

The doors of the Temple opened with a convention enlivened by a Silver Band, a large choir, a golden harp, and vocal and instrumental specials of great variety. Later, sacred operas and oratorios were composed and produced by Mrs. McPherson. Many who came to enjoy good music left their sins at the altar. The music and the program appealed to rich and poor, black and brown and white, rural and urban, cultured and rustic, young and old. Hollywood stars would kneel alongside skid-row derelicts in quest of newness of life. Some even came to jeer and stayed to cheer.

Opportunity for Christian Service

Many people came to the Temple with a desire to find opportunity for Christian service, such as hospital and prison ministry and rescue mission outreach. The Temple was involved in all these ministries with organized activities. Anyone who would prepare for or demonstrate qualification for such ministries could become occupied. Angelus Temple was a literal beehive of Christian social outreach. Aimee Semple McPherson, with her Salvation Army background, was dedicated to social service.

She did not preach the "social gospel," but she believed that the gospel of salvation had social implications.

A practical outreach was that of "shop meetings." Mrs. McPherson launched this activity in 1924 under the leadership of chaplain Lieutenant M. Arthur Spotts.[8] Noontime meetings were held each week for the employees of various shops, factories, and institutions. Assigned to this work were 350 trained workers in groups of seven who conducted fifty shop meetings each week. In most cases these meetings were conducted in a sheltered area where the employees could eat their lunches while they enjoyed the meeting. The service consisted in singing, strong personal testimonies, and a brief salvation message. Later on, these shop meetings were assigned to the students of L.I.F.E. Bible College. Through these opportunities, in addition to winning souls, future Foursquare ministers gained much practical experience.

A favorite of the young Crusaders was the street meeting. Some street locations were chosen at random after prayer. Others were held at set times in established places, like the Saturday night street meeting in Compton, California, which was sustained for several years. There were strong testimonies and an appeal; others held in set locations were more elaborate, including gospel singing to the accompaniment of a portable organ, guitar, tambourine, and wind instruments, followed by testimonies and a short sermon.

During and after World War II, churches began to discontinue, even frown upon, street meetings. Are they practical today? With the advent of the "Jesus People" movements in the 1970s, they started to reappear in many cities. In some areas permits are required, but no possible outreach for Christ should be abandoned in a time when every vile and satanic cause is heralded openly.

Publications

One of the most common avenues of witness was the distribution of tracts and other gospel literature such as books, Gospels, and Christian magazines. Aimee Semple McPherson began publishing the *Bridal Call* magazine in September 1917. It featured her very readable sermons and amazing healing testimonies. After the Temple opened, the magazine also included the radio schedule, occasional articles on special Temple activities, and later, news about the branch churches.

Among other books and booklets by Aimee Semple McPherson, all of which were helpful and inspiring for soul winners, were *This Is That* (1923), *Divine Healing Sermons*, *The Second Coming of Christ*, and *In the Service of the King* (1927). In 1927 the Temple opened a convenient bookstore called "Ye Foursquare Book Shoppe," operated by Mrs. Cooksey, wife of the 500 Room evangelist H. Wesley Cooksey. Their daughter, Olive, managed the book shop for more than fifty years, from the late 1930s until her recent retirement.

Almost all the Angelus Temple constituents carried tracts and Gospels. Those who rode the streetcars to and from church could be counted on to witness to the other passengers, leaving them with a tract of Gospel of John. How many people must have accepted Christ through channels of gospel outreach before ever attending Angelus Temple!

We live in the most literate age of history. Much attractive gospel literature is available to willing workers. With so much ignorance of truth and the availability of evil propaganda, it is to be lamented that more use is not made of this medium about which we have so clear an historic example.

The Prayer Tower

One of the best known activities of Angelus Temple was and is the Prayer Tower. It was staffed with 368 men and women who prayed around the clock. The following is a description of the vital activity written in 1923:

> The revival is growing so mightily, like a flame that refuses to be checked for a moment, that it has been necessary to keep the Temple open day and night. For many weeks the lights have never been out. The Watch Tower is the scene of continuous prayer. Men pray by night and women by day. Telegrams and letters are streaming in from all parts of the nation, desiring prayer; then streaming in again to testify to answered prayer.[9]

If counted, the prayer requests that have come to the Prayer Tower of Angelus Temple would number in the millions. Prayer, of course, is a soul-winning outreach available to any church or group.

The 500 Room

Almost as well known as the Prayer Tower is the 500 Room. It was so named because it had seating for approximately that number. However, since there was another room at the top of the first balcony called the 120 Room, the two taken together were reminiscent of two New Testament groups of the same numbers: those in the Upper Room on the Day of Pentecost, and the number of believers who were witnesses of the resurrection of Jesus.[10] Names Aimee Semple McPherson assigned to a facility or an activity often had to have some biblical significance.

The 500 Room served to put into practical application two of the cardinal doctrines of the Foursquare Gospel: divine healing and the baptism with the Holy Spirit. There were exceptions, but Mrs. McPherson normally did not pray for the sick in the public services until they had first been taught from the Word on divine healing in the 500 Room services. After several days of teaching, each was given a card admitting them to the healing line on Wednesday afternoons or Saturday nights. This assured that those who were anointed and prayed for in public had a reasonable and biblical basis for faith. Many were prayed for and healed in the 500 Room.

One who frequently attended the 500 Room in 1925 reported as follows:

> The daily afternoon meeting was the famous indispensable preparation of the many sick folks who are to be prayed for in the big meetings in the Temple by the minister that earnestly contended for divine healing as part of the "faith once delivered unto the saints" even years ago when it was nothing like so popular as now. Many sufferers, however, never have the anointing oil, for in the sacred institution older than the church they draw very near to the Lord, faith claims the inheritance provided by Him through "whose stripes we are healed," and the healed ones need simply to appear in public as witnesses that "Prayer changes things."[11]

The other ministry was that of teaching on the glorious experience of the baptism with the Holy Spirit. In the early days people believed in tarrying for the Spirit's fullness, just as the disciples of Jesus did before Pentecost. Most now teach that since believers are living on this side of Pentecost, there is no need to tarry; one needs only to receive it. Whatever the case, there is something to be said for the persevering prayer that helped to bring inner healing and cleansing. Thousands look back to the blessings received in the 500 Room.

Some great servants of the Lord were identified with ministry in that famous room: Rev. H. Wesley Cooksey, Rev. Kelso

Glover, and Rev. Mrs. Hal Smith, etc. The 500 Room also was the assembly room for the Bible institute before 1926, and a meeting room on Sundays for the men's Bible class.

The Angelus Temple Commissary

The outreach activity for which the Foursquare Church received the greatest civic acclaim was the Commissary. In 1927 thousands were pouring into Southern California. The community, whose principal business was tourism, had not yet become an industrial area.

At the same time, the industry that existed was beginning to experience depression. Local welfare was inadequate. City, county, and state charities required new arrivals to have six months' residence before help was available.

The Lord laid on Mrs. McPherson a burden to help the needy. She organized an activity that she called "The Angelus Temple Commissary," challenging the large constituency to bring non-perishable food and usable clothing to the services. The response was almost unbelievable. The Temple became known as "The Church with the Singing Heart and the Helping Hand."

An impartial observer of 1928 described a visit to the Temple:

> I've seen many a Sunday morning congregation file through the doors of churches, said a man outside Angelus Temple a few Sundays ago, but in all my experience never before have I seen a crowd of people carrying such an assortment of packages to church!
>
> Such seeming similarity of purpose, yet so diversely equipped; unusual I'll say!
>
> Unusual, yes—but thank God for the unusual, at least when it refers to those miracles of mercy that are being wrought in Angelus Temple today.

> The procedure that the stranger noted was not peculiar to the Sunday services alone. Watch any crowd as it gathers for a service at this great Foursquare Lighthouse. Each individual, almost without exception, carries a contribution, a little token of their appreciation of the work that love is performing.
>
> A man carries a bundle which holds an ill-concealed blanket!
>
> Under the arm of another is tucked a box so small that its obvious purpose is to protect a pair of wee shoes.
>
> Cans of corn!
>
> Loaves of bread—food of all sorts is brought to church. Army equipment, it might almost be, and surely, more than one problem confronts a forward moving army of soldiers of the Cross! Had the keen-eyed man followed the "package-carrying" crowd into the Temple, he would have seen the bundles deposited in the Lighthouse in the foyer and later taken into the basement of the Bible School, for there is located the department so often humbly referred to by Sister McPherson as the "Commissary."
>
> In it she sees the realization of her dream of some day being able to help others bear the heartbreaks and trials that cloud the skies of life's journeying pilgrims.[12]

The Commissary still exists today. Through the years it has fed and clothed over a million and a half needy people. Some of those, who at the time of their deepest material need found help at Angelus Temple, have later become substantial and even famous people. One became a movie star; another became the chaplain of the United States Senate. For years it was as important for a typical Foursquare church to have a commissary as it was to have the biblical motto, "Jesus Christ, the Same Yesterday and Today and Forever," displayed in the lobby or above the platform.

The City Sisters

Along with the Commissary, Mrs. McPherson organized a group of women called, "The City Sisters." These women followed up on the commissary help with love and spiritual guidance. A description of the ministry of these godly women is best described by an article in the *Bridal Call* of January 1929:

> The workers pray for the sick in their homes and in the hospitals, nurse the helpless, care for young mothers and babies, provide food for the hungry, give clothing to those in need, furnish work for the unemployed, call on the new converts, extend a hand of friendship to new members, secure homes and care for fallen girls, and conduct a nursery and kindergarten during the various church services so mothers can be free to receive help from the sermons...Boxes of groceries have been sent out to 32,349 people...We have furnished 25,650 pieces of clothing to the needy, helping 4,409 families to meet great problems. The City Sisters are following the motto: "Inasmuch as ye have done it unto one of the least of these ye have done it unto me."[13]

Many souls were won through this very effective army of evangelism. The memory of the work of the City Sisters inspired Lois Van Cleave and Edythe Dorrance, in 1954, to begin the organizing of Foursquare women into a nationwide cooperative women's fellowship, which they named "The United Foursquare Women." Their goal was to unite local church women with a view to helping missionaries, pioneer pastors, and the needy of every description. The UFW has been extended around the world.

Social Involvement

Angelus Temple, though never active in partisan politics, was strongly involved in civic and community affairs. Through Radio KFSG strong support was given to measures for the betterment of the police and fire departments and the general improvement of the community. In the early 1920s Angelus Temple entered floats in the Tournament of Roses Parade, earning a cup in 1924 and the Grand Prize in 1925. All effort was expended not for glory, but to make better known the revival center.[14]

Mrs. McPherson's social involvement became a potent force in the City of Los Angeles. During the 1920s the metropolis was a burgeoning, new West Coast community and the target of crime bosses from across the nation. It was during the prohibition era, and there was much illegal activity with the police department and other city offices. As men and women were saved out of such a terrible lifestyle, they would stand on the platform and testify. Officials were forced to take action.

This led to the now renowned kidnapping and to the resulting accusations against Mrs. McPherson. Misrepresented until this day by sensationalistic journalism, she was accused of an immoral tryst with a former employee of Radio KFSG. It must be known, however, that all charges were dropped due to lack of evidence, and Mrs. McPherson was found to be completely innocent of any such actions.

Actually, those who prosecuted her were later sent to jail for graft and civil corruption. Anyone desiring to read more about the entire episode may do so in the books *In the Service of the King*, by Mrs. McPherson herself, and *The Verdict Is In* and *Aimee*, both authored by Dr. Raymond Cox.

Public Prayer for Sick

The number of outreach arms that contributed to the permanence of the revival was almost numberless. But next to the general outpouring of the Holy Spirit upon the pulpit ministry was the public prayer for the sick. Miracles for healing drew crowds that filled the Temple almost to suffocation. Thousands were turned away, but they tuned their radios to KFSG or sought branch churches in their own communities where prayer was made for the sick. These miracles of healing were real and lasting, demonstrated by the fact that hundreds sent, in writing, their testimonies of miraculous healing to the *Bridal Call* editor, often verified by their physicians. Aimee Semple McPherson never claimed a special gift, nor did she give undue importance to the healing services that were held on Wednesday afternoons and Saturday nights.

Many were healed in the 500 Room before they got as far as the Temple platform. Mrs. McPherson did not pray for everyone who came for healing. A number of lines were formed with elders assisting at the head of each line. Faith built to the point where many were healed while sitting in their seats. To God was attributed all the glory. All the "corners of the Foursquare Gospel" were kept sharp.

A great vine always must put down strong roots in fertile soil, a soil filled with the nutrients that will keep the vine growing and producing luscious fruit. The Foursquare Church was rooted in revival, a revival that endured for years, a revival solidly based on Bible truth and inspired by a vision of world evangelization. For nearly seven decades the vine has prospered and shows no sign of withering. Better, it shows evidence of branching out with new abundance.

The Doctrinal Basis of the Foursquare Church

The basic doctrinal beliefs of the Foursquare Church have remained constant throughout its history; they are the beliefs of the founder, Aimee Semple McPherson. She prepared a doctrinal booklet called *The Foursquare Declaration of Faith*, which was adopted by the church at the time of its incorporation in December 1927. Since Mrs. McPherson had held credentials for several years with the Assemblies of God and was substantially influenced by the same sources as those that shaped the teachings of the General Council's leaders, her beliefs and theirs were, for the most part, identical except on church organization.[15]

It is a remarkable fact that as far as is known no Foursquare churches have seceded from the organization over doctrinal differences. Issues such as "Oneness" and "Latter Rain" that have divided other Pentecostal communions have stirred hardly more than ripples of curiosity on the Foursquare waters. The issue of "eternity security" through the years has provoked a few classroom debates in the Bible colleges, and arguably, the dismissal of one teacher. But this issue has never reached debate on the convention floor nor resulted in the reaction of what some call "eternal insecurity."

There are many differing views on forms of worship and on the location of the "Rapture" in relation to "The Tribulation," but no unity-shattering doctrinal debates on the convention floor come to the author's remembrance, which stretches back to 1926. This is not to deny that there have been procedural and organizational issues that have injected excitement into convention business. But this relative doctrinal tranquility can probably be traced to Aimee Semple McPherson's positive teaching and her position of moderation in all things; "in essentials unity, in nonessentials liberty, in all things charity."

Space will not permit an in-depth discussion of the entire *Declaration of Faith* or all forty tenets of the "Creedal Statements." After all, The Foursquare Gospel Church does have more than "four" doctrines. Mention will be made only of the major tenets and the distinctive positions.

1. *The Holy Scriptures.* In common with all Pentecostals and fundamental evangelicals, the International Church of the Foursquare Gospel believes in the plenary verbal inspiration of the original manuscripts of Scripture. The Foursquare Church has never yielded on the position of inerrancy (2 Tim. 3:16; 2 Pet. 1:20–21).

2. *The Triune Godhead.* The International Church of the Foursquare Gospel holds to the historic doctrine of the Trinity. It rejects the neo-sabellianism of "Jesus only," a reappearance of a heresy condemned by the church in A.D. 263 (Matt. 28:19–20; 3:16–17; 2 Cor. 13:14).

3. *The Deity and Humanity of the Lord Jesus Christ* (Phil. 2:5–11; John 17:5) and *The Personality and Deity of the Holy Spirit* (John 14:15–16).

4. *The Substitutionary Atonement.* The Foursquare Gospel Church believes that Christ's vicarious atoning work on the Cross purchases for the believer full salvation and that no human works can add to that finished work of redemption. Men and women are saved by grace and not of works; however, good works are the goal Christ sets before them as a result of salvation. People are saved by grace through faith, but are rewarded for works (Eph. 2:5–10; Rom. 3:23–28).

5. *Holiness and Sanctification.* Some would exclude the International Church of the Foursquare Gospel from the Holiness movement because it does not believe in entire sanctification as an instantaneous crisis experience separate from the born-again experience. Nor does The Foursquare Church believe in instantaneous Christian perfection. Aimee Semple McPherson states in her creedal statement, "We believe in the maintenance of good works and holy living, in Christian perfection and holiness through absolute surrender and consecration," clearly referencing an abiding commitment to holiness of life and purity of conduct.

   She defines this sanctification as progressive, not instantaneous:

> We believe that having been cleansed by the precious blood of Jesus Christ, and having received the witness of the Holy Spirit at conversion, it is the will of God that we be sanctified daily and become partakers of His holiness; growing constantly stronger in faith, power, prayer, love and service, first as babes desiring the sincere milk of the Word; then as sincere children walking humbly, seeking diligently the hidden life, where self decreases; then as strong men having on the whole armor of God marching forth to new conquests in His name, living a patient, sober, unselfish, godly life that will be a true reflection of the Christ within (Prov. 4:18; Rom. 6:4; Phil. 3:9–12; Heb. 6:1; 2 Cor. 7:1; 2 Pet. 3:17, 18).[16]

   John Wesley is adopted as the leader of those who hold to an instantaneous experience of sanctification resulting in Christian perfection. Wesley did not profess moral infallibility, though he believed in a perfection of "intention"[17] and Christian love.

Mrs. McPherson certainly was influenced by a Holiness background and believed in holiness as the believer's goal, even as John Wesley. But unlike Wesley, it was her belief that sanctification began with the born-again experience and continued progressively throughout the believer's life. She taught a holiness of "intent," "motivation," and "love of others," one that did not major in outward appearance.

In the Pentecostal outpouring at the turn of the century, some Holiness people discovered a crisis experience for power certified by speaking with tongues. They called that experience "the baptism with the Holy Spirit." Many added the Pentecostal experience to the sanctification experience, making three crisis experiences.

Aimee Semple McPherson was a student of men like Gordon, Finney, Simpson, Torrey, etc., "Holiness men" to whom sanctification and the Holy Spirit baptism were different names for the same experience. Yet, to her, Pentecost did not add up to three experiences; the baptism with the Holy Spirit was power for service and power for the victorious living that the blood of Jesus purchased. That the Holiness movement saw sanctification and the baptism with the Holy Spirit as synonymous is demonstrated by the fact that the Church of the Nazarene, one of the largest Holiness churches, used the word *Pentecostal* in its name until the advent of the Pentecostal movement. Let it be immediately said, however, that sanctification is such a blessing of God that any believers who seek it have the Foursquare Church's good will no matter when it is received.

6. *Healing in the Atonement.* The International Church of the Foursquare Gospel believes that the atoning work of Christ availed for the whole person, spirit and body. Christ came to destroy the works of the devil; sickness is one of the devil's works that Calvary heals through faith (Isa. 53:5; Matt. 8:16–17; 1 Pet. 2:24; James 5:13–15).

7. *The Initial Evidence of the Baptism with the Holy Spirit.* The International Church of the Foursquare Gospel believes that speaking in tongues is the initial evidence of the baptism with the Holy Spirit, as seen in Acts 2:4; 10:44–47; 19:6, where tongues are specifically mentioned; in Acts 8:14–19, where tongues are strongly implied; and 1 Corinthians 14:18, where Paul testifies to frequent speaking in tongues.

8. *The Second Coming of Christ.* The International Church of the Foursquare Gospel believes in the premillenial second coming of Christ. It also believes in the Rapture of the church, at which Christ comes for His bride (1 Thess. 4:17). The New Testament also mentions a coming with His saints, which event closes the "Tribulation" (Rev. 19). The view of Aimee Semple McPherson was that of a pre-Tribulation Rapture. Some theologians prefer to believe in a post-Tribulation Rapture, and a few hold to a mid-Tribulation coming. The majority view is that of a pre-Tribulation Rapture, but all three positions are tolerated. It is clear that

> Mrs. McPherson believed that the Rapture was "imminent."[18]

Indeed, the Foursquare vine was rooted in revival, one of the most powerful and enduring revivals in this century. But how long did the revival last? What form did it take? This is a story of a "vine" planted in revival soil that grew rapidly, sprouted many branches, and has produced ample fruit.

Chapter 2

THE FIRST BRANCHES OF THE VINE

1924–1933

CONCURRENT WITH THE building of Angelus Temple, Aimee Semple McPherson had planned the establishment of an Evangelistic and Missionary Training Institute. Within weeks after opening the Temple, fifty students were enrolled. At the end of June 1923, the number had increased to over one hundred. By the time summer of 1924 arrived, she had so motivated the trainees to soul winning that they could scarcely wait to cast out the net.

In anticipation of the unmeasured enthusiasm of her pupils, Mrs. McPherson had obtained several brown tents similar to those she had used in her early ministry. Also, Angelus Temple radio station KFSG had been on the air for several months broadcasting the revival message with occasional mention of the training institute. Spiritually hungry people throughout Southern California were becoming increasingly aware of the Holy Spirit revival that was happening in their midst.

By the time the first full term of the training institute ended in June 1924, invitations had flooded into Angelus Temple from a number of the communities, begging Mrs. McPherson and the elders to dispatch a tent and a group of students. Often the invitations included the generous offer of a vacant lot, along with physical and financial assistance. Mature workers such as Rev. Anna D. Britton were sent with the students to give guidance. By the end of summer, three fully established branch churches (Santa Ana, California; Alhambra, California; Pasadena, California) were in operation.

The fall term of 1924 began with reports of the eight summer tent meetings. The institute was faced with the problem of keeping the budding evangelists and missionaries in class long enough to get a diploma and ordination. It seemed more important to many of the students to fling themselves into the reaping of whitened harvest fields; a few were not restrained. By the summer of 1925, with the revival at Angelus Temple surging to ever higher crests, a tidal wave of evangelism was ready to inundate the environs of Los Angeles. Communities were ready for the inundation. Even civic leaders and prominent citizens joined together to invite Mrs. McPherson and the groups to bring to them the Foursquare message.

In June of 1925, sixteen students graduated and became licensed or ordained ministers, with more than one hundred eager students having gained one year of preparation for evangelism. Out they went with their Bibles, folding organs, guitars, tambourines, trumpets, trombones, and tracts, motivated by a desire to preach, teach, witness, sing, or just pray. They possessed an irrepressible burden for souls. When that event summer came to a close, there were thirty-three established branch churches, one in almost every sizable community of Southern California, and several in Central California. The Foursquare vine had climbed almost every available trellis in the immediate vineyard. One branch sprouted as far away as Ohio.[1]

The First Branches

The first branches were considered to be branches of Angelus Temple. In fact, in Santa Ana, California, and Long Beach, California, new members were taken in by Mrs. McPherson over the radio, with telephone response. She was their pastor, the local leader was an assistant. However, as soon as there was a sufficient number of ministers who had graduated from the training institute with ministerial credentials, these breathlessly awaiting pastors were installed in the established branches.

Some of the first pastors were: Anna Britton, Hazel Granvol, D. V. and Eva Alderman, Jack and Louise Richey, Wesley and Ruth Norgaard, Bessie Randall, Bert Bruffet, Harold and Ione Jefferies, Sidney and Helen Correll, Luther Plankenhorn, Arthur and Helen Wegner, Helen Isaker, Durward Myers, Gwendolyn Pittinger, F. C. Warren, Guy and Ted Tobey, Mrs. H. Short, Elizabeth Still, Eleanor Grigsby, Maybelle Reel, Iva Wallick, Claire Britton, Vera Overgaard, Essie Locy, Roy Grey, Earl and Edythe Dorrance, Roderick and Viola Morrison, Herman Mitzner, Alice Wilson, Arthur Pedersen, Mr. and Mrs. James Lynn, Eva Hale, etc.

It is often difficult to attribute the pioneering of a branch to a specific person because the tent meetings were conducted by groups. The above persons or couples pastored several of the new branches during the years before a denomination existed. Graduates from the institute continued pioneering more branches, and their evangelizing efforts were not restricted to the summer vacation periods. Each class that graduated added to the number of full-time evangelists and pastors.

By 1927 the number of branches had swelled above the century mark—105 to be exact. When the year 1933 came to a close, the seventh year of existence after incorporation as a denomination, there were 253 Foursquare churches in twenty-nine states.

The roll of ordained ministers numbered more than five hundred with an almost equal number of licensed preachers, most of whom were graduates of L.I.F.E. Bible College.

Of more than one thousand credentialed ministers, there were a large number of capable evangelists who helped the pastors maintain a high level of dedication in the local churches. Almost every church planned to have two or three special evangelistic campaigns during the year. In some areas the spiritual thermometer reading of churches was determined by how often they displayed a "revival" sign; there some that never took them down. Revival campaigns usually lasted from two to four weeks, depending upon their success in attendance, in souls won, or in believers healed and filled with the Spirit. Evangelists who had results in those categories were usually "booked" months or years in advance.

Some of the cities where these branches were located were: Santa Ana (the first), Pasadena (the second), Pomona, Riverside, Goodyear, Van Nuys, Alhambra, Long Beach, Whittier, Torrance, Willowbrook, Anaheim, Fullerton, Burbank, Lankersheim, Ontario, Inglewood, Ventura, Santa Paula, Santa Monica, Sawtelle, Lomita, Brentwood, South Gate, Garden Grove, Salinas, Hanford, San Diego (all in California), as well as New Philadelphia, Ohio, and Vancouver, British Columbia.

While many of the organizational revivals were held in tents, soon permanent tabernacles and church buildings were under construction by eager volunteer workmen. Often the pastor with a saw or hammer in hand was in the midst of the building activity. Obviously the growth of the vine was phenomenal.

How can such explosive growth be explained?

1. The large crowds overflowed Angelus Temple Sunday after Sunday. Many traveled to the Temple from every part of Southern California for the

midweek day and night services. Soon the distance became inconvenient, for if persons arrived a bit late, the Temple was already filled to capacity. How much better it would be if there were a local Angelus Temple.

2. Angelus Temple radio station KFSG began broadcasting in February 1924. It was the first all-religious radio station in the United States, the first station licensed to a woman, and in operation only three years after the first religious broadcast ever. Regular listeners to the broadcast services began to desire a local place of worship where the same Holy Spirit-anointed message would be preached and the same ministries would be available.

3. Los Angeles was ready for revival again. The Azusa Street outpouring, which lasted only about three years, was a distant memory; most of the fruits of Azusa Street were found only in upstairs and back street missions. People yearned for the old-time religion in an updated setting. Many have said that Aimee Semple McPherson moved Pentecost "from the back streets to Main Street."

4. The inroads of liberalism had made many of the historic denominational churches a spiritual desert. Many pastors were giving "book reports" on Sunday nights, if the Sunday night service had not already been discontinued. Many of the middle-aged and elderly people still had nostalgia for a remembered but largely unavailable atmosphere of Holy Spirit-inspired worship. They found in the Angelus Temple services all they remembered and more.

5. The students and graduates of the Angelus Temple training institute were Spirit filled and sufficiently prepared in the Foursquare Gospel to gain the public's favorable response. They had developed under a role model from whom they gained a clear message and an intense burden for lost souls.
6. There is no doubt that a sovereign God had prepared Los Angeles for a spiritual awakening and had provided the needed vessel through whom He could accomplish His purpose for the time.

The growth of a denomination cannot be measured entirely by the number of local churches. If the churches could double their membership, the movement would be doubled in strength even if no new churches were opened. Some of the evangelists pioneered new churches; others helped the local churches to grow in constituents. The Foursquare Church continued to increase in number of churches and members. The numerical growth at home made possible an increase in the number of missionaries sent and supported.

One cannot tell much about the branches of a vine without an examination of the vine itself. Denominations that are formed by the united effort and planning of a number of leaders can be structured from the start with a chosen form of church government. Leaders can sit down together and choose whether they want the church government to be episcopal, congregational, or presbyterian. But the Foursquare organization was not planned in advance.

The First Church Structure

The Foursquare Church emerged out of a great revival, the leader of which had no intention of founding a denomination.

Angelus Temple was intended as a base for evangelistic campaigns across the nation and around the world. It was viewed as "a place to go home to" after seasons of arduous reaping, a base that could be maintained during Mrs. McPherson's absence by her mother, a well-chosen board of elders, and other Spirit-filled evangelists.

The original plan was followed for a short while, but the response in Southern California was so overwhelming. All of a sudden the vine had sprouted so many branches that an arbor had to be erected, one designed to provide for the offshoots.

In 1927, when the branch church count had soared above one hundred, it became obvious that certain legal and organizational steps were necessary to accommodate the burgeoning growth. However, like John Wesley, Mrs. McPherson had no idea of starting a new denomination. Her vision was for "interdenominational worldwide evangelization," as the cornerstone of Angelus Temple declares. During the founding convention of 1923, all the speakers that were chosen were Spirit-anointed ministers from different historic denominations, such as: Dr. Keeney Towner, Baptist; Dr. Charles Price, Congregational; Rev. Charles Schreve, Methodist; Rev. Edward Leech, United Brethren; Dr. Gale, Baptist; etc. This interdenominational spirit was and still is the attitude of the Foursquare movement.

Articles in the *Bridal Call* magazine of 1923 and 1928 disavow any intention of starting a new denomination.[2] The Echo Park Evangelistic Association was an incorporation solely for the purpose of fulfilling the fiduciary trust of Angelus Temple properties. It was not set up to confer ordination or provide other necessary ecclesiastical relationships.

Furthermore, the branches were tied in spirit to Angelus Temple and consequently to one another. Many of the constituents at the branches were Angelus Temple members who prized the Foursquare fellowship and unity of vision. In order to conserve what had been accomplished by 1927, there seemed to be no other solution to the problem except to incorporate. The resulting form of church government, as it turned out, was borrowed from several historical forms of church order.

In December 1927 a religious corporation was formed and named "International Foursquare Gospel Lighthouses." Each local Lighthouse was incorporated with local trustees authorized by a charter and governed by the bylaws of the parent organization. The local Lighthouse pastors were selected by the local congregation from a requested list of qualified and available ministers received from the divisional officer. This was not always observed. There were occurrences, although rather rare, of mutual exchanges of pastorates between pastors with only the consent of the local church councils. The election of pastors was for one year, but the pastor could be reelected by the local congregation.

The First District Supervisor

More quickly than anyone had anticipated, there arose a need for oversight of the growing number of churches. The busy founding evangelist was, of necessity, too occupied with the revival center to respond in full to their supervision. A Supervisor (at first called Superintendent) was appointed.

In 1927, Rev. John Goben, an experienced independent pastor and evangelist from Iowa who earlier had been chairman of the Iowa District of the Assemblies of God, having been apprised of a Midwest evangelistic tour by Aimee Semple McPherson, invited her to conduct meetings in Des Moines, Iowa. The meetings were highly successful. When the ICFG incorporated, Mrs. McPherson invited Rev. Goben to Los Angeles to serve as the first superintendent of branch churches.[3] As the branches increased in numbers and entered many states, the superintendent became general supervisor, overseeing divisional and state superintendents.

From an early year issue of the bylaws, a glimpse of a local congregation or Lighthouse can be seen:

> The name of the organization (local) shall be the Foursquare Gospel Lighthouse of ______________ as duly organized and incorporated under the laws of the State of ____________.
>
> ARTICLE II
>
> Purpose
>
> The principle and objects of this organization shall be based on the Bible as the inspired Word of the living God. The purpose of this organization shall be the propagation and dissemination of the Foursquare Gospel as presented in the "Declaration of Faith" compiled by Aimee Semple McPherson, a copy of which is hereby presented, and which by reference is made a part hereof; and to hold such property as may become vested in and belong to this organization, and to administer the same and all revenues therefrom in accordance with the articles of incorporation of this lighthouse, these Bylaws, and a charter granted to said corporation by the International Foursquare Gospel Lighthouses, duly organized under the laws of the State of California, and having its principal place of business at 1100 Glendale Blvd., Los Angeles, California.[4]

These bylaws pertained to the local Lighthouse inasmuch as each branch was incorporated locally and its property held by local trustees. Each was tied to the parent, however, by a charter issued by the parent organization and by provisions of the local incorporation. Each agreed to preach the Foursquare Gospel as set forth in the *Declaration of Faith*.

Note section 2 on qualification to hold office in the local Lighthouse:

> Section 2. In order to be eligible to hold any office in this corporation (local) a person must be a member of this Lighthouse, in good standing, living a godly Christian life, and shall have received the Baptism of the Holy Ghost, or be an earnest seeker thereof. The board members and trustees shall be twenty-one years of age or over.[5]

The following from Article IX, Sections 1–5, has to do with the election of pastors of local Lighthouses:

> Section 1. No minister or pastor shall receive a call to this Lighthouse except through the office of the Divisional Officer of the International Foursquare Gospel Lighthouses.
>
> Sections 2–5. When this Lighthouse is to call a pastor, the official board shall proceed as follows: It shall apply to, and receive from, the Divisional Officer of the International Foursquare Lighthouses the names of ministers who are qualified and available for a call. These names shall be brought before the membership of this Lighthouse for vote after being called together for that purpose... When called to the pastorate of this Lighthouse a pastor shall fill such pastorate for the term of one year... A pastor may be called to serve as many terms of one year as the membership of this Lighthouse may desire.[6]

Two features of these original bylaws are of interest to many: (1) local church properties were held by local trustees within certain limits; and (2) pastors were elected by the local congregation and remained in office by an annual vote.

Formation of the International Church of the Foursquare Gospel

In 1930 a new corporation was formed under the name "International Church of the Foursquare Gospel." At first, under the bylaws, properties were held by three trustees with one of the trustees chosen by the international board of directors. But in 1934 provisions were made for all properties to be held by the parent corporation for the custodial use of the local church. In 1936 a new provision of the bylaws required that the pastors be appointed by the president and the board of directors on recommendation of the district supervisor.

Between 1927 and the convention of 1936 the basic bylaws were in a state of development and refinement. Though there have been several restatements through the latter years, the original concepts have been maintained.

Why was the appointive system chosen? First, there is no doubt that the founder of the International Church of the Foursquare Gospel, coming from a Methodist and Salvation Army background, preferred a strong central church government. Further, the original voting system resulted in pastoral changes being too frequent, causing insecurity of the pastors and undesirable local politics. A pastor, voted out by one congregation, found difficulty sometimes in gaining acceptance by another church. Settled pastors often felt they had to spend too much time catering to members' preferences instead of ministering by God's direction.

The holding of church property titles was changed to prevent some withdrawals of churches from the organization by a small number of trustees or elders, contrary to the wishes of those who had invested in the church as a Lighthouse of the Foursquare Gospel. A great advantage of the present system of holding title to assets has enabled Foursquare churches to obtain sizable financing for the acquisition of properties and the construction of churches, when such privilege has been denied to congregational types of churches who then had to seek less desirable means of procuring loans and trust deeds on the assets of single locations.

Such a pattern of church government has proved beneficial to the Foursquare Gospel Church. It has assisted in overcoming proprietorship that is experienced in many cases where local trustees are responsible for pastoral appointments and major property decisions. According to the Bible, ministerial leadership is not based on popularity but guided by the Holy Spirit. Foursquare pastors are allowed more freedom in presenting an uncompromised message (Acts 20:28).

Greater unity has been created by the holding of all church property in common and providing protection for the investment of the gifts and labors of the founding ministers and congregations. There were at that time many privately held churches that a minister would sell and the congregation was either out or would be forced to pay for the church several times over. It was vowed that no Foursquare congregations would lose their investment because of private interests. Consequently, great respect for the Foursquare system has been expressed by businesses, particularly lending institutions.

There are three or four major types of church government. And there are those who argue with logic in favor of each type. No human ecclesiastical system can claim to be perfect, but ICFG has a form of church government that has been changed in the past and has manifested openness to change in the future. All of the church's documents, such as the bylaws and manner of operation, are living and serving instruments. Present leaders declare their dedication to find ways to dress the vine to make it more productive. There are an increasing number of observers who express a great admiration for this system of ecclesiastical structure.

The officers of the new corporation were: (1) president, Aimee Semple McPherson (for her lifetime, with the privilege of appointing her successor), (2) vice president, (3) secretary, and (4) treasurer. The administrative bodies were a board of directors, an Executive Council, and the Annual General Assembly. Members of the board of directors were: (1) president, (2) vice president, (3) secretary, (4) treasurer (at the discretion of the board), and (5) general supervisor.

The first members of the board of directors were: (1) Aimee Semple McPherson, president/pastor; (2) dean of L.I.F.E. Bible Institute Harriet Jordan; (3) Dr. B. F. Gurden; (4) D. V. Alderman, who was the second general supervisor and the first Foursquare minister to receive Foursquare ordination; and (5) F. C. Warren.[7]

The first executive council was composed of persons appointed by the president whose purpose was to serve the president and board of directors in an advisory capacity. This council was subsequently comprised of members of the board of directors, the district supervisors, and the divisional officers who later became known as divisional superintendents.

Bylaw changes required the approval of the annual convention. The convention body was comprised of registered delegates who were pastors and qualified laymen from each local Foursquare Gospel church, chosen on the basis of one to each one hundred members, or fraction thereof. (Today, one delegate is allowed for each fifty members.)

The area administrators of the churches were called divisional officers. There were twelve in number, usually selected because they pastored the strongest and most respected church in the state or region. In 1931 they consisted of:

1. Northern California—Rev. William E. Opie, pastor in Fresno, California
2. Idaho, Oregon, Washington—Rev. H. W. Jefferies, pastor in Portland, Oregon
3. Western Canada—Rev. Anna D. Britton, pastor in Vancouver, British Columbia
4. Colorado—Rev. Herman D. Mitzner, pastor in Denver, Colorado
5. Montana, Wyoming, South Dakota—Rev. D. W. McCullough
6. Texas, Oklahoma—Rev. A. C. Wegner, pastor in Dallas, Texas
7. Kansas, Nebraska, Missouri—Rev. Frank Cummings, Omaha, Nebraska
8. North Dakota—Rev. Howard Ray
9. Iowa, Minnesota—Rev. John R. Richey, pastor in Des Moines, Iowa
10. Wisconsin, Illinois—Rev. Sidney Correll, Kenosha, Wisconsin
11. Michigan, Indiana—Rev. R. J. Turner, New Baltimore, Michigan
12. Ohio, Kentucky, Pennsylvania, New York—Rev. Bert Bruffet, Dayton, Ohio[8]

Most of the divisional officers had earned their leadership positions by arduous labors as soul-winning evangelists, having pioneered (started) the church they pastored as well as other churches. On the basis of their experience they were able to guide the newer arrivals to their areas in church planting and in pastoral ministry.

By 1933, however, it became obvious that the double task of pastoring a growing church together with area supervision was too demanding. Either the church or the area suffered some neglect. The solution to the problem was solved by the division of the United States, with the exception of California, into three large areas. Three officers were appointed from among the divisional officers and given the title of district supervisors. The remaining divisional officers became state of divisional superintendents working under the district supervisors. (NOTE: Some see in this officer structure a pattern borrowed from the Los Angeles county government.)

These new supervisors were salaried from general funds. Freed from pastoral responsibility, they were able to give full attention to the rapidly growing number of churches in their areas. The three highly capable men who were appointed to this new office at the convention of 1933 were: (1) Rev. Harold Jefferies (Northwest District), (2) Rev. Frank Cummings (Midwest District), and (3) Rev. Sidney Correll (Great Lakes District).

While California counted as many churches as the rest of the nation, it was a compact area by comparison. Therefore, it was placed under the newly appointed general supervisor, William Black, renowned evangelist and longtime trusted friend of Mrs. McPherson. Rev. Anna D. Britton, perhaps the most prolific planter of branch churches, who after 1927 and for many years pastored the Foursquare Church of Vancouver, British Columbia, Canada, was made the general supervisor of Western Canada.[9] That these appointments were wise and divinely guided is shown by the fact that every appointee continued in office for many years and they were greatly appreciated by the pastors of their districts.

Women in Ministry

Before leaving the story of the original branch churches, it must be noted that a great number of early branches were pioneered by women preachers. Of course, it was natural that a woman preacher of the talent, anointing, and fame of Aimee Semple McPherson would attract many other women to her ministry. Of the first students in the Foursquare Training Institute, at least three-fourths were women. Of the sixteen graduates in the first class, only two were men, John Wright and D. V. Alderman. It is not surprising that Rev. D. V. Alderman became the first L.I.F.E. graduate to hold the office of general supervisor.

While Aimee Semple McPherson only occasionally placed women in top leadership positions, women evangelists were given great encouragement. Many husbands and their wives, both of whom were graduates of L.I.F.E., pastored together. The promise of the Father, which the apostles were commanded to await (Joel 2:28–29), declared that He would pour out His Spirit on "all" flesh, and that sons and "daughters" would prophesy. Mrs. McPherson based her right to preach on the Pentecostal prophecy of Joel and the other example of other Bible women who were prophets and evangelists.[10] Since the modern Pentecostal outpouring after the turn of the century, almost all Pentecostal movements have had successful women preachers and evangelists.[11]

Of the many Foursquare couples who pioneered and pastored early Foursquare churches, the wife, at least at first, was the more effective preacher. Examples are Ione Jefferies, Bessie Bruffet, Alice Parham, Mrs. Hal Smith, Eva Hale, Vera Overgaard, Helen Myers, Ova Wallich, Frances Luddington, Ethel Heidner, Alice LaMar, Evelyn Thompson, Mrs. A. A. Carpenter, Marion Plies, Ethel Singleton, Martha Risser, Ada Teeple, and Nola Amos, to name a few.

In later years, there were Gladys Johnson, Juanita Smith, Frances Larson, Betty Hourez, Mabel Kirk, Dorothy McIntosh, Vonitta Gurney, Billie Francey, etc. Among these couples there was surprisingly little jealousy. When children came into the family, the man assumed the role of pastor or, at least, co-pastor.

Several single or widowed women became outstanding pastors, evangelists, or missionaries. Listen to this honored roll call: Louise Webster, Vivian Twyford, Paula Risser, Evelyn Taylor, Mary Jane May, Mary Young, Sylvia Erickson, Ruth Baker, A. A. Carpenter, Dorothy Jean Furlong, Juanita Conger, Edith Campbell, Ena Fanson, Judy Chavez, Fern Luther, Lovetta Conlee, Eloise Caldron, Leita Mae Steward, Virginia Cravens, Maybelle Cutting, Mildred Poole, Marie Trimble, Arleta Keck, Mary Lou Canata, etc. Among the above are women who have served as state or division superintendents, and several who have held responsible positions in the Bible colleges or the headquarters offices.

Outstanding women pioneers who started more than one church included Evelyn Taylor, Louise Webster, Anna Britton, Alice Wilson, Mrs. A. A. Carpenter, Ruth Baker, Mary Young, Ruby Moore, Isabelle Hall/Helmle, etc. When to these names are added those of women missionaries, the roll becomes extensive.

Vinson Synan writes the following paragraph about our Foursquare women preachers:

> By 1986 a new Foursquare church was opened somewhere in the world every six hours. Serving these churches is a ministerium of 4,856 pastors, evangelists and missionaries around the world. Of these, 737 are ordained women, many of whom serve as pastors. In fact, the 1986 minutes indicate that no less than 41 percent of all the ordained Foursquare ministers in the United States are women, one of the highest

> proportions of women ministers of any church in the world. This large percentage may reflect the fact that a woman, with roots in the Salvation Army, founded the church.[12]

This figure of 41 percent for 1986 is, however, somewhat deceiving. What the figure reveals is that a great number of women hold Foursquare credentials; it does not indicate to what degree our present-day Foursquare women are involved in public ministries such as pastoring, evangelizing, and church planting. The figure indicates that a large number of our credentialed men have married women graduates from the Bible colleges, or after five years in the ministry have obtained credentials for their wives, which privilege the bylaws permit.

Effective women evangelists, pastors, and spiritual leaders have been associated with the Pentecostal movement, such as:

1. Maria Woodworth Etter, one of the earliest of women evangelists who stirred the Holiness movement with her healing ministry, came to the Pentecostal movement in 1916. She was much admired by Aimee Semple McPherson.
2. Carrie Judd Montgomery of Buffalo, New York, headed a healing mission. She was one of the founders together with A. B. Simpson of the Christian Missionary Alliance. She later was baptized in the Spirit and with her husband united with the Assemblies of God in 1917.
3. Agnes Ozman is believed to be the first person to speak in tongues in the latter rain Pentecostal outpouring in 1900.
4. Evangeline Booth was the daughter of William Booth, founder of the Salvation Army. After the

death of General Booth, Evangeline became the commanding general of the entire Salvation Army. From the beginning of The Salvation Army, women and men held officer rank on an equal basis. Catherine Booth, wife of General Booth and mother of Evangeline, was said to have been an eloquent preacher.[13]

5. Florence Crawford, after being filled with the Spirit at Azusa Street in 1906, returned to Portland, Oregon, where she founded the Apostolic Faith movement, which had influence on many early ministers and laymen who later entered the Foursquare, Open Bible Standard, and Assemblies of God churches.
6. Kathryn Kuhlman ministered to multitudes across our nation with her remarkable healing ministry.
7. Freda Lindsay was originally from the Portland, Oregon, Foursquare Church. After the death of her husband, Gordon, Freda has carried the work of the Christ For The Nations Institute to ascending heights.
8. Marilyn Hickey of Denver, Colorado, ministers on 120 radio stations and thirty-five TV stations, teaching the Bible and promoting worthy projects in many countries of the world.

The above-mentioned women are included to demonstrate that, in spite of an apparent decline in leadership on the part of Pentecostal women, a significant number have been and are involved in vital public ministries.[14]

During the early years many women felt called to preach.

Today, very few do. It seems a bit strange that in a day when women are assuming leadership roles in politics, industry, and social services, Pentecostal women are less active in public ministry. What has happened? Why do many churches still deny ordination and public ministry to their women? Have leaders become so fearful by the activity of the women's liberation movement? Have they been intimidated by the books and tapes of some of the independent charismatics who disallow the ministry of women? Have some of Paul's writings, which were given to correct certain cultural problems in his day, been misinterpreted? Has the church ignored other passages of St. Paul that demonstrate or encourage women's public ministries?

A 1988 declaration concerning The Foursquare Church's positive attitude toward women in all ministries, written on request by Dr. Harold Helms, pastor of Angelus Temple, was unanimously passed by the board of directors and entered into the board's minutes.[15] The board's resolution read:

> The present and historical position of the Foursquare Church affirms the Biblical truth that women are called of God to roles of leadership and public ministry. We hereby reaffirm and encourage the ministry of women throughout the International Church of the Foursquare Gospel.[16]

A similar position has been taken recently by the newly merged Lutheran denomination. The following excerpt is taken from the Sunday religious section of the Whittier, California, *Tribune/News* (1989):

> Another action saluted the Twentieth Anniversary of the start of ordination of women in the three Lutheran branches merged into the present 5.3-million-member denomination. It has about 1,000 ordained women among 11,000 clergy. Congregations "that have not experienced the preaching,

> teaching or pastoral care of women" were encouraged to open doors to them. Active recruitment was urged of women for seminaries and ordination.[17]

On one occasion Mrs. McPherson was asked whether she liked to hear a woman preach. She answered, "No! Neither do I like to hear a man preach. But I love to hear God speak, whether the vessel is a man or a woman."

It will be very interesting to trace the history of the International Church of the Foursquare Gospel through the exciting second and third decades of the church's growth. However, before those important periods are chronicled, a look must be taken at the beginnings and progress of the Foursquare Bible institutes and colleges, as well as the ministries of youth and Christian education.

Chapter 3

THE BIBLE COLLEGES

Cultivating the Vine

It is to be expected that a vine will sprout branches. It is a phenomenon of nature. But the quality of the branches, their strength, growth rate, and fruitfulness depend upon the richness of the soil and the skill of cultivation. Applying this analogy to the Foursquare Gospel Church, the divinely sent revival at Angelus Temple provided the rich soil. The Bible colleges and the training institutes supplied anointed workers, making possible the phenomenal growth rate and the abundant fruitfulness.

An article written by a student editor in the 1927 *Carry On*, the yearbook of the training institute, by the time renamed International Institute of Foursquare Evangelism (I.I.F.E.), is inspiring:

> As we look back upon the past year, we have seen an enormous increase in the enrollment of the school. Students have come from all parts of the world to train as evangelists, pastors and missionaries. We have in our midst students from Australia, England, Scotland, South America and Germany. There are also students from nearly every state of the Union.
>
> We have seen the spreading of the Foursquare Gospel

> as never before. We have nearly gasped at the rapidity with which new branch churches have been started in new localities. Calls are coming in continually for students and workers, which shows that the world is hungry for the precious Word of God told in the Foursquare way...At the present time there are already over fifty branch churches, each one thriving in the love of God under the leadership of able and devoted pastors of the Gospel.
>
> We are not exaggerating when we say that we hope to see a branch church in every state of the Union.[1]

Mrs. McPherson expressed her eloquent evaluation of the training institute as a vehicle for the spreading of the gospel:

> The bugle has sounded! Its stirring notes have reached hearts far over the Rockies! Many scores have risen up to answer! They have come and are still coming by train, boat and auto. With cloudbursts of power and glory, with a mighty witnessing of the Spirit, with shouting and weeping and heavenly singing, the fall term opened (1923). A large company of consecrated young men and women with open Bibles and open hearts are studying the Word, that they may, upon entering the field show themselves approved unto God, a workman that needeth not to be ashamed, rightly dividing the Word of Truth. A Spirit-filled faculty teaching. The power coming down. The Lord hath need of workers, harken to the call!
>
> To the front the cry is ringing, to the front your place is there; In the conflict men are needed, men of hope, and faith and prayer.[2]

In the previous chapter the involvement of the Bible college in the founding of the first branches was described. This chapter will tell the story of the Foursquare institutes and colleges, their origins, leaders, faculties, curricula and alumni. While reading about triumphs, problems, and relocations, one especially recognizes the inestimable value of the institutes and colleges in carrying the Foursquare Gospel from coast to coast and around the world.

L.I.F.E. Bible College

Fourquaredom's principal ministerial training institution, now known as L.I.F.E. Bible College (L.I.F.E.), was conceived in the heart and mind of Aimee Semple McPherson during her revival campaigns abroad and throughout the nation. To the much sought-after evangelist, the most obvious need was for trained workers who could both evangelize and ground new converts in the Word. But when, where, and how? With the building of beautiful and spacious Angelus Temple, which opened January 1, 1923, these questions were answered.

No time was wasted. On the morning of February 6, 1923, classes in the Echo Park Evangelistic and Missionary Training Institute began, just five weeks after the Temple's opening. More than one hundred enrollees with barely controllable emotions marched into the institute's assembly room. A highly competent and deeply spiritual faculty awaited the students. The founder and president, Aimee Semple McPherson, would teach Bible and practical evangelism; evangelist Billy Black, a dynamic revival preacher, gospel singer, and longtime acquaintance of the founder, would serve as acting dean and assistant to the president, as well as teach practical ministry. Dr. Frank C. Thompson, compiler of the world-recognized Thompson Chain Reference Bible, would teach Gospels, Epistles, and Life of Christ. Lillian B. Yoemans, MD (University of Michigan), former physician and surgeon, taught Divine Healing and Church History. Rev. J. R. Harris, Spirit-filled Baptist, would teach Major Prophets and Pentateuch. Rev. A. E. Mitchell, noted artist, theologian, and missionary, would teach Doctrine and Philosophy of the

Cross. Organization of classes and curriculum were supplied by Rev. John Quincy, former Texas state educational director for the Baptist Church.[3]

A number of the original faculty remained with the institute for a number of years. Additions were made of teachers such as Dr. Claire Britton, Anna D. Britton, Dr. Fredrick W. Farr, etc. Visiting evangelists to the Temple, such as Paul Rader, A. P. Goethe, Smith Wigglesworth, Hardy Mitchell, and A. G. Garr, were invited to bless the students with their knowledge of practical evangelism and effective ministry.

At first the majority of the students attended the services of Angelus Temple with its multifaceted outreach. No greater instruction in practical ministry and ministry gifts of the Spirit could be found in all the world. While L.I.F.E. always maintained an adequate scholastic level, the principal objective was preparing devout men and women to win souls and to evangelize the unbeliever (non-Christian) and to minister to the body of Christ.

In 1924 the student body outgrew the available space. It became clear that an education building had to be added to the Angelus Temple complex. A school building project was begun to which the people readily responded. In December 1924 ground was broken; at the beginning of 1926 the institute moved from the parsonage and the 500 Room into a beautiful five-story edifice. For sixty-four years thousands passed in and out of L.I.F.E.'s famous and unforgettable "iron gate."

Additions to the full-time faculty in the 1920s and 1930s were Charles W. Walkem (Greek and Hebrew), H. Wesley Cooksey, Roderick Morrison, R. Hamilton Grey, Durward F. Myers, Watson B. Teaford, Ronald Holcomb, Mildred Holcomb, Elmer Gottschalk, Christopher Gabie, and Nathaniel M. Van Cleave. In the 1940s changes and additions brought to the faculty:

Thompson Eade, Vinton Johnson, Paul Royer, Charles Tate, William Cochrane, Dorothy Boosinger, and Orlando Shields. In the 1950s and 1960s the following faculty members were added: Clarence Hall, Kathryn Hall, H. P. Courtney Sr., Leland Edwards, Guy P. Duffield, Paul Hackett, Coleman Phillips, Ralph Hammon, Jack Hayford, Don Pickerill, Chester Allen, Raymond Becker, Dorothy Jean Furlong, Juanita Conger, Zoe Ann Hill, Mary Robertson, Herman Rosenberger, and Samuel Middlebrook. The faculty of the 1970s and 1980s will be covered in chapter 11, under the discussion of accreditation.[4]

The first permanent dean of the Foursquare Institute was Miss Harriet Jordan. Miss Jordan was well qualified for the challenging position. Her father was pastor of the First Presbyterian Church of San Diego. She was a graduate of a teacher's college.

Initially, Harriet Jordan was drawn to Aimee Semple McPherson because of a remarkable miracle of healing. Throughout her youth Harriet had been frail in health. After her college work, she became seriously ill with no hope of recovery. Having read of Mrs. McPherson's healing ministry and being told that the evangelist was holding a campaign in San Jose, California, Harriet persuaded a friend to drive her to the revival site. The campaign was being conducted at the invitation of the First Baptist Church, pastored by Dr. Keeny Towner.

When "Hattie" (as her friends called her) was prayed for, she was marvelously healed and filled with the Holy Spirit. A few months later Angelus Temple opened, and Harriet enrolled in the institute's first class. For the next thirteen years Miss Jordan was a devoted, inseparable friend of Mrs. McPherson. In 1924 Mrs. McPherson appointed her dean of the institute. Under her leadership the enrollment climbed from fewer than two hundred to one thousand students. The number of churches started by students who graduated during her tenure was over three hundred.[5]

In 1937 Miss Jordan tendered her resignation, which was accepted with reluctance. Concerned to fill the dean's chair with a worthy successor, Mrs. McPherson appointed Rev. Watson B. Teaford, pastor of the Long Beach, California, Foursquare Church, to the vacancy.

Rev. W. B. (Bert) Teaford graduated from L.I.F.E. in June 1928. He immediately launched out into pioneer evangelism, opening new branches in Arkansas City, Parsons, and Pittsburg (all in the state of Kansas); St. Louis, Missouri; and Muscatine, Iowa. In 1931 he assumed the pastorate of the Ventura, California, Foursquare Church, where he planned and began the construction of a beautiful new sanctuary patterned after the style of Angelus Temple.

Rev. Teaford was unable to finish the building project (completed by Thompson Eade), for in 1937, recognizing his outstanding leadership quality, Mrs. McPherson asked him to fill the position of dean of L.I.F.E. Bible College. Dr. W. B. Teaford served very successfully in that role for sixteen years, in recognition of which he was awarded the honorary degree of Doctor of Divinity. In 1953 he was appointed by Dr. Rolf McPherson to the co-pastorate of Angelus Temple.

The vacancy in the leadership of L.I.F.E. Bible College was filled by Dr. Clarence Hall. Dr. and Mrs. Hall were educated at Oberlin College and L.I.F.E. Bible College. They had served with distinction as pastors of the Vancouver, British Columbia, Kingsway Foursquare Church, at which time he was also dean of L.I.F.E. of Canada. In 1953, at the time he was asked to assume the deanship of L.I.F.E. at Los Angeles, Dr. Hall held the office of supervisor of the Northwest District of Foursquare Churches.

Going to Los Angeles was a difficult decision for Dr. Clarence

Hall, who loved the Northwest. But his decision to accept the position at L.I.F.E. was obviously justified inasmuch as he remained in that position for twenty-one years, the longest tenure of any of L.I.F.E.'s deans. During Dr. Hall's long term at the helm of L.I.F.E., he not only maintained a highly competent faculty and a solid Bible curriculum, but he greatly enlarged a very attractive correspondence program.

Upon retirement in 1974, Dr. Hall was invited by Dr. Paul Risser to serve on the staff of the Florence Avenue Foursquare Church in Santa Fe Springs, California, where his memorial service was held at his passing in 2002 at age ninety-six.

In 1974 the office of dean was changed to "executive director," then in 1977 to "president." The changes of title were closely connected to the college's goal of accreditation, which will be explained in a later chapter.

L.I.F.E. Bible College of Canada

The second Foursquare training institute to be established was L.I.F.E. Bible College of Canada. It opened its doors to eagerly awaiting students in June of 1928. The first graduating class of 1930 numbered five aspiring preachers, all of whom entered active pioneering ministry. By 1935 sixty-nine young men and women whom God had called to ministry earned diplomas from the Canadian school.

The first dean of L.I.F.E. of Canada was Rev. Anna D. Britton, pastor of Kingsway Foursquare Church of Vancouver, British Columbia. Rev. Britton also served as supervisor of the churches of Western Canada. Earlier she had pioneered at least four churches in Southern California before taking leadership in 1927 of the Vancouver church and the Western California District. Patterning after the founder of Angelus Temple, she opened a training institute in Vancouver as soon as possible.

The directors of L.I.F.E. of Canada have been: Anna D. Britton, B. A. McKeown, Water Mussen, Clarence Hall, Warren Johnson, Guy Duffield, Charles Baldwin, Harold Wood, John Holland, Art Wolfe, Roy Hicks Sr., Victor Gardner (president of the Foursquare Gospel Church of Canada from 1981–1992), and the current college president, Robert Buzza. All the above were also pastors of the Vancouver Kingsway church with the exception of Roy Hicks Sr. (a former Canadian supervisor), Water Mussen (formerly pastor of the Hastings church), Art Wolfe (former director of Canadian L.I.F.E.), and Robert Buzza. In 1972 Dr. John Holland began the construction of a new Bible college building, which was completed by Rev. Victor Gardner in 1975.

A local institute was operated for a time by the Foursquare Church of North Battlefield, Saskatchewan, pastored by Rev. and Mrs. J. E. Chartier.

Portland Training Institute

In 1930, one year after assuming the pastorate of the Portland, Oregon, Foursquare Church, Dr. and Mrs. Harold W. Jefferies opened a worker's training institute with the view to planting churches in the Northwest area. The school opened with sixty students. To graduate with ministerial credentials, the Portland Institute students were required to take a final semester at L.I.F.E. Bible College in Los Angeles. Some who did not finish at L.I.F.E. became key workers in Portland and surrounding churches. A number who did complete their work in Los Angeles became successful pastors and missionaries. One of them, Dr. Roy Mourer, became supervisor of the Northwest District of Foursquare Churches. The Portland Institute continued in operation for eight years.

Mount Vernon Bible College

Since all the Foursquare institutes mentioned above were located on the Pacific Coast, the eastern districts (Great Lakes, Eastern, and Southeast) in the 1950s began to feel a pressing need for an institute or Bible college east of the Mississippi. Los Angeles seemed to be too far away for many of the aspiring ministerial students to go. Likewise, the eastern states seemed too far away for the L.I.F.E. graduates to go for ministry after spending a minimum of four years in the Far West. As a result, the eastern area supervisors, suffering a scarcity of replacement pastors and pioneer evangelists, began to search for a college campus site in their region.

In the spring of 1957, a four-story building located on a 343-acre site near Mt. Vernon, Ohio, was discovered. The property, which had formerly been a home for the elderly, was purchased for $75,000. Over the years to follow, several hundreds of thousands of dollars were to be invested to develop the large edifice for school requirements. Foursquare people across the nation responded. Eventually, the allotment of a portion of missions offerings toward Bible college development and the selling of all the surplus land (except 167 acres) helped toward retirement of the debt. At first, the farm was intended to supply food for the college and work for some of the students. For the task of equipping the building for operation as a Christian college, the United Foursquare Women across the nation rendered inestimable assistance.

Before the fall semester of 1957, the attractive campus of Mt. Vernon Bible College was ready for occupancy. The enrollment for the first fall class of September 1957 was thirty-three. In later years faculty housing, a Vincent Bird Student Center, and a Kenneth Erickson Memorial Chapel were added to the campus.

The first dean of Mt. Vernon Bible College was Rev. Orlando

Shields. Rev. Shields had been converted under the strong ministry of Rev. Anna D. Britton, pastor of the Vancouver, British Columbia, Kingsway Foursquare Church. He was ordained in 1939 after which he pastored in Western Canada and the state of Washington. In 1947, on the basis of his excellent pastoral ministry, he was invited to the faculty of L.I.F.E. Bible College in Los Angeles where he served for ten years, the last three in the capacity of registrar. After three years as founding dean of Mt. Vernon, Dr. Shields returned in 1960 to the faculty of L.I.F.E. Bible College.

The first faculty of Mt. Vernon Bible College was composed of Dean Orlando Shields, Mrs. O. J. Shields, Vernon Holmes, Nettie Lopp, and William Mouer. Later additions to the faculty were: Opal Mouer, Harold Helms (dean of students), Winona Helms, Stanley Ellis, Marjorie Ellis, Vance Fordyce, A. E. Wolf, Florence Gamble, Elton Orewiler, M. E. Clark, Sylvia Clark, Donald Powers, Margaret Gomez, Benjamin Brackett, Clyde Greisen, Henrietta Holmes, Charles Middlebrook, Barbara Middlebrook, Hal Starr, and others.

In the fall of 1960, Rev. William Mouer was appointed dean of Mt. Vernon Bible College. Following his graduation from L.I.F.E. in 1944, he had been busily engaged in fruitful evangelism. In 1953 he and Mrs. Mouer were appointed pastors of the splendid Amherst (Ohio) Foursquare Church. Of the seven who have served as dean of Mt. Vernon, the Mouers had the longest tenure, from 1960 to 1978. Following Dr. Mouer in that position have been C. Marty Jenkins, Harold Muetzel, Howard Clark, Mark Ballard, and Sterling Brackett.

The general oversight of Mt. Vernon Bible College was assigned to a board of regents, which was comprised of the supervisors of the three districts east of the Mississippi River, three pastors (one from each district), and three laymen (one from each district). Among the first regents were: (supervisors) Vincent Bird, Warren Koon, A. B. Teffeteller, Glenn Burris Sr., M. E. Nicholls, Howard Clark; (pastors) Harold Meyers, Dennis Elder, Kenneth Erickson, Harry Hensen; (laymen) Brie Bradley, Jack Groves, Wallace Helms, and Joe Woodson.

There was great value in the location of a Foursquare Bible college in the eastern area of the nation. By 1970 a large percentage of the pastors of churches in the three eastern districts were graduates of Mt. Vernon Bible College.

Local Church Institutes

A very interesting and unique approach to ministry training was that developed by the "Ministries Institute" founded by the Eugene, Oregon, Faith Center Foursquare Church. Ministries Institute was not, at least at the beginning, a school open to the general public. It was conceived as a ministerial training program for the church's staff, all of whom had as a prerequisite a college degree and an established family life.

The Ministries Institute was initiated in 1973 by Rev. Roy Hicks Jr., whose church was ministering to several thousands. Since the institute was comprised mostly of staff members, the enrollment seldom exceeded thirty-five students. Subjects taught were systematic theology, basic Greek for Bible exegesis, practical theology, etc. Classes were held one evening, three mornings, and all day Saturday once each two months. Graduates from the institute pioneered seven churches in the city of Eugene, seventeen in the state of Oregon, and, in total, sixty congregations. The success of the institute was due to its being a part of the outreach and extension programs of the Northwest District. An institute unrelated to a great church and an organized program could not conceivably expect comparable results.[6]

In the early days of the Pentecostal movement many of its

leaders were reluctant to found ministerial training institutions. The colleges and seminaries had become suspect because of the infiltration of liberals into many of the better known learning institutions. However, when safeguards were discovered, the fear of higher education proved to be unfounded. The menace of biblical education was minor compared with the peril of false doctrine, shallowness, and instability. Today, all the major traditional Pentecostal denominations have accredited Bible colleges, liberal arts colleges, and some even have graduate schools.

The schools themselves are not a threat to Pentecostal orthodoxy or charismatic worship. However, the careful selection of faculty is crucial. There seems to be no scarcity of college- and seminary-trained persons among Pentecostals or vice versa. It cannot be doubted that the phenomenal growth and stability of the International Church of the Foursquare Gospel results from the early establishment of Bible colleges. Aimee Semple McPherson's vision of a training institute as an adjunct of Pentecostal revival clearly came as a result of the Spirit's anointing.

Chapter 4

THE TENDER SHOOTS OF THE VINE

Ministry to Children and Young People

THE FUTURE FRUITFULNESS of a vine depends upon the number and quality of the new shoots that sprout forth. Great care must be given to the tender branches. In the same manner, the future of a church lies in the nurture and training of its children and young people.

From the study of the Scriptures and guidance of the Holy Spirit, Aimee Semple McPherson, founder of the Foursquare Church, appeared to understand this principle. Simultaneous with the Angelus Temple revival, programs were launched for children and the youth.[1] Sunday school, children's church, and a Crusader Youth program became a part of the Temple's agenda from the very beginning.

Before the end of its first year (1923), the Angelus Temple Sunday school had over one thousand in regular attendance. By 1925 that number had doubled. In the January 1925 issue of the *Bridal Call*, Sunday school superintendent R. A. Powell wrote:

> Angelus Temple each Sunday morning is packed and jammed with the hundreds of boys and girls who come to learn the Word of God. During the past year the attendance

> has just doubled. Last January there were about one thousand in attendance each Sunday and today there are about twenty-two hundred (2200) each Sunday. In January there were about 47 classes with 57 teachers and officers, now there are 153...We are not a fair weather Sunday school either. On a Sunday a couple of months ago, when rain was pouring in drenching tourists, the building was filled with Sunday school members singing, "Get God's sunshine into your heart."
>
> Lately there has been a decidedly new innovation in our work. For some time there has been a class for Spanish speaking pupils taught by a retired missionary from Mexico. Also there have been added a class for Armenian children, and one also for Japanese...
>
> There is a teacher's instruction class held every Monday night, where various problems are discussed and counsel is given.[2]

By the end of 1926, the weekly Sunday school attendance had exceeded three thousand students.

But Angelus Temple's Christian education program did not stop with a thriving Sunday school. A highly successful children's church met on Saturdays, with the goal of teaching evangelism and church activity. Under guidance of the adults, the children conducted the entire services. They led the singing, ushered, offered public prayers, and even presented short sermons, including the altar calls. Sometimes the sermons were illustrated. The children organized their own orchestra and provided the musical programs.

Directing the children's church was Miss Estelle Jones. Often she took the children to branch churches where parents and families would attend in large numbers. It was not surprising that most of the branches eventually developed their own children's church ministries. In fact, some of today's Foursquare churches were actually started as a children's church. A good example is the Lankersheim branch, now known as the North Hollywood, California, Foursquare Church.

Some of those who were trained through this program became evangelists and pastors' wives, such as Carol Burnett, wife and co-pastor with her husband, Bill, of the growing Artesia, California, Foursquare Church; Halene Smith/Larrimore, evangelist and co-pastor; and Norma Teeple/Musgrove, evangelist and co-pastor.

Each summer a vacation Bible school was conducted as part of the children's church. Also, the children would visit tent revivals, conducting entire services. Children who had reached an age of accountable understanding, and who gave evidence of a genuine born-again experience, would preach and give an altar call to the other youth in attendance. Children who came to Christ in those meetings would later bring their parents, winning them to Christ. In 1925, Dr. William (Billy) Black reported that in response to those altar calls, ten to fifteen persons accepted Jesus as Savior. He also remarked:

> The children have made several trips to the hospitals carrying flowers and on one or two occasions have sung in the wards. Nearly every one of these boys and girls declare that they are going to be missionaries and evangelists.[3]

Most of the early graduates of the Foursquare Institute, and those who were the founders of the first fifty or so branch churches, had been members of Angelus Temple. The enthusiasm for Sunday school had been deeply imprinted in them. From this same group arose the early leaders of the Foursquare movement, which was incorporated in 1927. It is not at all surprising, therefore, that Christian education became an unmistakable Foursquare emphasis. One of the officers appointed by the pastor in every local Foursquare church was the Sunday school superintendent. At early conventions a typical greeting among pastors was, "What are you running in Sunday school?"

Creation of National Department of Youth and Christian Education

Because such enthusiasm was shared by almost every Foursquare pastor, it did not occur to the denomination's leadership to create a special department for the promotion of direction of Sunday school. In 1936 Rev. Harold Chalfant was appointed director of Foursquare Crusader Youth with the responsibility of organizing the youth nationwide, especially through summer camping programs. It was also felt that his office could oversee the development of Sunday schools.

However, by 1940, when the number of Foursquare churches had increased to more than 350 congregations in thirty-two states and four provinces in Canada, it became obvious that a central Sunday school office was needed to achieve uniformity of literature and guidance in enlightened methodology. A search for a willing, knowledgeable director began.

Prior to his graduation from the Foursquare Institute in December 1925, Bert Bruffet had been a member of the student group that had pioneered the Pasadena, California, Foursquare Church. He married another member of the group, Bessie Randall, who was a very capable evangelist. Following ordination and several years of evangelism, the Bruffets pioneered a thriving church in Dayton, Ohio; Bessie was the evangelist and soul winner, with Bert being the teacher, manager, and organizer. Bert's organizational skills were brought to the attention of the Foursquare leadership. And in 1942 he was chosen as the first national director of Foursquare Sunday schools, a position he held until 1946.

Rev. Bruffet's annual reports show visits to district conventions and Sunday school conferences, and ministry in at least one hundred local churches per year. His office also was responsible for the distribution of quarterlies and Sunday school manuals, as well as the promotion of an increasing Sunday school tithe. He laid a solid foundation for district Sunday school leaders.

By 1947 building strong Sunday schools became the concern of all evangelical churches across the nation. Most Bible colleges and seminaries offered courses for ministers and directors of Christian education. Larger Foursquare churches began to employ Christian education directors. In response, the ICFG board of directors authorized Rev. Harold Chalfant, who had been given the official title of International Director of Youth and Christian Education, to secure an assistant especially trained in Christian education.

Rev. Isabelle Hall was selected to fill that important office in the spring of 1947. She had graduated from Northwestern College and Seminary of Minneapolis with a major in Christian education. She had also graduated in 1928 from L.I.F.E. Bible College. Together with her husband, Malcolm, Isabelle had successfully pastored and pioneered throughout the Midwest sector of our nation, as well as created and supervised the newly established Atlantic Seaboard District. Malcolm passed away in 1950.

Isabelle Hall served with great distinction as the national director of Christian education from 1947 to 1963. Her achievements were outstanding. In the 1951 Convention yearbook, Dr. Chalfant pays Isabelle the following tribute:

> Without the inspiration and untiring efforts of Mrs. Isabelle Hall, our fine assistant and international secretary, the growth of the department could never have been what it is today. She has given months of her time on the

> field in the interest of Sunday schools and never counts the hours she spends in devotion to her work. There has been a tremendous increase in our Sunday School department since she has been assisting in this capacity. Her talents are many and varied as an inspirational leader, speaker and organizer.[4]

Rev. Hall was able to obtain from Dr. Cyrus Nelson, president of Gospel Light Publications, the finest Sunday school quarterlies available, modified for use by Foursquare churches and designed with Foursquare covers. In addition, she solicited faculty members from L.I.F.E. Bible College, such as Guy P. Duffield, Nathaniel M. Van Cleave, and Luther Meier, to write adult quarterlies, expounding on the denomination's *Declaration of Faith*. There were many editions of these lessons, and they are still available in more updated form.

Under Isabelle's direction the department created curriculum guides, vacation Bible school manuals, and many other helps. Between 1948 and 1952 distribution of the above-described materials increased 400 percent. In 1948 the materials were used in 265 churches; in 1952, by 490 churches. In 1952 the department distributed 176,903 copies of quarterlies, manuals, and helps.[5]

Rev. Hall's influence extended beyond her own denomination when she was appointed to the board of the National Sunday School Association. Through that channel she led the Foursquare Christian Education Department into involvement with the National Sunday School Association (NSSA). As a result of her involvement in NSSA, together with Dr. Nelson she was one of the founders of the Greater Los Angeles Sunday School Association (GLASS), and for several years the GLASS convention was conducted at Angelus Temple. Rev. Hall influenced L.I.F.E. Bible College to accept the materials and standards of the Evangelical Teacher's Training Association (ETTA), which in turn allowed certification to those students graduating from the college.

In 1954 Isabelle married Theodore Helmle, a businessman from Alhambra, California, who was a great encouragement to her. Nine years later, in 1963, she resigned yet continued to give laudable assistance to the L.I.F.E Bible College library and to the L.I.F.E. Bible College Alumni Association.[6]

Because of serious ill health, Dr. Harold Chalfant resigned from leadership of the Youth and Christian Education Department in 1959. He was succeeded by Dr. Vincent Bird, who for ten years had been the supervisor of the Great Lakes District. Dr. Bird's strongest burden had been for development of Christian education, as could be seen in the fact that from his district had come two of the nation's leading Sunday schools, namely Moline, Illinois, and Decatur, Illinois. This emphasis differed somewhat from that of Dr. Chalfant, whose principal interest had been in youth camping and in world missions.

When Dr. Vincent Bird assumed the Department of Youth and Christian Education, he appointed Jack Hayford to replace Lester Vollmer, who had served as National Youth Director. He named Robert Inglis to the position of National Cadet Director and Edith Campbell, who had previously served under Mrs. Helmle, to the office of National Defender Director. Other very important offices in the department were held by Eloise Clarno, Mary Lou Canata, Kathy Brachman, and Dora Glenn.

Jack Hayford had served for five years as a successful pastor in Ft. Wayne, Indiana; Edith Campbell, after a period of pastoral work, had served together with Miss Ena Fanson for two extended periods of time as assistant to Dr. Harold Jefferies of the Portland, Oregon, Foursquare Church. At that time the

Portland church claimed the organization's largest church and Sunday school. Eloise Clarno had held the office of Director of Youth and Christian Education in the Northwest District from 1959 to 1963. Mary Lou Canata had been employed in the international headquarters offices during her student days, and after graduation from L.I.F.E., Mary Lou, with her famous puppet "Tommie," had toured through several districts as a children's evangelist. Altogether, during Dr. Bird's tenure of eighteen years, a strong Christian education emphasis was maintained.

Vincent Bird was born in Elmwood, Nebraska, in March 1912 to George and Maude Bird. Under the influence of Pastor Paul Royer, Vincent accepted Christ as Savior and became a mature worker. It was in Sterling, Colorado, that he met his wife, Connie, when she became employed in a business in which Vincent was co-owner. In fact, they had their first date on the first day of her employment.

From his earliest involvement in church life, Vincent had felt impelled toward Christian service. After being filled with the Holy Spirit, he served as Crusader president, a member of the church council, and as church treasurer. And it was not long after their marriage that Vincent and Connie enrolled in L.I.F.E. Bible College. It is an interesting fact that a larger number of historic Foursquare leaders have come out of the Foursquare congregation in Sterling, Colorado, than from any other source outside of California.

Vincent and Connie Bird graduated from L.I.F.E. Bible College in January 1937. Immediately they accepted the pastorate of the Foursquare church in Burlington, Kansas. Later, having proved their ability, the Birds were assigned the challenging task of restoring a divided church in Parsons, Kansas, where they remained until 1944. Their excellent accomplishment in Parsons obtained for them the opportunity in 1944 to pastor the strong church in Topeka, Kansas, where Vincent also served as the state superintendent.

After twelve years of pastor experience and seven years of executive leadership, the Birds were invited to become the supervisors of the expansive Great Lakes District. The district encompassed the states of Iowa, Minnesota, Wisconsin, Illinois, Michigan, and Indiana. The youth and Christian education programs in the district were extremely aggressive and fruitful. Therefore, Dr. Bird's appointment to the office of International Director of Youth and Christian Education, in which he was also a member of the denomination's board of directors, was most appropriate.

Altogether, Dr. Bird directed the office for eighteen years, 1959–1977. Following his retirement in 1977, Dr. Bird joined the ministerial staff of the First Foursquare Church of Van Nuys, California, as staff pastor with Dr. Jack Hayford.[7] His position was filled by Rev. John Bowers.

Ordained in 1956, John and Betty Bowers pastored in Hanover, Pennsylvania; Harrisburg, Pennsylvania; and Mansfield, Ohio. While serving in Mansfield, John also served as district secretary and divisional superintendent (1960–1962). In 1962 he joined the staff of the Eastern District as full-time field secretary. In 1965 he was invited to take a position in the headquarters office in Los Angeles, during which time he also pastored the Alhambra, California, Foursquare Church.

Rev. Bowers was promoted in 1971 to the position of director of the adult division of Christian education. Upon Vincent Bird's retirement in 1977, he was chosen as National Director of Youth and Christian Education. As an untiring worker, and in spite of a serious health problem in the early 1980s, John overcame through faith and prayer to serve as assistant to the general supervisor with a seat on the international board of directors and later as corporate secretary.[8]

Since 1981, national Christian education directors have included Tim Peterson, John Whitman, and Rick Wulfestieg. The short tenures of Christian education directors of the 1980s have prompted some to ask whether or not the movement is de-emphasizing the role of Sunday school and other areas of Christian education. There are still some great Foursquare Sunday schools, and many hope that the appearances of de-emphasis are deceiving.

The Foursquare Crusader Covenant

Another Foursquare emphasis that stems back to the very beginnings of the movement is the accent on young people. As organized by the founder, ministry to youth in the International Church of the Foursquare Gospel was originally called "Foursquare Crusaders." At Angelus Temple an average of one thousand Crusaders would meet on Friday evenings to worship, witness, and exhort one another to dedication and service. They readily signed a "Crusader Covenant" in which they pledged themselves to a high standard of Christian living.

The central role that the Crusader Covenant played in the life Foursquare youth is summed up in an article by Dr. Clarence Hall, an early Crusader president:

> Not many people realize that in this modern day there is an organization of young people banded together for the cause of Christ, who have signed the pledge and covenant found on this page. Not many realize that there are young people who believe in "holiness" and live it as best they can. "The Crusaders for Christ" have signed this pledge and from day to day live accordingly.[9]

The Crusader Covenant to which Dr. Hall refers is quoted in part:

> Rejoicing that we have entered into Salvation through repentance and faith in the precious atoning blood of our Lord and Savior Jesus Christ; and seeing that Satan and his hosts are encamping 'round about us on every hand, and that he is constantly making his camps more attractive, inventing new weapons and increasing his methods of attack, so that daily, scores, yes, hundreds of our young people are allured and enticed into his snares, wounded by his deadly weapons, then bound body, soul and spirit, and cast into the pits of sin, and knowing that the "wages of sin is death" and that "Jesus Christ came into the world to save sinners."
>
> We now band ourselves together as Foursquare Crusaders...and going forth as He directs us, we will preach the Foursquare Gospel of Jesus the Savior, Jesus the Baptizer with the Holy Ghost, Jesus the Great Physician, and Jesus the coming King, our battle cry shall ever be "Onward Christian Soldiers."
>
> Furthermore, unless sent there as a messenger for our King, we will not at any time be found in the camp of the enemy, and knowing that Satan's weapons are a hindrance in the battle for righteousness, we will by God's grace, ever keep ourselves free from tobacco, from swearing, from giddy talk and idle gossip, from immodest dress, from vulgar stories, from backbiting and criticism, and from all forms or worldliness.
>
> Our most mighty weapon shall be a sharp, two-edged sword, the Bible which is the Word of the living God, with two other weapons, prayer and praise, and our shield of faith in Jesus Christ, we will go forth under the blood stained banner of the Cross to win other souls into the Kingdom of our Lord.[10]

In the passing of time there were many criticisms of the old covenant, many calling it "legalistic," and others declaring it outmoded. Coming to the defense of the covenant, others pointed out that nothing in it was contrary to Bible teaching. Whatever the consensus, it was finally abandoned by corporate vote, with a new covenant compiled in more modern terminology, which a majority felt set an equally high biblical standard.

To understand the covenant and the Foursquare Crusader movement, one must review its original vision under the commentary of a man who has taught and guided as many young people as any person in the International Church of the Foursquare Gospel. The first Angelus Temple president of Foursquare Crusaders was John Gleason. He was also the first to bear the title as national president. He was followed as the Temple president by Bert Teaford, Hubert Mitchell, Clarence Hall, and then "Mr. Foursquare Youth," Harold Chalfant.

When he graduated from L.I.F.E. Bible College in 1936, Harold was appointed by Mrs. McPherson as International Director of Youth, a position that he held until 1960. Also, in 1937 Harold Chalfant was given the additional charge of Missionary Field Director, in which endeavor he glamorized Foursquare missions for young and old alike.

Foursquare Crusader Camps

Harold's first unforgettable achievement, however, was the organization of Crusader camps. No one who attended camps in that era will forget the programs of Camp Radford and Cedar Crest, with Harold's sermons on "Science and the Bible," nor the skits by Harold and Ulphin Davis, "Cherry" Cheroski and Tom Matthews. Equally memorable were the "victory circles" around the campfire, where hundreds of youth cast pine cones into the flames, symbolic of their dedication and of their surrender to God's will. Many of these young people later became missionaries, pastors, and denominational leaders.

So successful were the Radford camps that similar programs were started in all the districts, remaining even to the present time. The summer Crusader camps not only became a Foursquare establishment, but also the building of Camp Cedar Crest in Southern California inspired other districts to purchase camping properties. There is "Crestview" in the Northwest; "Old Oak Ranch" in the Western District; "Pomme de Terre" and "Wondervu" in the Midwest; "Courtney" in the Southeast; "McPherson" in the Eastern District; and "Whispering Oaks" in the South Central District of the United States.

Harold Chalfant's dynamic leadership style was so vivid, a number of young men and women aspired to become youth leaders. Soon many were available to head Crusader units and camps. Listen to a list of some of these: Roy and Gladys Bell, Ulphin and Emma Davis, Art and Joy Larson, Lester and Hope Vollmer, Jack and Cappy Gwillim, Maurice and Cecilia Evans, Norman and Annie Smith, Everett and Ruth Dennison, Harold and Mary Williams, Roy and Marianne McKeown, Earle and Eileen Williams, Victor and Dorothy Gardner, Jerry and Helen Jensen, Billy Opie, Max and Carolyn Siesser, Charles Duarte, Victor and Mary Samples, Ron and Joyce Mehl, Curtis and Maxine Correll, Earl and Ruth O'Connell, Jim and Mary Lou Ritch, Orville Broker, Paul Talbot, Roy Lane, Evelyn Wilson/McGowan, Helen Mitchell, Ben Larson, Jack and Lavonna Hopkins, Eloise Clarno, Roy Hicks Jr., and the list continues today.

In the beginning the district youth and Christian education directors were supported in the denomination's budget. Therefore, these men and women were able to devote full time to the respective district's Crusader and Sunday school ministry. But at the 1954 International Convention in Moline, Illinois, their positions were terminated. Many reasons were given for the decision.

Some conjectured that the exposure these youth and Christian education directors sustained to the local churches posed a threat to the district supervisor in the sense of divided authority. Still others felt that a few individuals had overextended their tenure as youth directors. Budget problems were also blamed for the termination.

Looking back, one must question whether it was a wise decision. Wouldn't a better solution have been to correct the difficulties rather than terminate the ministries? Almost immediately some of the districts suffered a de-emphasis on youth and Christian education. Most of the districts were able to find leaders for these areas of ministry through giving district support or using part-time workers. Whether or not the 1954 decision was wise, the camps continued to grow in popularity, even to the extent of taxing the facilities.

Later new leadership, inspired by the memory of Harold Chalfant, brought new enthusiasm to Foursquare youth. At the international level, successors to Harold Chalfant have been Vincent Bird and John Bowers. On a national level, leaders have included Lester Vollmer, Jack Hayford, Paul G. Jones, Jim Hayford, Dan Ussery, Ed and Ivy Stanton, Tim Peterson, and John Whitman.

National Youth Director Gregg Johnson was backed by a representative Youth Council. His position was created by a vote of the convention body, and his ministry was devoted entirely to the national youth. Gregg brought a renewed enthusiasm to the program that has been strengthened by new, energetic plans for the future. These developments are shared in the concluding chapter of this history.

Foursquare Christian Day Schools

An important phase of Christian education is the Christian day school. In the United States, the first Foursquare Christian day schools were those located as Escondido, California (founded by Rev. and Mrs. Arthur Thompson), Harbor City, California (founded by Rev. Marion Plies), and Bellflower, California (founded by Rev. Pete Nyenhuis). There are many fine preschools and primary and secondary Christian day schools throughout the movement, including Florence Avenue, Azusa, La Puente, Hesperia, San Diego, Prairie Avenue, Santa Barbara, Santa Maria, Lemon Grove, Simi Valley, and Crescent City in California; Las Vegas and Boulder City in Nevada; Grand Junction and Durango, Colorado; Dallas and Lubbock, Texas; New Castle, Indiana; Salina, Kansas; Roanoke, Virginia; Augusta, Georgia; and Anniston, Alabama. A complete list may be found in the annual reports of the denomination.

Leaders in the burgeoning day school ministry have been Evelyn Thompson, Harold Wood, John Holmes, Paul Risser, Elmer Nelson, Fred Dawson, Marjorie Kitchell, Jack Hicks, George Johnson, Charles Hollis, Ken Wright, Ken Bland, etc. Some pastors and church leaders are strong advocates of church-related elementary school programs; others oppose the parochial school philosophy. Some efforts at day school ministry succeed; others fail. What makes the difference?

Some experienced and knowledgeable leaders in parochial school work advance the idea that schools fail generally because they are launched with the wrong motivation. It is advised that a pastor not launch a Christian elementary school unless there are qualified laypeople who are able to carry out the day-to-day operation. A neglected church cannot provide the necessary backing for a successful school.

A school should not be operated out of desire for financial gain. And simply because many public school conditions have a bad influence on children, purportedly teaching atheism, evolution, or secular humanism, should a church day school program be instituted? A school should be started only if the sponsoring church is able to give the pupils a good, all-around education, as well as solid Bible teaching.

Some criticize the Christian day school, contending it insulates pupils from the real world that they must eventually face in life. On the other hand, many parents are high in the praise of the Christian school, avowing that their children are well ahead scholastically of the neighbor's public school children, free from violence and temptation to drug or substance abuse and able to study and learn in a healthier environment.

There is no doubt that a well-equipped Christian day school with trained Christian teachers and directors, operating with a sound philosophy of Christian education, can be a great asset to any community. Such schools fill a great need in our modern society. On the contrary, if the Christian school teachers are only poorly equipped "babysitters" for parents who can't or won't provide Christian leadership in the home, the schools' value is doubtful.[11]

Foursquare churches wishing to explore the possibility of Christian schools should first consult with the national church office of the denomination, which has helpful guidance material on the subject. Another important source of guidance is the Association of Christian Schools International, P. O. Box 4097, Whittier, CA 90607.

Chapter 5

THE VINE GROWS

The Branches Cover the Nation

A WELL-WATERED VINE WITH deep roots in good soil will eventually cover the land. The International Church of the Foursquare Gospel was a very good ecclesiastical vine, planted deep in the excellent soil of Holy Spirit revival. It became a vine that expanded across deserts, mountains, plains, and basins of America, preparing itself to reach across national boundaries to the outstretched hands of awaiting lands.

The psalmist had said about the children of Israel:

> You have brought a vine out of Egypt; You have cast out the nations, and planted it. You prepared room for it, and caused it to take deep root, and it filled the land. The hills were covered with its shadow, and the mighty cedars with its boughs. She sent out her boughs to the Sea, and her branches to the River.[1]

Like the growth described by the psalmist, the growth of the Foursquare Gospel was to be expected. The vine was vital and the garden was waiting.

During the very first summer after the founding of Angelus Temple in 1923, eight branch churches were put forth. By the end of the second summer the number of branches was thirty-two. All but a very few of these were in Southern California. However, by the time the vine and the branches were incorporated as a denomination in 1927, there were 128 branches located in twenty-five states of the nation.

The name that was adopted at the time of incorporation was "International Foursquare Gospel Lighthouse." Three years later, in 1930, the name was changed to "International Church of the Foursquare Gospel" (ICFG). (It is interesting that the "L" in the name of L.I.F.E. Bible College, standing for "Lighthouse," did not change.)

In 1930 the number of Foursquare churches had become 216, with 109 in California and 107 in other states. But in 1933, only five years following incorporation, the International Church of the Foursquare Gospel had grown to 278 branches, with 112 congregations in California and 166 in the rest of the nation. The Foursquare Church was no longer a predominantly "California Church." Not only had the vine spanned the nation, but it had already grown over the garden fence to many other nations. But that is a story told in our next chapter.

Factors of Growth

What were the factors in the vine's rapid and consistent growth?

Beyond question, the initial growth resulted from the Bible institute (college). During the first three years after the founding of Angelus Temple, the branches were started from student groups who evangelized with the famous "brown tents." An unquenchable thirst for soul winning had been inspired by the Word of God through the anointed lips of Aimee Semple McPherson and a Spirit-filled faculty. The first thirty branches of our denomination had been started by students, many of whom had not yet earned a diploma.

The influence of the media was another factor. Thousands of subscribers to the *Bridal Call* were reading monthly about the revival at Angelus Temple. They were also being informed about the Foursquare Evangelistic and Missionary Training Institute. If students were being trained to preach the Foursquare Gospel, why not invite them to preach it in each subscriber's community?

With the commencement of radio station KFSG in 1924, the air waves were filled with the message of Jesus: Savior, Baptizer, Healer, and Soon-Returning King. There remained no Southern California community unaware of the nearby revival that was spawning students trained to preach that message wherever there was an open door. Invitations poured in; students poured out![2]

Touching the wider range was the nationwide evangelistic ministry of the founder, Aimee Semple McPherson. Long after the planting of the Foursquare vine and the organization of its branches, Mrs. McPherson continued to make evangelistic tours to the nation's largest cities. Between June and October of 1928, city-wide campaigns were held in Oregon, Washington, Idaho, and Montana, including a Northwest convention in Portland, Oregon, where a new branch was established.[3] These revivals were followed with a campaign in New York City and a historic meeting in London, England, in the famous Royal Albert Hall.

In 1929 an evangelistic tour by Mrs. McPherson concentrated on Detroit, Michigan. This resulted in the planting of fifteen new Foursquare churches.[4] In like manner, cross-country campaigns in 1932, 1933, and 1934 enlarged the number of Foursquare branches and prepared the fallow ground for follow-up pioneer efforts by Foursquare evangelists and newly graduated students who eagerly followed God's call.[5]

There is no question that the Foursquare Gospel message itself was a significant factor in the church's growth. The nation was ready for return to apostolic power and practice, as set forth in the Book of Acts. The Foursquare Gospel focused on the fourfold emphasis of Jesus' redeeming ministry, proclaiming "Jesus Christ, the Savior, Baptizer in the Holy Spirit, Healer, and the Soon-Coming King." It was a message that met the needs of every person, wherever they lived.

The Term "Foursquare"

The term "Foursquare" was given by inspiration to Aimee Semple McPherson during her evangelistic campaign in Oakland, California, in 1922. It was not a new concept, for before the turn of the century, A. B. Simpson and others had described the same fourfold ministry of Jesus, except that for them the third aspect, "Baptizer with the Holy Spirit," referred to Jesus as the Sanctifier. Many teachers before the 1900 Pentecostal outpouring in Topeka, Kansas, and Azusa Street in Los Angeles were using the term "Sanctifier" as a synonym for "Baptizer with the Holy Spirit," assuming that empowerment was an attribute of holiness.

Mrs. McPherson used the terms "Foursquare" and "Baptizer" instead of "Fourfold" and "Sanctifier" for two reasons. First, the term "Foursquare" was more biblical (Ezek. 40:47; Rev. 21:16; KJV, RSV, NRSV), while "Fourfold" (to describe a structure) was not. Furthermore, she believed it to have been given here by the Spirit's anointing to describe the Full Gospel.

According to Foursquare doctrine, sanctification is imparted with regeneration initially, and in three ways progressively. The process of sanctification is brought about through (1) the indwelling of the Spirit, (2) the devotional reading of the Word, and (3) the cleansing blood of Christ.[6] The use of the name

"Baptizer with the Holy Spirit" does not imply an oversight of sanctification, but focuses on the need of empowerment for service. It implies that sanctification is a "work" of both regeneration and the Spirit's continuous indwelling. The balanced presentation of the Pentecostal message accompanied by the Spirit's power found responsive ears.

The Foursquare Gospel, however, is not a four-note melody. Rather, it is a four-point, Christ-centered emphasis with a many-faceted doctrine. It shares with the entire classical Pentecostal movement the truth of the baptism with the Holy Spirit with the initial evidence of speaking with tongues and in bodily healing in the atonement. Furthermore, it shares with all Bible-believing churches the full range of biblical and fundamental, evangelical truth:

> The Foursquare Church believes:
>
> 1. In the verbal inspiration of the original Scriptures.
> 2. In the absolute trinity of the eternal God-head.
> 3. In the deity of our Lord Jesus Christ.
> 4. In the personality and deity of the Holy Spirit.
> 5. In the reality and personality of the devil.
> 6. In the natural depravity of the human race.
> 7. In the substitutionary atonement.
> 8. In the propitiation for sin only by the blood of Christ.
> 9. In the full salvation by grace through faith and not of works.
> 10. In Divine Healing through the atonement.
> 11. In the anointing with oil and prayer for the sick.
> 12. In the personal Baptism with the Holy Ghost as received by the apostles.

13. In the necessity of the new birth.
14. In water baptism by immersion at an age of accountability.
15. In the one and only true church composed of all blood-washed believers.
16. In the evangelization of the heathen and all the nations of the world.
17. In a middle-of-the-road policy in public worship, between extreme fanaticism and ultra-ritualism.
18. In obedience to civil government.
19. In divorce only on New Testament scriptural grounds.
20. In church government, loyalty and obedience to those in authority over us in the Lord.
21. In tithing as God's financial plan.
22. In restitution for past wrongs whenever possible.
23. In the open table at the Lord's supper.
24. In the free moral will power of man, who can backslide, apostatize, and be lost.
25. In the maintenance of good works and holy living.
26. In the victorious life over sin, self, and bad habits, by Bible study and incessant prayer life.
27. In Christian perfection and holiness, through absolute surrender and consecration. [Christian perfection here does not imply moral infallibility, but should be interpreted in light of section VIII of the "Foursquare Declaration of Faith" on "Daily Christian Life".]
28. In Christian modesty in the matter of dress, wearing apparel, and jewelry.
29. In keeping the Lord's day as a matter of privilege, rather than law.

30. As regards recreation—liberty of conscience and a Godly example to the world.
31. In the immortality and conscious existence of the soul.
32. In the resurrection of our literal bodies, the just and the unjust.
33. In a literal heaven and life everlasting for all true believers.
34. In a final day of judgment for the incorrigibly wicked.
35. In the everlasting punishment of the impenitent.
36. In the personal, literal, bodily, pre-millennial coming of Jesus Christ.
37. In a future, literal, on thousand years reign of Christ on earth with all His saints.
38. In the judgment seat of Christ where the saints will be finally rewarded for their deeds of commission and omission.
39. In Christian tolerance toward all denominations of the Christian faith.
40. "In essentials—unity, in non-essentials—liberty, in all things—charity."[7]

The constant growth of the vine and the multiplication of the branches were not hindered by the Great Depression that began with the stock market crash in 1929, in 1927 in California.

In those years the average pastor received a salary that ranged from a "love offering" to $150 per month. Thousands of hungry people stood in long bread lines for hours. The farmers' crops of wheat, corn, or oats were not worth enough to bother reaping. Innumerable businesses went bankrupt. Yet The Foursquare Church and many other Bible churches marched on. Clearly the Lord through His Spirit implemented the enlargement of His kingdom. Through His enablement, Foursquare churches not only survived, but they also maintained commissaries to help the poor and hungry, following the example of Angelus Temple.

Formation of Districts

At first, the center of growth activity had been Angelus Temple and the founder's evangelistic campaigns. With the creation of districts and the appointment of district supervisors who were supported by headquarters' funds, the number of centers became five instead of one. The pattern for growth also changed.

Each district developed a strategy of growth. The supervisors charted their areas, selecting certain population centers for pioneering activity. The selections were based on requests from residents, surveys, or upon the direct leading of the Holy Spirit. Then, at each annual "international convention," the supervisors would invite a number of the latest graduates from L.I.F.E. Bible College to evangelize in their districts. Sometimes the evangelists would act upon their own leading and burden for a specific area, perhaps their family home community. The motivational influences for church growth manifestly multiplied.

Techniques for church planting were several. Some districts owned a tent in which meetings might be held. Auditoriums, women's club houses, lodge halls (after cigar smoke and stain and odor were washed from the walls and ceilings), empty store buildings, mortuary chapels (the spiritually dead were brought to life), armories (which witnessed a new warfare!), school buildings (where Bible lessons were taught!), large homes, and even the open air sites such as street corners, parks, and bandstands were used as available.

Means of publicity might have been the newspapers, distribution of handbills, radio spot announcements, door-to-door visitation, large signs and street meetings. In later years, when there were families sympathetic to the gospel residing in the locality, home Bible studies would be launched.

More recently, the activity known as "church planting" has been used—larger established congregations taking on the responsibility of birthing another church in a nearby city, or even across town. At times these "mother churches" would encourage a portion of their members to transfer to the new church. Many fine churches have been planted by the "mothering plan"; however, the method has not received the attention of application it deserves. When special guidance or encouragement is needed, there is a supervisor, a divisional superintendent, or a fellow pastor who has oversight of a portion of a district, not far away.

Who were some of the early "pioneers" of Foursquare churches? Who were some of the pioneer preachers who left the Golden State of California with its flowers and oranges to start churches "from scratch" beyond the desert and the mountains?

One was an entire family—the Corrells.[8] The family consisted of Sidney and Helen, R. H., Stella and Maxine, and Caroll and Inez. In 1927, after a brief pastoral experience, the family returned to Colorado, their original home state. There they opened churches in the communities of Sterling, Trinidad, Lamar, and Cortez. When permanent pastors were secured, the Corrells continued opening churches farther east: Fairfield, Iowa; Kewanee and Decatur, Illinois; and Kenosha, Wisconsin.

In Kenosha, Sidney and Helen Correll found a home. They built a strong church in that city, became superintendents of the states of Wisconsin and Illinois, and eventually were appointed as supervisors of the Great Lakes District.

Another was Rev. Anna Britton, a close friend and coworker with Aimee Semple McPherson, who had been responsible for starting a number of branch churches in Southern California.

For several summers she had directed student groups that conducted tent revivals. Some of those churches include Santa Ana, Long Beach, Pasadena, and Santa Monica.

In 1927 Rev. Britton moved to Vancouver, British Columbia, in Canada where she built a small group of believers into a congregation of nearly 1,000. She opened a Bible institute that later became L.I.F.E. Bible College of Canada. Her vision prompted her to extend the Foursquare Gospel to the three western provinces of Canada, over which she served as supervisor for many years.

Yet another early pioneer family extending the Foursquare message beyond California was Rev. and Mrs. Harold Myers. When they retired, they held the record for the longest pastorate—a tenure of more than thirty years in Gettysburg, Pennsylvania. Yet before pioneering that strong church, they had pioneered several churches throughout the Eastern District.

An irrepressible church planter was Rev. Floyd Dawson (lovingly called "Pop" Dawson). He started a church in Lubbock, Texas, which he built into one of the strongest in that region of the country. He was not content, however, until he had raised up four other churches in the Lubbock area. His was one of the most stimulating examples of the "mothering" system.

Rev. Watson B. Teaford, who later became dean of L.I.F.E. Bible College and pastor of Angelus Temple, left immediately after graduation from Bible college to pioneer churches in Kansas, Missouri, and Iowa, including Parsons, Kansas; Pittsburg, Kansas; and Muscatine, Iowa.

Several of the district supervisors themselves pioneered solid branch churches. Among these were Vincent Bird, Frank Cummings, Fred Beard, Harold Jefferies, and Earl Dorrance.

Among the most successful pioneer church planters were several capable women preachers. Rev. Mrs. A. A. Carpenter opened new works in Roanoke, Virginia; Rockford, Illinois; and another in Iowa. Rev. Isabella Hall started churches in Urbana, Illinois; one in Iowa and two in Minneapolis, Minnesota. Rev. Hall later became the architect of the denomination's Christian education program.

Other women pioneers included Hazel Granvol, later a missionary to Panama. Evelyn Taylor pioneered Cape Girardeau and St. Joseph, Missouri, later becoming state superintendent. Rev. Louise Webster planted a church in Phoenix, Arizona, out of which were started several others. For many years Rev. Webster was state superintendent of Arizona.

Noteworthy pioneers in the eastern sector of our nation were: Eugene Kurtz, later a general supervisor, Floyd Brock, Paul Krebs, and David Holland, effective in the New England area. Among church planters in Canada must be mentioned James and Evelyn Chartier in North Battleford, Saskatchewan; Ruby Moore in Calgary, Alberta; and Ruth Baker and Mary Young.

Cross-Cultural Ministry

God had given a world vision to Aimee Semple McPherson. She possessed no racial prejudice, nor in any of the entities of the Foursquare movement was there discrimination on the basis of color, race, or national origin. Thus, when the term *ethnic* is used, it is only to distinguish services that are conducted in a non-English language. Services in the United States that are conducted in a foreign language and shaped to suit a national culture are in a separate but certainly not inferior category. They are grouped as "cross-cultural" because special knowledge of their culture is necessary on the part of those who minister to them.

Cross-cultural ministry has been an important part of ICFG's growth. Any California-based church is obviously now located in an area with a large Hispanic population. The same is true for churches located in the Sun Belt and in the larger U.S. cities.

Aimee Semple McPherson was a friend of the great Mexican evangelist Rev. Olazabel. Very early in our history a Hispanic church was sponsored in East Los Angeles, California, pioneered by Antonio Gamboa. For decades the church sent many students to L.I.F.E. Bible College. This church, Pleasant Avenue, known today as "Inglesia del Buen Pastor" (Good Shepherd) regrettably is not part of the Foursquare Church. No one seems to recall why it became separated, but the ICFG has by no means diminished its interest in the Hispanic community nor its friendship toward that congregation.

In the Southern California area there are approximately seventy-five Hispanic congregations. Some of the early Spanish-speaking Foursquare pastors were Patricio Lopez (Canoga Park, California), Richard Ramirez (San Gabriel, California), Angelo Arbizu, Robert Aguirre, Jose Alba, Helen Mata (East Los Angeles, California), Ricardo Grijalva, Pete Zuniga (San Gabriel, California), Robert Espinosa (San Fernando, California), Julia Hoskins (Los Nietos, California), Helen Gorospe, Pauline Martinez (Pasadena and El Cajon, California), and L. Aubuchon (West Los Angeles, California).

When the area around Angelus Temple began to have a growing Hispanic population, the "mother church" initiated Spanish language services in Angelus Auditorium, which seats approximately twelve hundred people. From the start the work grew, but under the pastoral ministry of Raymundo Diaz from Monterrey, Mexico, the central Spanish church has grown to twelve hundred on Sunday mornings and large crowds at evening services.

In 1992 there were more than six Hispanic Foursquare churches in the Southern California District, with Dr. Enrique

Zone and Rev. Luis Ramos serving as Hispanic superintendents. There were twenty Hispanic congregations in the Southwest District.

A strong and fruitful minister among Hispanic churches in Colorado was Carry McCormack, who maintained a Bible institute for Spanish workers for many years. The Midwest District now counts many churches whose services are conducted in Spanish, with several Hispanic churches in the South Central District. Emigration from Mexico, Central America, and South America will make it expedient for the Foursquare Church to place greater emphasis on that outreach.

Preparation for Hispanic and other cross-cultural evangelism has made excellent strides in Southern California with two strong Bible institutes, Facultad de Teologia—located in Montebello, California, and directed by Enrique Zone; and Angelus Bible Institute—conducted in Angelus Temple and directed by Dr. Harold Helms and Rev. Raymundo Diaz. Both institutes have graduated men and women into successful ministry.

The growing Oriental communities in Southern California have been touched by expanding Foursquare ministry. Foursquare Korean churches are located in Harbor City, California (pastored by Dr. Daniel Park), Los Angeles, California (Pastor Kwon Sunwoo), San Gabriel, California (Pastor James Hwan Yi), Lynwood, California (Rev. Paul Kee Kang), Arleta, California (Rev. and Mrs. Jae-Duc Ko), Van Nuys, California (Pastor Gie Tae Hwang), and Angelus Temple (Rev. Jacob Oh). There are two Taiwanese Foursquare churches: one in Los Angeles, California, pastored by Rev. and Mrs. Ken Hong, and another in Torrance, California. Filipino churches include Los Angeles, California, pastored by Rev. and Mrs. Veronico Suan, and the Highland Park Foursquare facility, pastored by Rev.

Michael S. Alonzo. The Pasadena Asian Foursquare Church is pastored by Rev. David Ephraim.

A Bulgarian church congregation meets in Angelus Temple. An Iranian church meets in the facility of "The Church On The Way" in Van Nuys, California, and a Russian congregation has recently been established in the state of Oregon. In this arena of cross-cultural ministry, special honor should be attributed to James Roper, Arizona Hawes, Vernon Mericle, Ray Wilson, and other faithful pastors/evangelists who have given years of ministry to the North American Indians.

Most of the people who attend the above-mentioned churches do so because they are first-generation immigrants to the United States. People who understand English or prefer to attend an English language Foursquare church are, as Rev. Milton Ellithorpe used to say, as welcome as "the flowers in May."

Also, churches once classified as "Hispanic" because of language are no longer designated when the media of their services is changed to English. Those who prefer or need to conduct special services shaped to their own particular language and culture we unavoidably classify, but in love and brotherly respect.

Because such full and accepted integration of black and white people has become so appropriately normal in the United States today, our main "black" congregations have not been reported in a special category. The annual Foursquare Yearbook no longer designates any churches as "black." Blacks attend all Foursquare churches, where they are unreservedly welcome. Further, many Caucasians attend the so-called "black" churches by preference.

Corporate Leadership Developed

In chapter 2 details were started concerning the original structure of the denomination. The first general supervisor, divisional officers, and district supervisors were identified. However, more must be said about the pioneer leaders of the International Church of the Foursquare Gospel.

In 1927 John Goben, a former officer in the Assemblies of God and independent pastor in Iowa, became the first general supervisor. After three years he found it increasingly difficult to adjust to the Foursquare structure and vision. He resigned at the end of 1929.

Filling the vacant office was D. V. Alderman, graduate of L.I.F.E. Bible College and pastor of the strong Foursquare church in Riverside, California. Because of his strong attachment to the Riverside church, he alternated in the office with Charles Rosendahl. Finally, in 1933, when he could not return to that congregation that was now pastored by William Wildman, he withdrew from the movement. The full story of his secession will be recounted in a later chapter.

The first general supervisor of extended tenure was the beloved Irish evangelist and singer, Dr. Billy Black. Dr. and Mrs. Black, longtime friends of Mrs. McPherson, had assumed oversight of the first branch churches at an earlier period, prior to incorporation.[9] He was appointed to the board of directors in 1932, becoming the general supervisor in 1933, where he served until 1938.

One of the strongest and most controversial leaders was Dr. Giles Knight. He and Dr. Black were the first persons to be awarded an honorary doctor of divinity degree by L.I.F.E. Bible College.

In his earliest ministry Dr. Knight was a pastor in the Christian Advent Church. He had been attracted to The Foursquare Church in 1933, taking pastorate of the Pomona, California, church. He came to the special attention of Mrs. McPherson because of his education on business law, in which he later earned a LL.D. degree.

Because of his assistance to Mrs. McPherson, he was appointed to the board of directors in 1934, becoming executive secretary and business manager of Angelus Temple in 1955. Because of the heavy cost of the commissary and that of the defense against a wrongful litigation against the church, Angelus Temple faced a financial crisis. Dr. Knight came to the rescue and restored financial solvency.

In 1936 Dr. Knight became supervisor of the Southern California region; in 1937 he was appointed vice president of the corporate church. His portfolio expanded to include: secretary and treasurer (1938) and general supervisor and director of foreign missions (1939). In 1940 Dr. Rolf K. McPherson replaced him as secretary and treasurer, but Dr. Knight continued to hold the other offices until 1944, when he retired. Dr. Howard P. Courtney Sr. was appointed to fill the vacancy as general supervisor and director of foreign missions.

Dr. Giles Knight made a great contribution to the International Church of the Foursquare Gospel. He as an astute businessman who laid a strong foundation in organization and financial management. He also served as a strong role model for Rolf McPherson in his preparation for leadership.

Unfortunately, due to Dr. Knight's managerial philosophy, tension was created with others, and, in time, there arose growing opposition. In 1943 Mrs. McPherson began to feel physically stronger. She began to deeply sense the urge to resume revival campaigns. But by that time Dr. Knight had become very protective of her and opposed her desire. Realizing her son, Rolf, had become fully capable of conducting the business of the corporate church, Mrs. McPherson asked Dr. Knight to step down and called upon Dr. Courtney from the Great Lakes District to assume Dr. Knight's responsibilities as general supervisor and director of foreign missions.

Rolf McPherson was appointed to the offices of secretary, treasurer, general manager of Angelus Temple, editor of *Foursquare Magazine*, and vice president of the International Church of the Foursquare Gospel. At the death of the founder, Aimee Semple McPherson, Rolf became president, a position that he would hold until May 1988.

In 1938 Rev. Myron Sackett, who had done well as pastor of the Cedar Rapids, Iowa, Foursquare Church, was appointed to the office of supervisor of Southern California. He served there until 1943, when Dr. and Mrs. Earl Dorrance followed him in that role. They held the office of supervisor for twenty-five years, until 1968, the longest tenure of any Foursquare district supervisor.

Earl and Edythe Dorrance had pioneered the Burbank, California, Foursquare Church, as well as pastored with success in Santa Monica and East Los Angeles, California. In addition, Dr. Dorrance was a member of the board of directors for a number of years, a position he held until 1952.

New Districts Emerge

The Great Lakes District extended from Iowa to the Atlantic Ocean. When Dr. and Mrs. Howard P. Courtney Sr. left the district to assume the office of general supervisor, the region was divided into two districts. Dr. Herman Mitzner, early pioneer and leader, was appointed to oversee the Great Lakes District, including the states of Iowa, North and South Dakota, Minnesota, Wisconsin, Illinois, and Indiana.

The Eastern District, which was comprised of Ohio, Pennsylvania, New York, New England, and the area known as the Atlantic Seaboard District, was assigned to Dr. Warren Koon. Dr. Koon had formerly pastored with distinction the

Omaha, Nebraska, Foursquare Church and occupied the position of state superintendent of Nebraska.

The Midwest District, supervised by Dr. Frank Cummings from the formation of districts in 1933, was originally comprised of all the middle and southern area from Arizona to Florida. In 1939 it was decided that the Midwest District was too large for one person to supervise. (Frank Cummings knew it all the time!) Therefore, all the southern area from Texas to Florida was made a new district called the Gulf States and assigned to Rev. and Mrs. Charles Gaines, who had pastored the growing San Diego, California, Foursquare Church. That area was to again be divided and will be discussed later.

In 1945 Dr. Cummings was given an important new assignment at Foursquare headquarters. His office as Midwest District supervisor was filled by Rev. Frank Beard, pastor of the Foursquare church in San Antonia, Texas, and superintendent of that state. Frank Beard had distinguished himself as a successful pioneer of churches. With his wife, Edna, he held the office for twenty-four years.

The vine continued to grow and to sprout branches. As the number of churches grew, new districts were created. New servants of God were called to minister in their supervision. That belongs, however, to a period of Foursquare history that present-day members will remember.

Before advancing in the development of The Foursquare Church in the United States, it is important to go back and pick up the story of Foursquare world missions, an area of ministry of high priority in the mind and heart of the founder whose "battle cry" was "Around the world with the Foursquare Gospel."

Chapter 6

TRANSPLANTS OF THE VINE

A LIVING VINE DOES not remain within the fences. It fastens itself wherever there are planned or receptive supports. That the International Church of the Foursquare Gospel quickly began to be transplanted in lands beyond its borders of origin is not surprising. The church's founder, Aimee Semple McPherson, began her ministry with a missionary call and a missionary experience.

Following a brief apprenticeship under the guidance and sponsorship of William Durham, pastor of the North Avenue Mission in Chicago, Illinois, Robert and Aimee Semple boarded a ship in January 1910 for the British Crown Colony of Hong Kong on the borders of China. From there they continued on into China to the city of Poon Yu, where they began missionary service.

Before the year ended, Robert contracted malaria, and on August 16, 1910, having been returned to Macao and then Hong Kong, Robert died. His death occurred just one month before Aimee and Robert's first child, Roberta, was born. Soon afterward, finding herself with scarce financial support and the care of her young daughter, Aimee returned to the United States. Nevertheless, she never lost her profound burden for the untold multitudes who, concerning the gospel, "were yet untold." With the opening of Angelus Temple, Aimee Semple McPherson's slogan was "Around the world with the Foursquare Gospel."

It appears that a missionary passion, as in the early church, accompanies all genuine outpourings of the Holy Spirit. Many of those who were filled with the Holy Spirit at Azusa Street in 1907 carried the Pentecostal message to other lands. Mrs. Florence Crawford's Apostolic Faith Church in Portland, Oregon, is credited with sending forth the first "Pentecostal" missionaries.[1] Shortly afterward, from William Durham's North Avenue Mission in Chicago, Illinois, known as the "Azusa Street of the Midwest," other Spirit-filled missionaries were sent.

Among early Pentecostal missionaries were Daniel Berg—founder of the Assemblies of God in Brazil; Luigi Francescon—pioneer of the Pentecostal movement in Italy; and A. G. Garr—who carried the Pentecostal message to India and China. During a visit to the United States in 1906, T. B. Barratt of Oslo, Norway, was "baptized in the Spirit." He took the Pentecostal message back to Europe where he influenced several of those who would become Europe's great Pentecostal leaders, including Lewi Pethrus of Stockholm, Sweden, who pastored the largest Pentecostal church on that continent.[2]

The importance of world missions in the beliefs and behavior of Pentecostals is seen in the fact that the sending, financial support, and wise direction of missionaries were among the principal motives in the founding of the Assemblies of God 1914.[3]

Pentecost and world missions are inseparable. A Pentecostal movement is a missionary movement. The command to tarry until filled with the Spirit is accompanied by the promise in Acts 1:8 (NKJV):

> But you shall receive power when the Holy Spirit has come upon you; and you shall be witnesses to Me in Jerusalem, and in all Judea and Samaria, and to the end of the earth.

The founding of Angelus Temple in 1923 as a center for "interdenominational and worldwide evangelism" made possible the fulfillment of a long-enduring and inescapable dream of its founder. Simultaneously with the Temple's opening, the Bible institute was started. Informed by fifteen years of experience in winning the lost, Mrs. McPherson well knew that capable workers must be properly prepared in the Bible, soul winning, and spiritual maturity. While eager to send out workers to the "uttermost parts," she recognized that they must first be selected and trained.

Philippine Islands—1926

It was in late 1926, nearly a year prior to the incorporation of the Foursquare denomination, that the first official "Foursquare missionary" was commissioned. That first missionary was Rev. Vincente DeFante, a graduate of the Foursquare Bible Institute. He would become the founder of the Foursquare ministry in the Philippine Islands.

Vincente had grown up in a Christian home. But, desiring to see the world, he left the influence of his godly mother and joined the Navy. His mother passed away, and Vincente soon drifted away from his Christian upbringing.

Finding his altered lifestyle increasingly frustrating and in search of fulfillment, Vincente wandered into Angelus Temple where, on his first visit, he accepted Christ. He enrolled in the Bible institute, and while he was a student, God called him to take the Foursquare message to the Filipino people. On January 11, 1927, he embarked en route to his native land, the land of his divine call.

Rev. DeFante gave many years of faithful ministry to the people of the Philippines, stationing himself mainly in the city of Iloilo on the island of Panay. In 1929 he was joined by Rev.

and Mrs. Ilauan, who served in Manila, on the main island of Luzon. In 1942 Rev. and Mrs. Santos Tuzon assumed direction of the Manila congregation.

In 1949, following World War II, Rev. and Mrs. Everett Dennison were sent to the islands as the first non-Filipino missionaries. They served in that nation from 1949 to 1956, as well as a further term in the late 1970s.

The importance of the Foursquare work in the Philippines is illustrated by the fact that some of our denomination's finest leaders have spent one or more terms overseeing that work. They were and are: Rev. and Mrs. A. B. Chavez (1955–1972), Rev. and Mrs. Arthur Thompson (Davao City in Mindinao, 1955–1966), Rev. and Mrs. Allan Hamilton (1956–1960), Rev. and Mrs. Don McGregor (1958–1973), Rev. and Mrs. Jack Richey (1959–1975), Rev. Wilma Wright (1966–1970), Rev. and Mrs. Phil Starr (1969–1979), Rev. and Mrs. William West (1970–1975), Rev. and Mrs. Ralph Elmore (1975–1978), Rev. and Mrs. Gary Loop (1977–1989), Rev. Eloise Clarno (1979–1983), and Rev. and Mrs. Greg Romine (1988–1990).[4] Also serving in the Philippine Islands were Rev. and Mrs. Don Nicholson, and Rev. and Mrs. Fred Horner.

In 1975 leadership of the Philippine work was placed entirely under the leadership of the national church. At the 1975 Philippine convention, Rev. Ernesto Lagasca was elected president; Rev. Veronico Suan was chosen as general supervisor. Since that time the number of churches has increased from 279 to 616, with hundreds of meeting places.[5]

1928 Missionary Convention

With the sending of the first "official" Foursquare missionary and the incorporation of the Foursquare movement, there resulted a new surge of interest in and enthusiasm for evangelizing the world. The vision for world evangelization is expressed in an article in the Foursquare *Bridal Call*:

> Angelus Temple is opening one of the mightiest missionary enterprises that has ever been started. Nothing short of establishing missionaries and mission stations in every land and among every kindred, tribe and tongue, will satisfy these earnest, enthusiastic and consecrated followers of the Foursquare Gospel.
>
> "The field is the world," is their motto, and "Around the world with the Foursquare Gospel" is their slogan. The spirit of the Foursquare Gospel is that of the true pioneer.[6]

The above quote might sound exaggerated; however, it should be noted that within two years following that statement, twenty-two Foursquare missionaries had been sent out to ten foreign countries.

In January 1929 the *Bridal Call* published "The Sun Never Sets on the Foursquare Gospel." It began like this:

> DO YOU REMEMBER?
>
> As though one of those assembled thousands who stood there in Angelus Temple at the 1928 New Year's Convention—stood there with uplifted hands and tear-drenched, love-inspired faces and the light of heaven shining in their eyes, could ever forget that moment!
>
> That epochal moment when the slogan of the Convention, which became the slogan of the year rose instinctively and simultaneously to every lip:
>
> "The Foursquare Gospel around the world in 1928." . . . How near have we come to the realization of our dream, the fulfillment of our pledge? Take a deep breath and get ready to shout![7]

The fifth annual international Foursquare convention in January 1928 at Angelus Temple was the greatest convention to that date. Statistically, the greatest number to that date of ministers and official delegates registered.

Since it had been noised abroad that the Foursquare Gospel lighthouses had been incorporated in late 1927, many independent Pentecostal pastors, evangelists, and workers traveled to Los Angeles for the conclave. Added to this number were several hundred pastors and workers from Angelus Temple and the "branches." Ministers and local laymen jammed the building for every service.

It was a great convention spiritually; the Lord poured out His Spirit in service after service. Listen to this description:

> Never has Angelus Temple been so busy as during this great conclave—the convention which far overshadowed all previous conventions... From the early morning prayer meeting that began each day at six o'clock in the morning, on through the fleeting hours, oftentimes far into the night, the crowds surged into the Temple doors almost unceasingly.
>
> They came from every state in the Union and from many countries across the seas; they represented all walks of life—the rich, the poor, the educated, the uneducated; bankers, doctors, professors, and laborers, ministers and laymen. All came that they might take away with them even more of the divine Spirit who made them come... Hundreds were converted, hundreds healed, hundreds filled with the mighty power of the Holy Ghost. Shouts of praise ascended to the throne of grace like sweet incense.[8]

The 1928 convention was great strategically; at that historic gathering a missionary agenda was put into place that has yielded abundant fruit for six decades. Dedicated missionaries were appointed and during the year sent, who founded the mission stations that have remained some of Foursquaredom's strongest foreign fields until this day. The convention launched men and women who ministered to every part of the world, so that it could be said, by 1930, that "the Sun never sets on the Foursquare banner."

However, before getting ahead of the story, there must be a closer look given to those "missionary pioneers" who laid the foundation for our global expansion.

China—1928

One of the appointments made at the 1928 convention was that of the Lawler family—Mother Emma Lawler, daughter Beatrice and son Ronald. The Lawlers had already served for nine years in Shanghai, China, as independent missionaries. They had come to the convention with the goal of becoming part of the Foursquare revival.

Almost at first sight, Mrs. McPherson felt a love for the Lawlers, partly because she still felt a strong burden for China.

> Aimee Semple McPherson always has had a particularly imperative yearning upon her heart for the unnumbered millions of unsaved souls in the foreign missionary field of China. Ever since her own girlhood call there, ever since her widowhood and mother in kaleidoscopic Hong Kong and her sorrowful return to her native land, she has ever had an impelling desire to go back to gather in the Chinese sheaves.
>
> Now unable to go herself because of the multitudinous duties as president and pastor of the huge Foursquare movement, she nevertheless still hears the call. And so, in answer to it, the Foursquare Gospel is sending as its own Missionaries to China, two workers who have already had the invaluable experience of nine years spent in Christian

> endeavor in the Orient, Emma B. Lawler and her daughter, Beatrice Lawler, who sail on January 30th.[9]

The Lawler family, encouraged by Mrs. Sun Yat Sen, widow of the first president of China, planted a strong work in the largest nation in the world. They served under the Foursquare banner for a number of years. However, under the stronger corporate requirements, they withdrew from official representation of the denomination. This is no way lessened their personal love for Mrs. McPherson or for the Foursquare Gospel, which they preached until their passing.

Rev. and Mrs. Max Dykstra joined the Lawlers in 1929. Rev. Dykstra established his base of operations in the northern part of China, where he raised up fifty mission stations by 1938. He was a charismatic worker with a strong anointing of the Holy Spirit, and revival broke out throughout the area. Max was able to travel into war zones where other foreigners had been forbidden to go.

Because of a miracle in his life, reportedly being raised from the dead, Max felt led to change his name, in 1934, to Paul Stephen Dykstra. He was greatly respected as a missionary exerting strong influence on the home field while on furlough. Because of World War II, followed closely by the revolution in China, which ended in 1949, though there has been some limited contact, it is not known what became of these missionary stations under the Communist government.

Hong Kong—1936

A third area of China opened to the Foursquare Gospel in 1936, under the ministry of Rev. and Mrs. Edwin Lee. Edwin and Beulah directed the work in the British Crown Colony of Hong Kong, where Aimee Semple McPherson had been called and had suffered the trying loss of her husband. A number of churches were planted in South China.

The Lees served in Hong Kong until their retirement in 1973, establishing churches, the Semple Day School program, and an orphanage. The work in Hong Kong became the only Chinese Foursquare mission field, following the Communist takeover of China in 1949.

Edwin and Beulah Lee were joined in 1949 by Rev. and Mrs. Carl Lucht and Rev. Billy Charles. However, in 1952, the Luchts and Billy were transferred to Japan to open a new work in that nation being reconstructed after the war. After a period of pioneering in Japan, the Luchts returned to Hong Kong to serve in Christian social concern ministry, while Miss Charles came to the United States in 1955 to marry Mr. Jack Francey. In 1956 Rev. and Mrs. Francey returned to Japan. In 1961 Rev. and Mrs. George Britt were appointed to and served in Hong Kong for two years of missionary service.

In 1969 Rev. and Mrs. Ron Williams and family were assigned to the mission in Hong Kong. Their assignment was to be trained under Edwin Lee to assume supervision of the work, following Rev. Lee's retirement. The Williams family served the Foursquare Church in Hong Kong for sixteen years, returning to the United States in 1985. Ron assumed the role of editor of the *Foursquare World Advance* magazine and ultimately was appointed to fill a seat on the denomination's board of directors.

While in Hong Kong, Ron and Carole Williams introduced a number of new ministries: establishing new congregations, formulating and publishing bylaws for the operation of the churches, forming a national board, receiving of regular missionary offerings for the support of works in other Asian countries such as Sri Lanka, reorganizing the Semple Memorial School System, and discipling of a new generation of Chinese pastors and local church leadership. With the reopening of the doors to China in 1979, Rev. Williams had contact and served with Christian groups in the People's Republic of China.[10]

Joining Rev. and Mrs. Williams, upon Rev. Lee's retirement in 1973, were Rev. and Mrs. Gary Loop, and in 1976, Rev. and Mrs. Duane Chumley, whose service was terminated by the death of Duane's wife, Luanne, sister of Jack Hayford. They were replaced in 1979 by Rev. and Mrs. Larry Six. The Six family served in Hong Kong for a number of years, taking over leadership of the work for 1985 until the appointment of Rev. and Mrs. Gary Cooper. Until fall 1990 Rev. and Mrs. Cooper directed the Foursquare Gospel Church in Hong Kong. Other missionaries serving in the British Crown Colony were Dr. and Mrs. Greg Romine.

Panama—1928

Another missionary appointee to leave for the field immediately following the historic 1928 convention (on January 29) was a former banker from Morgan Hill, California, Mr. Arthur Edwards. Mr. Edwards accepted Christ on what was to have been his deathbed, through a vision that God gave him in answer to prayer. In 1921 Mrs. McPherson held one of her greatest tent meetings in San Jose, California. It was there that Mr. and Mrs. Edwards first heard the teaching of the baptism with the Holy Spirit and divine healing and witnessed miracles in answer to prayer. In 1922 the Edwards family was present at the historic meeting in Oakland where Mrs. McPherson first used the term "Foursquare Gospel." When Angelus Temple opened shortly thereafter, the Edwards family was there.

Arthur Edwards was completely dedicated to the Lord's service. He so strongly felt God's call to full-time ministry that at a dedication service he donated his entire bank account to the Lord's work. Arthur not only gave of his means, but when he received a missionary call to Panama in 1925, he and Mrs. Edwards enrolled in the Foursquare Bible Institute, graduating in June 1927. They began preparation to leave for the field immediately after the 1928 convention.[11]

God's call upon the Edwards family was confirmed in many ways, not the least of which has been the success of the Panama Foursquare field. At their retirement, twenty years later, the Foursquare Church in Panama had become the strongest Protestant church in the republic, with more than one hundred churches.

Another confirmation of Arthur Edwards' call is an interesting story. His missionary call came in the form of a vision. In his vision, Arthur saw an aged man with a white beard, holding his hand over his brow as if looking for someone to assume his labors of plowing, planting, and reaping. Months later, after Rev. Edwards had established the work in Panama, he made a trip to the town of Citre. There he was requested to visit a dying man in the Gorgas Army Hospital. As he leaned over the aged white-bearded man, he heard the gentleman speaking in tongues. At once, Arthur recognized the man as the aged figure in the vision of his call.

Later, Rev. Edwards learned that the man had been Presbyterian missionary. He visited the home of the deceased missionary and, to his surprise, discovered a picture of Aimee Semple McPherson and a number of issues of the Foursquare *Bridal Call* magazine. In a diary, there was an entry dated at the exact time Arthur had received his call. It read, "God, you know that I am advanced in years and my health is failing, please put your hand on someone else that will come to pick up the plow and continue the task."[12]

Dr. Arthur Edwards was assisted by his two sons and their

wives. Donald graduated from L.I.F.E. in 1932, after which he and his wife, Edith, served in Panama until 1947, especially on the Atlantic coast, opening several churches. Leland and Barbara were very strong in youth ministry, radio, and youth camps.

Dr. Arthur Edwards was succeeded by his son Leland, who gave strong leadership to the field until late 1959, when Dr. and Mrs. Leland Edwards were appointed to the office of assistant director of Foursquare Missions.

Leland and Barbara Edwards, as supervisors of the Church of the Foursquare Gospel in Panama, were followed in 1960 by Rev. and Mrs. Vinton Johnson, who had already spent ten years of missionary service in that nation. The Johnsons were appointed to the field of Argentina in 1967, and Rev. and Mrs. Edgar Coombs assumed the position. Other American leaders of the Foursquare ministry in Panama have been Rev. and Mrs. Loren Edwards (third generation of the Edwards family), Rev. and Mrs. Lewis Richey (son of Rev. and Mrs. Jack Riche, who served in the Philippines and in Ecuador), and Bonita Schwartz, who until recently served in Christian education ministry, coordinating four Bible institutes.

An interesting aspect of Foursquare ministry outreach in Panama was the evangelizing of the primitive Choco Indians of the Darien Province. Through work begun by Rev. and Mrs. Vinton Johnson in 1950, the Foursquare Church has provided a Bible in their native language.

The first task for the Johnsons was that of learning the Choco "spoken" language. The tribe had no written language, and the Johnsons worked diligently to grasp the sounds and begin translation of the Scriptures. However, before the work could be completed, Vinton and Verna were moved to Panama City to succeed Dr. and Mrs. Leland Edwards.

God had prepared Rev. Dick Scott to take up this monumental task. Dick had completed the course in linguistics offered by the University of Oklahoma. After appointment and a season of orientation in Panama, Dick and Dian Scott moved to the Darien to carry on the work of Bible translation. Dick spent several years learning the Choco language.

A very valuable helper named Jose Cabrera was raised up to assist Rev. Scott. Jose, a Choco Indian who had been wonderfully converted and delivered from alcoholism, became Dick's linguistic assistant.

After fourteen months of continuous, long hours of reducing the language to a written form and then translating the Bible to the new medium, the Gospel of Mark was completed. It was published in 1969 by the United Bible Society. Since that time, other books of the Bible have been published, and by 1985 the entire New Testament had been translated and published in the Choco language. Dr. Dick Scott continues to refine and to enlarge his work.

Other missionaries who have served in Panama are: Carl and Rosemary Thompson, Canal Zone; Rev. and Mrs. T. J. Tuttle, pastors of the Colon Church; Hazel Granvoll, former pioneer pastor in Santa Ana, California, serving in Chiriqui Province and married Mr. Payton Shelley in 1941; Rev. and Mrs. Frank Moncivaiz, pastoring in Panama and later pioneering the Foursquare work in Monterrey, Mexico, in 1942; Rev. and Mrs. Joseph Knapp, who also pioneered the Foursquare work in Barrancabermeja, Colombia, in 1949; Rev. and Mrs. Claude Updike—they pioneered in Guatemala in 1959, and his revival campaigns helped to open new works in several Central American provinces; Rev. Mattie Sensabaugh, who served many years afterward in Honduras; Rev. and Mrs. Robert Aguirre, later ministering in Ecuador, Venezuela, and Spain; Rev. and

Mrs. Dean Truett (the daughter of Rev. and Mrs. T. J. Tuttle), who also ministered in Honduras and Puerto Rico; Rev. and Mrs. Michael Frederick (a daughter of missionaries Ed and Vonitta Gurney). Others serving in Panama were Rev. James Nicholls (1940), Rev. and Mrs. Elmer Darnall, and Rev. Mary Frost, who later served in Colombia.

As can be seen by the above paragraph, Panama is strategically located to be a training base for ministry to all the Central and South American countries. Many Foursquare missionaries received their preparatory experience there under seasoned veteran missionaries.

Bolivia—1928

Among Foursquare missionaries, there is none more widely recognized than the Anderson family who have served for sixty-eight years in Bolivia and Colombia. Rev. Thomas Anderson had already served for five years as an independent missionary to the Quechua Indians in Bolivia before being appointed at the landmark convention in 1928. That same year Thomas and Fannie Anderson left with their family (Paul, Jack, Rachel, and Jenny) to return to Bolivia. There they carried the gospel to the savage jungle Indians near the Bolivian headwaters of the Amazon River.

The Andersons located their mission base in the city of Trinidad, which bordered on the not yet penetrated jungles of Bolivia and Brazil. Trinidad was situated on the Mamore River, which joined the Guapore River, part of the Western border of Brazil, emptying into the Amazon River near the city of Manaus.

After founding a church in Trinidad under the pastoring of Mrs. Anderson and Rachel, the men of the family established a jungle base on high ground about fifty miles to the east, called Ebiato. From there they made excursions into the jungle in search of unreached Sirionos Indians who had never heard the gospel. The Indians scarcely knew of civilization.

A number of Sirionos were won to Christ. The missionaries joined them in forming a colony at the jungle base where there was shelter, consistent food supply, and freedom from attack by hostile tribes. The colony also provided health care, instruction in crafts, basic learning, and gospel teaching for all, and in particular, for the children.

Stories of the jungle evangelism were brought to the U.S. Foursquare churches by international youth director Harold Chalfant. Great missionary interest resulted in a movie—*Beyond the Bells*—filmed of a jungle excursion and of life at the jungle camp. Large sums of money, earmarked for the Bolivian work among the primitive people, enabled the purchase of a large tractor for agriculture, the development of a mission compound, a church facility, a fully accredited day school, and an airstrip.

In the late 1930s the Andersons were joined by Tressie Neal, Virginia Colbert (a niece of the Andersons), and Rev. Claire Martin. Paul Anderson married Tressie, and Claire married Virginia. Later the Paul Andersons and the Claire Martins left Bolivia to pioneer works in Bucaramanga, Colombia, and Cartagena, Colombia, respectively. Rev. Thomas Anderson passed away in 1943. While on furlough in 1950, Jack Anderson was married in Angelus Temple to Darlene Ziegler, daughter of Rev. Frank Ziegler, missionary to South Africa. Others who served in Bolivia were Rev. and Mrs. Harold Williams, Rev. and Mrs. Lloyd Dickerson, and Rev. Valerie Baker.

Peru—1955

In 1939 Rachel Anderson was married to Ramon Perez, a Bolivian government official who had sought her hand for many years. The Perezes assisted the Andersons in Bolivia for a time, giving new strength to the jungle work. They then moved on to serve in the nation of Chile, and in 1955, Rev. and Mrs. Ramon Perez opened a new Foursquare work in the nation of Peru. In 1983 the church in Colombia sent a national to open churches on the border with Peru, among three Indian tribes. This work spread into Iquitos, the major city in Peru on the banks of the Amazon. In 1989 Rev. Charlie Finocciaro and Rev. Steve Galvan were sent to Lima to open a church. Steve returned to the United States, and Charlie remained with the church for a time.

The Congo/Zaire—1928

The great missionary convention of 1928 launched another dedicated couple to pioneer a territory new to Foursquare. Rev. and Mrs. Merrill Sigler, graduates from the International Institute of Foursquare Evangelism in 1927, sailed for the Congo (Zaire) on the continent of Africa. They stepped foot in that nation in December 1928. Following a long journey down the Kasai River, beset with many dangers and an extended attack of malaria fever, the Siglers reached the village of Luiza, where they were to build their compound for ministry to the Basal Mpasu people.

Earlier in Merrill's youth, while reading of David Livingstone's experiences, the name of a place in Africa fastened itself in his mind. Later, as both a missionary and a government official suggested the name for a place to locate a mission, he knew God was confirming his call.

One day, shortly after the Siglers had built the mission compound, Merrill was called upon to pray for an aged man who was dying. He asked the man if he was a Christian. The man related his conversion thirty years before. He also informed Merrill that for many years he had prayed that God would send a missionary to minister to his tribe. The Siglers then had double assurance of God's call not only to Africa but to the very people to whom they were ministering.

The work in the Congo prospered greatly. A number of preaching stations were established. The number of personnel expanded as well. In 1933 Dr. and Mrs. H. C. Kramer, Revs. Gladys and Vada Pinnel, Rev. Joe Henderson, and Rev. Dorothy Davis added new strength to the growing work. Two years later, Rev. Frances Forbes arrived.

In 1937 Dr. Kramer became the supervisor of the African Congo field. Dr. Kramer's daughter, Gladys, and her husband, Paul DeBosere, were added to the staff. In 1939 Rev. and Mrs. Ralph Cobb came to minister. In 1945, due to political developments, it became necessary to withdraw American personnel from the Congo field.

In 1987 elderly members of that same tribe contacted the director of foreign missions, who sent Mitchell Belobaba, coordinator of the African field, to that site, and the work was reopened with national leadership; there are now several churches, including one in Kinshasha.

South Africa—1930

Rev. and Mrs. Frank Ziegler graduated from L.I.F.E. in 1928. They returned in 1930 to their native land—the Union of South Africa, locating their mission in the region of the Transvaal. There they built a strong work that continues to the present. They were assisted by their children—Lewis, Emegene Manthe, Darlene, and Bernadine. After graduation from L.I.F.E. Bible College, Lewis and Arlene Ziegler began to assume the leadership of the mission. Lewis was appointed as supervisor of the field in 1961.

During the ensuing years the work spread as far south as Cape Town and into other parts of South Africa, including churches among the Zulu tribe. In 1989 Rev. and Mrs. Ziegler retired from the field; Rev., and Mrs. (Terry) Howard Manthe assumed the direction of the work.

Howard Manthe is the grandson of the founding missionaries of the Foursquare mission in South Africa, Frank and Dorothy Ziegler. Howard met his wife, Terry, while a student at L.I.F.E. Bible College. He graduated from L.I.F.E. in 1977. Before assuming the direction of the South Africa field, Howard directed the mission work in England for four years between 1981 and 1985.

Nigeria—1957

After assisting the Zieglers for a short period, in 1957 Rev. and Mrs. Harold Curtis were appointed to a newly developing work in Nigeria, West Africa. The Nigerian Foursquare Church, with many churches and a large Bible college program, has become Foursquare's largest in Africa. The nation also serves as a base for outreach into several other countries on the continent. Rev. and Mrs. Curtis were assisted by Rev. Audra Sowersby and Rev. and Mrs. Bonnie Jones.

In 1963 Faye Curtis suffered a stroke, requiring them to retire from the leadership of the Nigerian church to seek ministry in a less severe climate. The direction of the Nigerian mission passed to Rev. and Mrs. Joseph Babcock, under whose leadership the national church was established with a national board and with a national supervisor, Rev. Samuel Odunaike, who also served for several years as the chairman of the Association of Evangelicals of Africa and Madagascar. The Babcocks were assisted by Audra Sowersby, Margaret Season, and Rev. and Mrs. Jim Kitchell.

The strength of the Nigerian Foursquare church has been in part due to very strong and faithful national leadership that

God has raised up over the years and the Nigerians who carry on the work today.

Other successive directors from North America have been Rev. and Mrs. Larry Six, and Rev. and Mrs. Mitchell Belobaba. Assisting missionaries from North America have been Rev. and Mrs. John Barton; Rev. Dana Holland; and Rev. and Mrs. William Kieselhorst, who were the advisors to West Africa. Rev. David Metsker served as director of L.I.F.E. Bible College of Nigeria from 1984 to 1987 and was then appointed to the field desk of the entire Foursquare work in Africa.

At the time of this writing, Foursquare works have been planted in Sierra Leone, Kenya, Tanzania, Ghana, Liberia, Zambia, and Ivory Coast. The churches in Zambia were established by Edgar and Darlene Coombs, who had given many years of skilled service in Venezuela, Panama, and in the International Missions Office. Their missionary service came to an end when Edgar was killed in 1988 in a tragic accident while serving in Zambia.

India—1928

On their way to China in 1910 Robert and Aimee Semple visited India. From that time on Aimee carried a burden for that nation. It is not surprising, then, that she responded readily to the Lindens and Kleinschmidts who testified to a strong call to that land of Hinduism, pantheism, and an inflexible caste system.

Thus, at the convention of 1928, approval was given to Rev. and Mrs. A. L. Kleinschmidt and Rev. and Mrs. Carl Linden to go as Foursquare missionaries to India. Their effort to evangelize that nation was not long lived. However, in more recent years, the door has been reopened through gifted national Indian leaders. Rev. and Mrs. John Gnanaolivu, under whose leadership a national church was duly registered and a national board appointed, have organized churches in several provinces. With strong moral support and limited financial assistance, they are doing a very credible work.

Other 1928 missionaries were Rev. Martha Leising, a graduate of the first class of L.I.F.E. who was sent to Hawaii; Rev. Gussie Booth, who was sent to Japan; and Rev. Albert Yellen, who went out to his native land of Czechoslovakia, where he died after only a brief term of ministry. Rev. and Mrs. William Kay, following graduation from the institute, returned to their native country of Australia.

PUERTO RICO—1935

In the early part of the decade of the 1930s, Rev. and Mrs. E. E. Adams, with their daughter, Rhenna, pioneered a church in San Juan, Puerto Rico. In 1935 Rhenna was married to a Puerto Rican, Jose Ubarri. Soon afterward Jose and Rhenna came to the United States to attend Bible college. When the Adamses became increasingly legalistic in their view of sanctification, obligating all the young people, including Rhenna, to comply with an impossibly extreme dress code and lifestyle, Jose and Rhenna were alienated. This led to the separation and divorce of Jose and Rhenna. The Adams family then withdrew from the Foursquare denomination.

Rev. Ubarri remained loyal to The Foursquare Church, ministering outside of San Juan. However, when he remarried, his credentials were surrendered upon request. Rev. and Mrs. Lloyd Goodman were appointed to serve in Puerto Rico in 1941 but, due to ill health, resided there a little more than one year.

Much discussion ensued about closing the Foursquare work in Puerto Rico. But because Mrs. McPherson held strong feelings toward the "Emerald Isle," a U.S. possession, Rev. and Mrs.

Nathaniel Van Cleave were asked to assume direction of the mission. Nathaniel and Lois resigned from their faculty positions at L.I.F.E. Bible College, as well as the pastorate of the Pasadena, California, Foursquare Church, and flew to Puerto Rico with their two children, Robert and Lavonna, in one of the last "China Clippers." They arrived in San Juan in September of 1943.

Six months were given to language study and frequent visits to the two remaining Foursquare churches on the island, in Caguas and Aibonito. In April 1944, a new headquarters church was pioneered in the city of Ponce (named for Ponce de Leon). A large congregation resulted, followed by the establishment of a Bible institute. In late 1944 Rev. and Mrs. Eldon Easter joined the Van Cleaves and were assigned to Caguas. Under the training program, Rev. Carlos Lopez was discipled to take over the Caguas work. Rev. and Mrs. Lopez succeeded in building a strong church, which still endures.

During a visit by Rev. Harold Chalfant to Puerto Rico in 1945, a new church was established in the city of Mayaguez. Rev. and Mrs. Howard Gandy, new missionary appointees to Puerto Rico, took the pastorate. Three additional churches were opened in Ponce, one in Aibonito, and one in Caguas.

In 1946 Dr. Van Cleave was appointed supervisor of the West Indies. That same year, groups of churches in Cuba and Jamaica joined the Foursquare family. The Cuban work was directed by Rev. Francisco Rodriguez; the Jamaican churches by Rev. Cleveland Battieste.

When the Van Cleaves were assigned by Rev. Rolf K. McPherson to a special mission in the United States in 1948, Rev. and Mrs. Donald Edwards were transferred from Panama to Puerto Rico. One year later, Rev. Edwards moved the West Indies Office to Havana, Cuba. Rev. and Mrs. Norman Smith, who had been serving in Puerto Rico for two years, were appointed directors of the Puerto Rican churches, where they remained until 1955.

Other North American missionaries to Puerto Rico have been: Rev. and Mrs. Herbert Seale (1955), Rev. and Mrs. James Tuckness who moved the Puerto Rican headquarters to a new church in Bayamon in 1965, Rev. and Mrs. Vance Fordyce (1969), Rev. and Mrs. Joseph Knapp (1975), Rev. Angel Torres (1977), Rev. and Mrs. Dale Downs (1982), Rev. and Mrs. Dean Truett (1984). In 1989 the Truetts completed the construction of a new headquarters church building, seating six or seven hundred. Rev. Truett served also as supervisor of West Indies.

In addition to Puerto Rico and Jamaica, the Foursquare work in the West Indies includes churches in Haiti, the Dominican Republic, and Trinidad and Tobago. A very active work was done in Trinidad by Rev. Peter Hosein, a national evangelist whom God especially anointed in preaching and in praying for the sick. At the time of this writing, the Trinidad and Tobago field has eighteen churches and eighteen regular meeting places.

Cuba—1947

The Foursquare Church entered Cuba in 1947, when Rev. Francisco Rodriguez, a Puerto Rican worker ministering in Havana (Parraga), sought affiliation with the ICFG. Nathaniel Van Cleave visited a convention of Rev. Rodriguez's churches in Havana and was deeply impressed. ICFG Director of Missions Dr. Howard P. Courtney Sr., together with Rev. Van Cleave, visited the Cuban work again that same year, at which time the proper documents for affiliation were expedited.

In 1949 Rev. Donald Edwards moved the West Indies headquarters to Havana. The field grew to nearly forty churches. A Bible institute was organized, a Cuban board of directors was chosen, and bylaws were registered. Problems arose in 1951, when Rev. Rodriguez withdrew from the denomination, but most of the churches remained loyal to ICFG.

In 1960 Fidel Castro came to power. Becoming the Communist dictator in Cuba, he began to oppress those churches that would not align themselves with his political policies. The Foursquare churches went underground; the missionaries and many of the ministers were forced to leave the country for Florida, Mexico, or Los Angeles. One of these Cuban families, the Braches, became one of the founding families of the Hispanic congregation at Angelus Temple.

Jamaica—1947

As stated earlier, the Foursquare Church in Jamaica emerged by the affiliation in 1947 of a group of independent churches led by Rev. Cleveland Battieste. The union fared well for several years but finally became strained, due to the inability of the Missions Department to satisfy the ever-increasing requests for financial support. When it was discovered that Rev. Battieste was seeking and receiving financial assistance from other sources, Rev. and Mrs. Joseph Knapp were sent to Jamaica to oversee the work. Rev. Battieste withdrew, together with a number of his original churches.

Dr. Knapp moved the Jamaican headquarters to Kingston, where he pioneered a strong work. The Knapps were assisted by Revs. Orlen and Sarah Robinson. Knapp was followed by Rev. and Mrs. Howard Curtis (previously missionaries to Nigeria).

Under the leadership of Rev. and Mrs. Harold Curtis, new branches were initiated through a program of branch Sunday schools. Evangelistic teams from the United States helped the growth with the winning of many converts. A beautiful new headquarters church was built in the city of Kingston, with much of the construction done by nationals from the Bible training school. Other assistance was given by groups of "lay builders" from Foursquare churches in America.

The Curtises were assisted by Rev. Anna Maria Shalla. But in 1978 Mrs. Curtis suffered another severe stroke (the first in Nigeria), and the family was forced to leave the field. Supervision was assigned to a national minister, Rev. Neville Davis.[13]

Greece—1930

By the year 1930, the number of mission fields—twenty-nine missionaries to fourteen countries—began to stretch the denomination's budget. The Great Depression was beginning to be felt. Missionary ardor had not cooled, but thousands of people were unemployed. While remaining adequate to support those missionaries already sent, missions budgeting gave warning against increase at the same rate of 1928–1929. Consequently, only one new missionary was approved during 1930.

That year Rev. and Mrs. Costas Athans and son, Leo, were appointed to Athens, Greece, their native homeland. Since they were sent to minister to their own people, it was assumed that the work would soon be self-supporting. On the other hand, because the Greek Orthodox Church was so much a part of the fabric of Greek culture, winning converts was not easy. A small but loyal congregation was established.

Relatives of Rev. Athans, Rev. and Mrs. Theodore Davis, took charge of the work in 1958, and some progress was made. When the Davises retired in the late 1960s, George Patsaouras, a convert and disciple of the Rev. Davis, assumed the pastorate of the Athens church. For a time, the Ernie Denos family assumed the work. In 1982 Rev. and Mrs. Brooks Bryan, former youth ministers at Angelus Temple, were sent to Greece for a limited tenure.

The current overseer is Rev. George Patsaouras, under whose

leadership the Foursquare Church in Greece has become the fastest-growing church in that nation.

Mexico—1943

During the decade of the 1930s, most of the missionary growth had been in the addition of personnel to already existing fields, especially in Panama and Bolivia. As the church entered the decade of the 1940s, new fields were opened, such as Colombia, Mexico, Brazil, Cuba, Jamaica, and Cuba.

The extension to new fields was made possible by the larger incomes of the war and post-war eras. Moreover, the war had created a new world vision through the experiences of servicemen and a general enlarged awareness of world needs.

In 1943 Rev. Frank and Juvenita Moncivaiz, who had served for over ten years with the Edwards family in Panama, were sent to their native country of Mexico. By law, only Mexican nationals were permitted to perform ecclesiastical ordinances or serve as permanent pastors. Since the Moncivaizes were Mexican citizens, they were ideal missionaries to that country.

Frank and Juvenita located in the third largest city of the nation, Monterrey, where they soon had a substantial congregation. Rev. and Mrs. T. J. Tuttle were sent to Monterrey to construct a large central church building, which also housed a Bible institute. The Tuttles remained in Mexico as missionaries for a period of time.

Following his graduation from L.I.F.E. Bible College, Rev. Daniel Moncivaiz, the son of Rev. and Mrs. Moncivaiz, joined them. Danny assumed the central pastorate, permitting the parents to pioneer a number of branch churches in surrounding towns and villages. By 1967 the Foursquare Gospel Church in Mexico had grown to more than fifty churches. More recently a sizable work has developed in Baja California.

After the retirement of Rev. and Mrs. Moncivaiz and the coming of Danny to a church in Los Angeles, Rev. and Mrs. Floyd Frutiger assumed leadership. The supervisor of the Foursquare Gospel Church in Mexico was then Rev. and Mrs. Humberto Paz. Humberto is a convert and disciple of Rev. Frank Moncivaiz. Another outstanding product of the Moncivaiz family influence is Rev. Raymundo Diaz, who with his wife, Pam, pastors the Hispanic congregation of Angelus Temple.

Colombia—1943

The nation of Colombia in South America was opened in 1943. At first, it was a very difficult country in which to make progress. Protestant evangelicals were not welcomed in a country ruled alternately by rulers steeped in Roman Catholic culture or by leaders sympathetic to Communism. Missionaries endured severe persecution. One Foursquare missionary, Rev. Mary Frost, was struck by a large rock hurled by persecutors; several Foursquare national workers were shot and killed. On a number of occasions, churches were closed and padlocked by police, Later, however, The Foursquare Church in Colombia became one of the fastest growing Protestant groups in the nation.

The missionaries who pioneered The Foursquare Church in Colombia were Claire and Virginia Martin, together with Paul and Tressie Anderson. Paul, son of Thomas Anderson, had lived in Bolivia for thirteen years; Claire went to Bolivia in 1938, where in 1940 he was married to Virginia Colbert, niece of the Andersons. All were seasoned missionaries accustomed to hardship.

Due to a comity agreement among Protestant churches, the Andersons and Martins opened their work in Bucaramanga, Colombia. In spite of persistent opposition, a vigorous work was pioneered. After a period of time, Claire Martin's doctor recommended they find a more suitable climate on the coast. The Martins chose the island of Boca Chica, where a church was planted. Leaving the island church in the hands of a national pastor, Claire and Virginia pioneered a church in Cartagena, an important coastal city on the Caribbean.

Trained for a period by the Arthur Edwards family, Rev. and Mrs. Joseph Knapp moved to Colombia, where in 1945 they pioneered a church in the oil industrial city of Barrancabermeja. They were in for as severe opposition and persecution as pioneer missionaries ever suffer, but they were ready. The story of the preparation merits retelling.

It was in the 1930s that Joseph Knapp, a beer truck driver in Portland, Oregon, stalled one Sunday night in a snow storm. He went into the Portland, Oregon, Foursquare Church to phone for help. While waiting for help that didn't come, he sat in the service being conducted by Harold Jefferies. At the altar call he accepted Christ as Savior. His life and purpose were completely transformed.

Soon afterward, he enrolled in Bible college, graduating in 1940. Rev. and Mrs. Knapp pastored in Columbia City, Oregon, and then offered themselves for the mission field. They were the type of fearless, rugged, and unwavering people that were needed to break through a wall of Satan-inspired hostility to deliver the gospel to the hungry thousands in Colombia.

Joe Knapp's ministry raised up a large congregation in Barrancabermeja, as the result of a genuine revival. They built a large auditorium that was constantly filled. They suffered every variety of opposition. When the police would padlock their doors, they would go underground with meetings in private homes. In every case, when the church building was reopened, the congregation had grown larger than it was before the closure. This continued in spite of the fact that several of their national workers were shot and killed. The lives of the missionaries were saved several times by miraculous intervention.

After their years in Barrancabermeja, the Knapps pioneered a church in the city of Medellin, and in later years they served as directors of the churches in Jamaica and Puerto Rico.

Other missionaries to Colombia have included Rev. Mary Frost, Rev. and Mrs. Ramon Perez (Mrs. Perez is a daughter of the Andersons of Bolivia), Rev. and Mrs. Lloyd Dickerson, Rev. and Mrs. John Firth, Rev. and Mrs. Dan Larson, and Rev. and Mrs. Ray Vincent. Drug wars in Colombia have created a new menace for the missionaries.

John and Jean Firth were instrumental in writing a distinct chapter in the history of the Colombian church. After having served for a number of years in Colombia with an evangelical mission, they were baptized with the Holy Spirit under the encouragement of the Knapps. In 1952 they were sent back to Colombia, to the city of Barranquilla at the mouth of the Magdalene River, to work under the Foursquare banner.

Persecution was rampant when the Firths entered Barranquilla to pioneer the Foursquare work. They were forbidden to pass out tracts or advertise in any manner and were even stoned in the street. But God performed a miracle of healing on one of their neighbors for whom they had prayed. A revival ensued, and through prayer, fasting, and miracles of healing and deliverance, multiplied thousands entered the kingdom of God and The Foursquare Church. A very large church edifice was built, and hundreds of branch churches emerged. Soon the two largest Protestant churches in Colombia were Foursquare.

Prior to their retirement, the Firths pioneered a church in an affluent section of Bogota, the capital city. For the first time in the Foursquare Church in Latin America, a congregation was pioneered composed almost entirely of the upper economic class. A brother of the president of the country was, for a time, a member of the congregation. (In most every country, through the years, missionaries and nationals have ministered to the affluent and to political leaders, but never before had this class comprised an entire congregation.) Mrs. Firth was even invited to bring a series of teachings on the Holy Spirit at the cathedral in Bogota, influencing many Catholic charismatics. Under the guidance of John and Jean Firth, the Iglesia Quadrangular (Foursquare Church) became the fastest-growing religious organization in the nation of Colombia.

Brazil—1946

The year 1946 marked the beginning of the phenomenal work in Brazil. It was to become the largest national Foursquare church in the world. In 1990 the Foursquare Gospel Church in Brazil counted more than nine thousand pastors and thousands of chartered churches. In addition, there are literally thousands of meeting places scattered across the nation.

In the beginning, however, rapid growth was not occurring. Rev. and Mrs. Harold Williams had been called at first to Bolivia where they arrived in 1945. Soon afterward, feeling that the Bolivian work was well staffed, Rev. and Mrs. Williams sensed a deep moving to relocate in neighboring Brazil, which could be reached by boat down the headwaters of the Amazon. They proceeded to the city of Belen, then south to Santas, and finally made their headquarters in Sao Juao de Boa Vista, estado de Sao Paulo. Their first task was to learn the Portuguese language.

Seeking help in language study, Rev. and Mrs. Williams found many Brazilians eager to learn English. By providing English lessons, they discovered an open door to witnessing. A number of converts were made among the English-language students. However, when Harold and Mary returned to the United States for furlough in 1950, only one small church in a small had been established.[14]

Before returning to Brazil, Rev. and Mrs. Williams were advised that unless more progress was made, the Brazilian work would be closed. The director of missions, Dr. Herman Mitzner, suggested to Harold and Mary that they fast and pray for a God-sent revival. His advice was taken seriously, and as a result, God did send a mighty Holy Spirit outpouring.

Soon Rev. Williams was addressing large crowds with hundreds of converts. A tent crusade in Sao Paulo is reported to have yielded nine thousand converts with scores of miraculous healings. Tents were then erected in many large communities. At one point in time there were forty tents in use. Persecution arose with many national workers jailed, but because of the popularity of the revivals, the workers were not kept in jail for long. The greater the persecutions, the greater the revival. Before long, churches sprang up in scores of Brazilian cities.

A need for workers led to the establishment of a Bible school. New missionaries, Rev. Marguerite Hawley and Rev. Louise Aerl, were sent to provide teaching. Rev. Marguerite Hawley remained as director of the headquarters Bible school until her retirement in 1983. In 1959 Rev. Marie Johnson, daughter of Thomas Johnson, who himself was a charter member and renowned musician of Angelus Temple, was sent to teach in the Bible school and to direct the Sunday schools. She had been a teacher in the California school system. She continued as director of Sunday schools in Brazil until her death on the field in 1974.

The need for organizing the rapidly burgeoning work led to a Brazilian national Foursquare church named "Cruzada Nacional de Evangelizacao." However, when the Brazilian church was officially registered with the government, it was established as the "Igreja Quadrangular no Brasil." At the first convention Rev. Harold Williams was elected to the presidency. By 1960 the number of churches reported at the fifth annual convention was nearly one hundred. During the next two years the number doubled to two hundred.[15]

In the early 1960s Rev. Williams, according to some, began to embrace and propagate the teachings of the "Latter Rain" movement, teachings that were creating problems for all Pentecostal denominations.[16] While the "New Order of Latter Rain" sounded a call for return to the original Pentecostal power, elements within it became divisive in practice and unscriptural in its teaching on spiritual gifts and "a restored order of Apostles." The Brazilian church became alarmed over the purported teaching of their president and requested a change.

In 1962 Rev. and Mrs. George Faulkner, who had served as supervisors of Foursquare churches in Chile, Argentina, and Uruguay, were appointed to succeed Rev. and Mrs. Williams. He instituted a program of leadership training for national workers and a program of district Bible institutes. That grew to eleven three-year Bible colleges and twenty one-year institutes. To meet the demands of growth, a correspondence Bible school was begun under the direction of Rev. Gary Royer, who also served as national youth director.

Church planting in the early years was accomplished by use of large tents. Later open-air meetings were preferred over the tents. In large cities the pattern of pioneering calls for the use of large auditoriums in which experienced evangelists conduct protracted campaigns. Radio broadcasting has been employed extensively in Brazil for evangelism and Bible teaching.

Brazil has been divided into five districts and 125 divisions with corresponding leaders. Good organization has facilitated the rapid but steady growth. Dr. Faulkner attributes the local and nationwide expansion in Brazil to a "mind to work" attitude motivated by the spirit of revival. In 1982 Rev. and Mrs. Dale Downs were sent to Brazil to assist George and Jane Faulkner. In the year of 1984, 525 new churches were reported.

With the retirement of Dr. Faulkner, Rev. Dale Downs was appointed advisor and ex-officio board member. Rev. Eduardo Zdrojewiski, an experienced Brazilian pastor and leader, was elected president of the national board and Rev. Josue Bengtson as executive secretary.

The Brazilian church has also become a missionary-sending community, commissioning Rev. Alberto Idivan to French Guiana and Rev. Guido Sangiorgi to Italy. In addition, the Brazilian church has sent missionary personnel to Uruguay and Paraguay, solidly establishing a national church in each nation. As of this writing, the Foursquare Church in Brazil numbers nearly 11,476 churches and meeting places with 787,504 members and adherents.

The Resurgence of Foursquare Missions

The decade of the fifties was the "Decade of Resurgence" for Foursquare missions. The Great Depression had restrained growth in the 1930s; World War II in the 1940s. Only six new fields were opened between 1931 and 1950.

During the 1950s, sixteen new fields were entered. The postwar era brought new opportunity, new finances, and new vision. The following is part of the convention missionary report for 1955, given by the director of foreign missions Dr. Herman D. Mitzner:

> Never in the history of our organization have the Foursquare fields been set ablaze with great revivals as we are experiencing today...In 1955 the total missionary giving was

> $577,450. This amount far surpasses any previous year in the history of our organization; however, our missionary funds for 1955 have been practically exhausted in order to keep moving at the extreme rapid advancement of four foreign fields.[17]

In addition to revivals experienced by the missionaries themselves, seven gospel teams were sent from the United States to various areas of the world with a commission to conduct evangelistic campaigns in strategic cities. These included one team of women, sent in 1954. In most cases the teams were headed by a district supervisor from the United States, aided by missionaries. Supervisors who headed teams were Harold Jefferies, Earl W. Dorrance, Fred D. Beard, Frank A Cummings, Charles Gaines, and Harold Chalfant.

Honduras—1952

The first major field to be pioneered in the 1950s was that of Honduras. In 1952 a gospel team was sent to Central America, headed by Dr. Fred Beard, Midwest district supervisor. Two members of the team were Rev. and Mrs. Edwin Gurney. Rev. Claude Updike, a missionary who had been working in Panama and who had experience in the area, joined the team for revivals.

With Rev. Updike as the principal evangelist, the team conducted nightly meetings for four weeks in the city of Tegucigalpa, capital of the nation. Great crowds attended, many converts were made, and miracles of healing accompanied prayer for the sick. A strong church resulted, pastored by the Gurneys.

The revival continued, branch churches were opened, an effective radio ministry was initiated, and a Bible institute was established. With the help of Rev. Updike, a church was pioneered in San Pedro Sula, the country's second largest city. It was pastored for many years by Rev. Mattie Sensabaugh. (Years earlier Mattie was the first member to join the church in Roanoke, Virginia, and the first to be filled with the Spirit under the ministry of Mrs. A. A. Carpenter.)

Guatemala—1955

In 1955 Claude and Juanita Updike moved to Guatemala City to pioneer a church. Since there were no suitable facilities available for meetings, they decided to step out on faith and build a tabernacle before there was a following. A large building was erected that seated one thousand people and located on a main highway. For the next six months, nightly revival meetings were conducted, at the end of which time the "Foursquare Tabernacle" was filled to capacity. Approximately one thousand people joined the church. Other activities and ministries expanded the work: a radio broadcast, a day school, and a Bible institute. The growing membership soon counted a number of prominent citizens, army officers, and government leaders.

Since the Updikes, other missionaries to Guatemala have been Rev. Jackie Coppens, Rev. and Mrs. Irvin Espeseth, Rev. and Mrs. Jerry King, Rev. and Mrs. Joseph Knapp, Rev. and Mrs. Michael Weilein, Rev. and Mrs. Lee Schnabel, Rev. and Mrs. James Walker, and more recently, Rev. and Mrs. Kent Beahler.

Venezuela

The work in Venezuela was started only indirectly by missionaries from the United States. A Colombian couple, Obdulio and Digna Estupinan, while living temporarily in Colon, Panama, were converted under the ministry of Rev. Donald Edwards. Obdulio attended the Bible school in Panama and, following graduation, returned to Colombia, where he assisted with the Foursquare work in Bucaramanga. Needing employment, he obtained a job from the Venezuelan government in San Cristobal, which was only a short distance from Bucaramanga. Since there was no Pentecostal church in San Cristobal, he began holding services in his home.

Obdulio suffered great persecution, being injured in an attack on his life. Needing assistance, he petitioned the Missions Department to send a missionary to Venezuela. Rev. and Mrs. Edgar Coombs were sent but arrived shortly after Obdulio's death.

The Coombses were also persecuted. But through miracles of healing the Lord performed, property was donated to the congregation. In 1964 Rev. Dorothy Buck, who had been in Nicaragua, was sent to assist in Venezuela, particularly in the area of Christian education. She also developed a Bible institute. Through her education program, many capable workers were trained for ministry.

In 1968 Robert Aguirre was sent to succeed Rev. and Mrs. Coombs. Being a capable evangelist, Rev. Aguirre held revival campaigns and was able to plant churches in several cities. In the city of Rubio, reports show more than two thousand people were converted.[18]

Unfortunately, personal problems terminated Rev. Aguirre's ministry. Consequently, in 1974, Rev. and Mrs. Loren Edwards were sent to head the work in Venezuela. One of the early accomplishments was the moving of the national headquarters from San Cristobal, which was rather isolated, to the capital city of Caracas. This resulted in the planting of churches in several important cities. When the Loren Edwards family was transferred to Panama in 1979 (the third generation of Arthur Edwards family in Panama), Rev. and Mrs. Gary Royer were moved from Brazil to Caracas. In 1990 the David Stone family was appointed to that nation and served with the national church pastors in leadership development.

Costa Rica—1952

In 1952 and 1953 seven approved missionaries with a burden for South and Central America were sent to language school in San Jose, Costa Rica. Upon graduation three ladies, Ruth English, Nelwyn Palmer, and Lucille Hicks, with the help of evangelists Claude and Juanita Updike, established a small work in Escazu, a suburb of San Jose.

At first the work grew slowly, due to severe opposition. One of the young converts, Jorge, was a member of one of the opposing families. Yet he stood firm in spite of their persecution.

One day Jorge's niece became ill with little hope of recovery. Blood for a transfusion could not be found until Nelwyn Palmer, one of the missionaries, donated the needed blood. The opposition soon ceased. Holy Spirit–inspired love is stronger than satanically inspired hatred and unbelief.

In 1954 Rev. and Mrs. Updike held a three-month campaign in Puntarenas, Costa Rica's principal seaport on the Pacific Ocean. A potent work called "the miracle church" was established, together with a Bible institute. The three women missionaries moved from Escazu to Puntarenas to operate the school. Rev. Escudero, from Panama, assumed the pastorate and served there for ten years.

The Updikes also held a revival campaign in Limon. In 1955 this was the main port on the Caribbean. A thriving church resulted. At the same time workers from the Chiriqui Province of Panama crossed the southern boundary of Costa Rica to evangelize a large area. They were unable to remain in the country, so some of the new converts were trained to pastor the resulting churches.

When Rev. and Mrs. Maurice Tolle graduated from the language institute in 1955, they were appointed as supervisors of Costa Rica. A central church was opened in San Jose, the capital. After two years, substantial growth required a larger building, which also housed a Bible institute.

The Tolles, however, had to leave the filed in 1958, due to illness. They were succeeded by Rev. and Mrs. Elmer McCammon. Under the leadership of the McCammons, a number of new works were established, which required increased concentration on the training institutes. In 1959 Nelwyn Palmer, who had married Charles Gosling while on furlough, returned, and the pair assisted in training national pastors.

When the McCammons assumed leadership in 1960 of the Foursquare Church in Nicaragua, they were followed in Costa Rica by Rev. and Mrs. William Pritchett. Bill and Betty directed the work for eighteen years, greatly expanding the work through worker training programs. A six-week open-air revival campaign in 1963 more than doubled the San Jose church membership.

The rapidly growing field called for additional, seasoned assistants. The following missionaries were sent to assist the Pritchetts: Rev. and Mrs. Dean Truett (1961–1964), Rev. and Mrs. Arthur Gadberry (1965–1966), Rev. and Mrs. Floyd Frutiger (1969–1970), and Rev. Dorothy Buck (1970–1974). Dorothy Buck ministered in the Central Institute, and in 1973 she opened a new school in the southern border region, later directed by Rev. Jackie Coppens.

In 1977 Rev. and Mrs. Pritchett retired, and Rev. and Mrs. James Walker were sent to assume leadership. There was a need in San Jose for building a compound, and besides being a dedicated missionary, James Walker was a skilled builder. The needed building was constructed. James and Shirley served in

Costa Rica until 1987 when they were succeeded by Richard and Margaret Taylor. The Walkers assumed leadership of the churches in Guatemala.[19]

Nicaragua—1952

Foursquare missions work in Nicaragua was initiated by an evangelistic campaign with government approval. Conducted in 1952 by the third gospel team—Dr. Fred Beard, Rev. Edwin Gurney, and Rev. Claude Updike—crowds in excess of fifteen thousand gathered. Hundreds were healed, and during the crusade more than ten thousand accepted Christ. Unfortunately, there was no missionary available to follow up the revival. When Rev. and Mrs. Allen Tolle arrived in Managua, some time later, opposing forces had influenced the government. While many friends awaited, unbelievers persisted in persecuting those who had been converted.

The Tolles had initial success, but soon the government closed the church. While opposition continued, however, the church was reopened after a time, with an evening attendance of 1,000. In 1956, 281 converts were reported, and a Bible institute and two day schools were started.[20]

Following interim stays of one year each by Dean Truett and Elmer McCammon, Charles and Nelwyn Gosling replaced the Allen Tolles, who had left the field in 1960 due to illness. They experienced eight fruitful years and left a field with seven established churches and twenty preaching places, all with national pastors. Later Mr. and Mrs. Floyd Frutiger served for two years.

In 1972 the country was devastated by a major earthquake, which killed over ten thousand people and destroyed the central church. In 1974 Rev. James and Shirley Walker were appointed resident missionaries. The Walkers located new property inasmuch as the government had condemned the old property due to its location between two major faults. A new central church was built with sufficient property for a Bible institute and a parsonage. When Rev. and Mrs. Walker were appointed to Costa Rica, the Bible institute had been reestablished and ten churches with national pastors were in operation.

In 1976 Rev. and Mrs. Jerry King were sent to the country to complete the church compound. However, due to the ill health of their daughter and the outbreak of civil war, Rev. and Mrs. King were forced to leave. The Walkers filled in for a four-month period, but in 1977 Rev. and Mrs. King returned to Nicaragua. They remained for two years, but finally, after the Sandinista revolution, their residence was ended.

This left the field without a missionary. However, the national leaders, under a national board, have continued the work with notable success. The Foursquare Church of Nicaragua is now fully registered with the government, having grown immensely, even through difficult circumstances.

Chile—1941/1950

An official Foursquare mission in Chile was recognized in 1950. Actually, Rev. Lillian Hemsley, a 1938 graduate from L.I.F.E. Bible College, had gone to Chile in 1941. She had solicited her own support in order to minister among the Mapuche Indians.

Several circumstances enabled her to establish a solid foundation. A ninety-five-year-old Indian chief, killed in an accident, was raised from the dead in answer to believing prayer by the missionary. As a result, Lillian was overwhelmingly received by the Indians.

After a major earthquake, Rev. Hemsley was enabled to do outstanding relief work among the homeless, resulting in great favor by the government, including a permanent visa. Her day schools for the Indians gained wide respect in the community.

In 1949 Lillian became ill from overwork, necessitating a furlough in the United States. While home, she appealed to the Missions Department for recognition and support. In response, Valerie Baker, who had been serving in Bolivia, was sent to Chile to assist. At Miss Baker's request, Rev. and Mrs. Ramon Perez from Bolivia were also transferred. The new team moved the headquarters from Trihueco to Temuco, a much larger city.

Ramon Perez invited Evangelist "Tommy" Hicks to hold an evangelistic campaign in the new headquarters city. All Christian groups cooperated in the city-wide meetings. At the final service the attendance reached twenty thousand persons. In 1953 Rev. Josephine Toon joined the staff in Chile, where she organized the Sunday schools, vacation Bible schools, and Crusader programs.

In 1956 a group under the direction of Rev. Angelo Arbizu, an alumnus of L.I.F.E. Bible College, requested union with the Foursquare mission in Chile. The merger was consummated in 1959, bringing the number of Foursquare churches in the nation to fifty-two. Their location stretched along the three-thousand-mile border from north to south.

In 1958 Rev. Leland Edwards was sent from Panama to meet with the personnel. He and his wife, Barbara, served there one year, during which the merger was consummated, the national bylaws were drawn up, and a national board was organized. Mr. and Mrs. Lloyd Hall, Foursquare laymen from Lancaster, California, who had gone to Chile to work with Rev. Arbizu, stayed on the field and served as Foursquare missionaries for a period of time.

Rev. and Mrs. George Faulkner transferred from Uruguay to Chile in 1959. In 1962 the Faulkners were called upon to assume leadership of the great work in Brazil, and Rev. and Mrs.

Elmer McCammon arrived in Chile. Development programs for national workers and leaders brought substantial growth.

In 1964 Rev. and Mrs. William Von Hoff were sent to Chile to assist with the Bible institute operation. In 1966 a new institute building and headquarters offices in Santiago were dedicated.

The year 1972 saw the direction of the Chilean field, with the exception of the supervisor Rev. Sheila Ransford, placed into the hands of the national leaders and pastors. Missionaries served as advisors and as teachers in the institute. More recent missionaries have been Rev. and Mrs. Glenn Pummel (1975–1982), Stan and Molly Doland (1986–1990), and Rev. Sheila Ransford (1972 to this writing).

Ecuador—1956

Rev. and Mrs. Arthur Gadberry were sent to Ecuador in 1956. They pioneered a Foursquare Gospel mission in the city of Guayaquil, at that time the principal seaport of Ecuador, with nearly one million people. Situated just south of the equator, its hot and humid climate was all the less hospitable by reason of primitive sanitary conditions. The social and religious culture was not inviting to evangelical teaching.

Street meetings and services in a rented building brought measured success. An evangelistic meeting on a vacant lot yielded little more response. By 1962, through perseverance, two small congregations were established, one in Guayaquil and one in a smaller city.

In 1962 Rev. and Mrs. Robert Aguirre, experienced pastors of Hispanic descent and who had served in Panama, were sent to replace the Gadberrys who were returning on furlough. After furlough Rev. and Mrs. Gadberry returned to the field, opening a new work in Quito, Ecuador. Rev. Aguirre invited Evangelist

Robert Espinosa, a Hispanic pastor from California, to conduct a revival campaign in the local bull ring.

The crowd was small at first. But in answer to prayer by the evangelist, a widely recognized crippled girl who regularly sat by the local post office was miraculously healed. The newspapers carried prominent notice of the healing. Soon the bull ring was filled with crowds, reported to be twenty thousand to forty thousand people. At the close of the six-week campaign, fifteen hundred people were baptized, and six hundred members were added to the Guayaquil church rolls.[21]

Because of the phenomenal growth, a larger building was required. A large property was obtained over which a mere roof was erected until a central church could be built. As a result of the revival, twelve new churches were started. Two later campaigns held by Evangelist Espinoza in 1965 and 1971 brought continued growth.

Such rapid expansion of the work in Ecuador called for the training of pastors and workers. When the number of congregations reached eighty, Rev. Dick Scott was sent to Ecuador to train leaders. A visit to Guayaquil by Rev. Leland Edwards from the office of the director of missions resulted in the dispatch to Ecuador of several additional missionary couples: Edwin and Vonitta Gurney (1965–1973), Dick and Dian Scott (1968–1969), Leslie and Dorothy Cole (1965–1971), and Henry and Dorothy Davis (1968–1973). Later missionaries were Elmer and Marjorie McCammon (1973–1975), John and Penny Douglas (1974–1989), and Jack and Aline Richey (1976–1985). Supervisors after Arthur Gadberry were Robert Aguirre, Edwin Gurney, Elmer McCammon, Jack Richey, and John Douglas.

When Rev. and Mrs. Henry Davis went to Ecuador in 1968, they located in Quito, the capital. In a year, the mountain churches around Quito grew in number from five to fourteen.

While conducting a service in the federal penitentiary, Henry discovered that many of the children of the inmates lived in the prison. There they received no education.

Rev. Davis became burdened for the youth and soon rented several buildings for the children whom he began to reach. He called these buildings "Houses of Happiness." Before long, Davis' orphanage work received recognition by the government, which donated fifty acres of land on which to erect more such housing. The Davises were awarded a special Medal of Recognition by the president of Ecuador. The "Houses of Happiness" have become famous in social and religious circles, in and out of the Foursquare Church.

Argentina—1955

One of the rapidly expanding missionary fields of the Foursquare Church is that of Argentina. The first effort to plant Foursquare churches in that nation was made in 1955 by a Chilean layman, Hugo Castro. A number of small churches were started by Castro and other laymen from Chile. However, disagreement between workers from the two countries finally nullified the effort. By 1966, when Rev. and Mrs. Vinton Johnson arrived in Argentina, all that remained of the aborted effort was a building in Buenos Aires, housing a small congregation.

The Johnsons, former faculty members of L.I.F.E. Bible College, soon founded a Bible training institute. One of their pupils started another Bible school in a place called Neuquen. The training of workers resulted, as usual, in the planting of new churches, which Rev. Johnson organized into divisions.

Rev. and Mrs. Michael Frederick, son-in-law and daughter of the Edwin Gurneys, were appointed in 1970 as supervisors of the Foursquare work in Argentina. Bylaws were prepared and a national board organized. To prepare for wide expansion, a beautiful new headquarters church and offices were built in Buenos Aires. Rev. Frederick established a T.E.E. program (Theological Education by Extension). Jackie Coppens, who had taught the program in Guatemala, was sent to carry the program further. Within three years T.E.E. was being taught in eighteen locations with 250 students enrolled. Rev. and Mrs. Frederick later returned to the United States where they pastored a church.

In the 1980s a wave of evangelism characterized by miracles of healing was centered in the province of Mendoza, under the leadership of the president of the Foursquare Gospel Church in Argentina, Roberto Prieto. Many new churches resulted, bringing Argentina's total number of Foursquare churches to more than six hundred congregations. Efforts were made by unsympathetic authorities to close the Mendoza work, but the proliferation of converts and churches overcame the opposition. The revival in Argentina began to have the earmarks of that in the nation of Brazil.[22]

Other missionaries working in Argentina have included Edwin and Vonitta Gurney (1973–1981; 1985–1986), Jim and Alice Tolle (1983–1987), and Denny and Brenda Truett (1987–this writing).

Japan—1949

Foursquare missionary interest in Japan goes back to the end of World War II. In an interview given in 1949 to Dr. Howard P. Courtney Sr., director of Foursquare Missions, General Douglas MacArthur expressed the urgent need for missionaries to Japan to fill the spiritual vacuum created by the military defeat. Suitable candidates were selected and prepared, and the department sent Rev. and Mrs. Carol Lucht and Rev. Billie Charles.

Initially they worked primarily with Youth for Christ, as

well as the U.S. Army chaplaincy in interdenominational evangelism. However, Billie was able to pioneer a small Foursquare congregation that built a church building in the section called Oizumi, near Tokyo. The congregation purchased the property; the Foursquare churches in the United States provided money for the construction of the building.

During Rev. Charles' furlough in 1952, Rev. and Mrs. Clifford Barrett were sent to Japan. Many evangelistic campaigns were held in various parts of the country. Roy Hicks Sr., T. L. Osborn, and the fifth gospel team, consisting of Clifford Barrett, Water Mussen, Kenneth Erickson, and Everett and Ruth Dennison, conducted the meetings.

While on furlough, Billie Charles married Rev. Jack Francey. When the newly married couple returned to Japan, they started two new churches, one of which was pastored by Timothy Ashida, a disciple of Billie.

In 1960 Rev. and Mrs. Francey returned to the United States after appointing Rev. David Masui, a Japanese graduate of L.I.F.E. Bible College, as pastor of the Oizumi church. An independent congregation in Hakodate, on the northernmost island of Hokkaido, sought affiliation with The Foursquare Church. Rev. Masui accepted the church and became its pastor.

At first the work in Hakodate grew very slowly. But after David Masui experienced a personal spiritual renewal through prayer and fasting, as well as an emphasis on worship, the Foursquare church in that city has become one of the largest congregations in the entire nation. In 1980 Rev. Masui was appointed supervisor of the Foursquare Church in Japan, relinquishing the Hakodate church to Rev. Mike Kamiya. As supervisor, Masui has planted several new churches. The Foursquare Church in Japan has now become a missionary-sending church, supplying workers and funds.

A significant beginning in other areas of Japan also began through the influence of the Hope Chapel Foursquare works in Hawaii under Rev. Ralph Moore's leadership.

Other North American missionaries to Japan have been Walter and Ina Mussen; Harold and Sherri Muetzel, who helped organize elders to care for the churches; and Wilma Wright, who assumed the pastorate of another independent church that had become Foursquare. The Japanese Foursquare churches are now fully staffed with national pastors and workers. In 1986 Bill and Carol Paris went to Japan to serve in a special support ministry.

Okinawa—1954

Another part of the work in Japan was carried out by several missionaries on the island of Okinawa, in the Ryukyu island chain. In 1954 a Canadian couple, Creston and Florence Ketchum, were sent to Okinawa. They had previously served in China.

North Americans were not well received in Okinawa, but the Ketchums gained the confidence of the people when, after a destructive typhoon, they were able to provide food and clothing for the homeless. This act of charity was reported by the media.

Rev. Ketchum had a great love for the sea. He envisioned carrying the gospel by boat to all of the surrounding islands. A boat was provided, which he named "The Island Evangel." He took the gospel to a number of the islands, but unfortunately the boat was destroyed in a storm. Another boat was purchased for the island ministry, but it also sank in a 1961 storm. Because of illness, the Ketchums returned to Canada, after they founded a church in Naha, Okinawa's principal city.

In 1964 the Franceys were appointed to direct the mission

in Okinawa. After tent meetings, through a radio ministry, book publications, and worker training, the work was solidified. When they left, nearly six years later, the work had been established under national leaders and workers.

Australia—1929/1953

A Foursquare church was planted in Australia in 1929 by Rev. and Mrs. William Kay. They were invited by a small group of people who had been converted during a campaign in Australia by Aimee Semple McPherson in the early 1920s. Over the years the work remained small but persistent. When Elmer and Jean Darnall arrived in Perth in 1953, a nucleus of fourteen Foursquare people remained to back a work in an area called Victoria Park.

Through the miraculous healing of a paralyzed man, a number of new converts were added to the group. With the help of the U.S. Missions Department, they purchased property and built a sanctuary. A correspondence school was organized to train and provide workers, resulting in the opening of several additional churches. In 1957 Rev. Billy Adams conducted a revival campaign in which two hundred souls were won added to the church in Perth.

The Darnalls accomplished much through a network of radio broadcasts. Correspondence courses were also carried out through radio. These brought considerable growth and stability. The Western Australia Foursquare churches began to have a vision for the world. In 1959 they sent their first missionary to New Guinea. Rev. Ian Van Zuilacom, having had medical training as a doctor's assistant, gave much-needed help to Rev. Mason Hughes. At the twenty-fifth anniversary celebration of the Foursquare churches in Papua New Guinea, it was revealed that the Foursquare churches in Western Australia had sent twenty-one missionaries to that country.

Later missionaries to Western Australia were Rev. and Mrs. Weldon Mickel and Rev. and Mrs. Robert Tracey (1959), who served as supervisors until the passing of Mrs. Tracey in 1968. They were assisted in the Bible school for four years (1964–1967) by the James Kitchells. In 1967 Rev. and Mrs. Fred Cowan went to Australia to assist with the youth and camping programs. Rev. Cowan later became the supervisor, serving until 1983 when the work was placed under totally Australian leadership. Rev. William Pope, pastor of the Morley Foursquare Church, was selected as supervisor and chairman of the board.

At first, the Western Australia Foursquare Church avoided using the name "Foursquare." This was because an already existing group in Sydney, Eastern Australia, had incorporated under the name "Elim Foursquare Church." The Elim group had originated in England.

When the Darnalls went to Perth in 1953, the Elim group, which had been established in Australia since 1931, numbered seven churches. At the twenty-fourth annual convention of the Elim group, they invited Rev. Darnall to be their special speaker. Affiliation with the International Church of the Foursquare Gospel was discussed. One year later, ICFG general supervisor Howard P. Courtney Sr. was invited to Sydney to be the principal speaker. At that convention the delegates voted unanimously to unite and to change their name to International Church of the Foursquare Gospel of Australasia.

In 1955 Australian-born Don Baker entered L.I.F.E. Bible College, graduating in 1958. Returning to Australia, he pioneered Calvary Chapel Foursquare Church in Greenacre, Sydney, which is now one of the largest Pentecostal churches in Australia. At the time of this writing, there were twenty-four

Foursquare churches in Eastern Australia, with Don Baker serving as supervisor and president of the board of directors. The churches in Eastern Australia have sent thirty-four missionaries to Papua New Guinea, among whom are Graham and Irene Baker. (Graham is Don's brother.)

Papua New Guinea—1956

Of the three or four mission fields most interesting to Foursquare membership, one is that of Papua New Guinea (PNG). PNG occupies the eastern half of the largest island south of the Equator and directly north of Australia. For decades it had been governed by Australia. When the Mason Hughes family went to Papua New Guinea in 1956, there was a population of about 1.2 million in the entire nation. At that time, a missionary wishing to start a work in PNG was required by the Australian government to have an invitation from a resident within the country. The necessary invitation was supplied by Rev. Ron Teale, who had resided in PNG since 1939. Rev. Teale is at this writing credentialed by the National Foursquare Church in PNG.[23]

The majority of the inhabitants of PNG were primitive natives, some of whom still practiced cannibalism and head-hunting. While there were three official languages, English, Pidgin, and Hirimoth, the many tribes who were frequently at war with each other spoke hundreds of dialects. Most of the tribal people could neither read nor write. Untouched by civilization, they worshiped evil spirits, under the control of sorcerers. A challenge lay before the Christian missionary.

For the first year Mason Hughes devoted most of his time to learning Pidgin. He then purchased a used army Jeep in which he made a number of trips into the interior, looking for a site to locate the Foursquare mission station. On a trip through the Dunantina Valley, God spoke, saying, "This is where I want you." Mason returned to get Mrs. Hughes and the children. He remembers, "The first trip into the valley was faced by many anxious moments as Virgene and the children saw for the first time the people who had so recently been fighting and eating one another."[24]

Immediately Rev. Hughes began holding services in the yard of their home. The natives of the area cautiously began to attend to hear about Jesus and His love. After six months of patient witnessing, a prominent native named Tabiak stepped out of the crowd dressed in his loin cloth and feathered headdress, carrying his bows and arrows. He said, "I want to try what you have been telling us about." Immediately, by the power of the Holy Spirit, his whole life was transformed. Soon, after closely observing the life of Tabiak, the whole village came to Jesus.[25]

Mason taught the men how to use saws, with which they cut timber to build a mission compound. The Good News went from village to village. Soon a Bible school and a medical clinic were added.

God also added faithful workers. At the first outpouring of the Holy Spirit in 1963, a young man named Inagori was filled. He has played an important part in the history of Foursquare missions in Papua New Guinea.

The work grew so large that many helpers were needed to staff the scores of works that sprang up. Many missionaries were sent from the Foursquare churches in Western and Eastern Australia, including a number from the Christian Revival Crusade (C.R.C.), directed by Pastor Leo Harris of Adelaide. In a meeting between Dr. Rolf K. McPherson and Pastor Harris, an agreement was reached for the Foursquare Church and C.R.C. to work together in Papua New Guinea. During a period of twenty-five years, seventy-four missionaries from the four sending sources have participated together in the evangelization of the nation. The first missionary to join Mason Hughes was Rev. Ian Van Zuilecom, a medical doctor's assistant, who arrived from Perth, West Australia in 1959.

A powerful work has been done in Papua New Guinea by the churches of Eastern Australia, supervised by Rev. and Mrs. Don Baker. Rev. and Mrs. Graham Baker (a brother of Don) pastor the largest church in PNG, which has around two thousand in regular attendance. He also supervises eighty other churches.

The first missionaries sent to PNG from the Eastern Australia Foursquare Church were Rev. and Mrs. Albert Booth, who arrived in 1957. They were followed by Rev. Graham Baker in 1963, who went to PNG to build housing for a station and school. In 1967, after furlough, Graham and Irene Baker returned to New Guinea to build a medical clinic. While Graham ministered the Word, Irene worked in the clinic helping to deliver babies (three hundred in the first three years). The clinic serves a community of around ten thousand people. About two thousand outpatients per month pass through the doors.

In 1971 the Bakers moved from the mission station in the town of Fore to the large city of Madang, center of the present combined Foursquare Mission. In addition to the Hughes family, missionaries from ICFG in North America have been Paul and Darlene Palmer (1966–1970), who supervised the work during the Hughes family's first furlough; Larry and JoAnn Six (1970–1973), who formerly had served in Nigeria and later in Hong Kong; Phil and Diane Franklin (1977–1983); Phil and Millie Starr (1979–1981), who after ten years in the Philippine Islands served as supervisor of PNG and later would serve in the Missions Department in Los Angeles; Tim and Claudia Kelton (1981–1983); Lloyd and Claire Post (1983–1988), who served as supervisor; and present supervisors Frank and Kathy Greer (1983–to this writing).

Rev. and Mrs. Hughes moved to the city-nation of Singapore in 1982, where they pioneered a new Foursquare work. From there new fields throughout Southeast Asia have been opened to the International Church of the Foursquare Gospel, including Thailand, Burma, and Malaysia.

South Korea—1969

The Foursquare Church in South Korea resulted from an invitation. In 1969 Mr. and Mrs. S. O. Ahn requested that the International Church of the Foursquare Gospel send missionaries to that nation. The Ahns, former refugees from Communist North Korea, had migrated in 1952 to Daejon, South Korea. There they founded a Christian high school, which by1966 had grown to six schools involving hundreds of students form several faiths.

Desiring to win the students to Christ, Mrs. Ahn followed the leading of the Holy Spirit and came to the United States to study. In a dream she saw an unknown man who awarded her with a certificate of ordination. One year later, she met Dr. Rolf K. McPherson, whom she recognized as the man in her dream. She enrolled in L.I.F.E. Bible College, requesting that Dr. McPherson send missionaries to Daejon, Korea.

In response, Rev. and Mrs. Arthur Thompson, who had been very successful missionaries in the Philippines for fifteen years, were sent to Daejon. The Thompsons began an evangelistic ministry to the students of the school, preaching in chapel services that had already been initiated by Mr. and Mrs. Ahn. Many were won to Christ, and an evangelism training program was developed among the students.

In 1970 evangelism throughout the schools, with the help of trained students, won over six thousand students to Christ. Most of these had been Buddhists. When Mrs. Ahn returned to Daejon in 1971, a piece of ground was purchased and a Foursquare church was erected. In 1972 a second church in the city was started.

When the Thompsons returned to the United States in 1972, Rev. and Mrs. Harold Muetzel, Foursquare missionaries to Japan, were given the additional responsibility of supervising the Foursquare work in South Korea. However, in 1974 the Muetzels moved to Daejon to give full-time to the work in Korea, concentrating on Bible school development and the training of workers, including T.E.E. (Theological Education by Extension).

In 1978 Rev. and Mrs. Ron Myers, who had been serving in Korea for five years, were made supervisors, succeeding the Muetzels. Later, Rev. Myers moved his headquarters to Seoul, where a church had been pioneered by Chang Do Oh. A severely restricting law passed by the Korean government in 1980 forced the closing of the Bible institutes. To prepare Foursquare teachers to comply with the new standards, four men were sent abroad to study. One of these was Yeol Soo Eim, who attended and graduated from Fuller Theological Seminary with a doctoral degree in missiology. In fulfilling his dissertation, Dr. Eim wrote a fine thesis on the history of Foursquare missions, a work for which we are all indebted to him.[26]

When a national board was formed in 1985, the elected president was Rev. Mrs. Seen Ok Ahn. Since that time, missionaries have acted in an advisory capacity. One who has been an outstanding blessing and deeply loved by the Korean believers in Rev. Pat. Conrad. Until her retirement brought on by ill health, Pat worked closely with Mrs. Ahn in the training of Foursquare workers.

Sri Lanka—1976

An exciting missionary work is being accomplished in the nation of Sri Lanka, formerly known as Ceylon. The founding dates back to 1976 when Mr. and Mrs. Richard Kiser, dedicated members of the Kokomo, Indiana, Foursquare Church, retired from management in the steel industry. They began to search for another part of the world to start a second career. For a lengthy period of time, Richard had felt an intense burden for the nation of India.

During a residence in the nation of Sri Lanka, they invited people to their home for Bible study. The studies developed into gospel meetings, which led to the establishment of a church. When news of the new church was reported, Richard and Betty were appointed as Foursquare missionaries.

God also led Richard into contact with a young Sri Lankan named Leslie Keegel, who, as a boy, had been healed of a terminal illness. Leslie had already been preaching and had witnessed many come to the Lord. Richard Kiser sensed the aptitude of the clearly gifted youth, who had also received a good general education. He sent the lad to the Philippine Islands to study in the Foursquare Bible colleges there.

Following graduation with a Bachelor of Theology degree in 1981, Leslie returned to Sri Lanka with his newly married Filipino wife, Belen. When Richard Kiser returned to the United States in 1984, Leslie was made supervisor of the Foursquare Gospel Church in Sri Lanka.

Under Keegel's leadership, the growth of the Foursquare Church in Sri Lanka has literally skyrocketed, in spite of civil war and widespread demon possession. According to reports, during a recent two-month period, there were 614 converts, 80 baptisms, 155 people baptized with the Holy Spirit, and 836 people miraculously healed. Nearly 100 students were in training for ministry to the multiplying new churches. It is reported that the Foursquare Church in Sri Lanka is the fastest-growing church in the country.[27]

Other Asian Foursquare missions are located in Borneo, Sumatra, Java, Myanmar (Burma), Pakistan, Nepal, and Taiwan. A very fine national church has been established in India headed by John and Vijaya Gnanaolivu and consists of a number of churches pastored by nationals. The work is mostly self-supporting.

EUROPE

As of this writing, Foursquare churches are now located in seven European countries. These churches, largely self-supporting, could hardly be considered as missionary churches in the usual concept. However, since most of them were pioneered by U.S. personnel and initially supported by the North American Foursquare Church, they will be included in this chapter.

The first European Foursquare church was one of our earliest. The church in Athens, Greece, began in 1930 and has already been discussed.

Our next enterprise in Europe was the Foursquare church in Spain, pioneered in 1974 by Robert and Alva Aguirre. More recent missionaries to Spain have been Bill and Betty Pritchett (1978–1979; 1982–1983); John and Donna Verbarendse (1979–1990); Tim Lamb and supervisors, Stan and Molly Doland. In the city of Madrid there is a central church and meeting places, as well as a Bible institute.

Michael and Jill Picone pioneered the Foursquare church in Paris, France. Michael, a member of the Eugene, Oregon, Foursquare Church, went to Paris to further his studies. While he was there, a group of believers was organized for Bible study. Mary Ann Winter served with the church there, as well as expedited a program of correspondence Bible courses for use by Foursquare leadership in French-speaking sections of Africa.

Jorg and Elke Schmidt supervised the Foursquare Church in West Germany and pastored in the city of Hanover. Foursquare missionaries Marc and Kathy Shaw pastored a growing congregation in the industrial city of Frankfurt. With the tremendously surprising changes in Eastern Europe in 1989 and the demolition of the Berlin Wall, the time was ripe for great revival.

The Foursquare church in Stathelle, Norway, was pastored by John Henry Nosen. He was also supervisor of the Foursquare work in that nation. A program of evangelism was carried out in Odense, Denmark, by the Foursquare congregation under the pastoral leadership of Kai Patterson. Several congregations in Southern England are being supervised by Ian Walker. The British churches now support missions in Pakistan and Sierra Leone.

The *Foursquare World Advance* reported plans made by the church in Hoogblokland to pioneer three new churches in the Netherlands in 1990. The supervisor, Rev. Hank Rothuizen, pastors an aggressive church that envisions one hundred churches by the year 1995.

New fields are opening in Eastern Europe, about which information will be given in the mission department's information guide.

United Foursquare Women—1955

Another aid to Foursquare missions was the organization of the United Foursquare Women. Mrs. Lois Van Cleave, who had served together with her husband as a missionary, viewed at close range the usefulness of a well-organized women's group. After returning from the mission field, Lois and her husband pastored at Moline Gospel Temple and, later, at the Long Beach,

California, Foursquare Church. In each of these congregations she participated in women's group activities, which were a great blessing to the missionary fields. It seemed a pity to her that while many churches had a local "Dorcas" society, there was no united action or knowledgeable choice of projects.

Mrs. Edythe Dorrance, wife of the Southern California District supervisor, observing the limited work of her ladies' groups, began to be likewise concerned about how to make such church groups more useful and productive. The two women got together to discuss their concerns for the potential of organized women.

In 1954 Dr. and Mrs. Nathaniel Van Cleave were appointed to the newly created Southwest District. The region of their responsibility was adjacent to the district supervised by Dr. and Mrs. Earl Dorrance, making possible a bi-district united women's organization. Permission to organize was given by the ICFG president, Dr. McPherson, and the board of directors. In late 1954 the United Foursquare Women became a reality, with Mrs. Elmer (Billie) Card chosen as the first UFW president. At the next annual international convention the United Foursquare Women became a worldwide women's organization.

During the first ten years of the UFW's work, 88,072 pieces, 56 boxes, and 1 barrel of clothing were sent to mission fields. Forty-two thousand eight hundred sixteen articles and 6 boxes of clothing were given to missionaries on furlough. Through a fund called "Dollars for Darlings" the women provided financial help for foreign orphanages. Hundreds of books were provided for missions schools, etc.[28] Such early beginnings paved the way for habits of ministry, which UFW graciously continues today.

Foursquare Missions Press

The story of Foursquare missions would not be complete without a report of the important work of Foursquare Missions Press. Foursquare Missions Press became a viable part of the Missions Department as a special project on May 1, 1981. Churches and individuals rallied in a phenomenal manner to provide equipment and personnel for the publication of tracts and booklets for distribution on the mission fields. At this writing, Foursquare Missions Press operates a fully equipped printing plant with three large presses, located in the city of Paramount, California, about fifteen miles from the Foursquare Church's central offices in Los Angeles.

In the decade between May 1, 1981, and May 1, 1991, Foursquare Missions Press supplied foreign missions fields in fifty countries with 58,325,775 pieces of literature, consisting of tracts and booklets in nineteen languages. This literature brought the gospel message to millions of people and helped to train thousands of pastors and workers.

At home, Foursquare Missions Press supplies material for use in jails, juvenile halls, and rehabilitation centers. The work and growth of Foursquare Missions Press is the result of the persistent effort and leadership of Karl and Leona Williams and the help of scores of volunteer workers and contributors.

Directors of Foursquare Missions International

During the 1920s, 1930s, and early 1940s, the missionary programs of the International Church of the Foursquare Gospel was directed by the founder, Aimee Semple McPherson, with the assistance of her mother, Mrs. Kennedy; Dr. Billy Black; and Dr. Giles Knight. As in the early years of all Pentecostal denominations, great dependence was placed upon prayer and the direct guidance of the Holy Spirit for the selection and support of missionaries.

With the passing of the founder, direction of the missionary program became the responsibility of Rolf K. McPherson, Dr. Howard P. Courtney Sr., and Dr. Herman D. Mitzner. Drs. Courtney and Mitzner cared for the details of missions, but a very active hand in most major decisions was that of Dr. McPherson, who had inherited the deep love of world evangelism from his mother.

Dr. Herman Mitzner, who gave years to the office of Director of Foreign Missions, was a man of prayer. He prescribed prayer and fasting for almost every missionary problem. Though he seldom visited the fields, he daily spent time on his knees praying for the missionaries. When he did visit a field or a church, his first interest was in how many were receiving the baptism with the Holy Spirit. He was deeply loved by the missionaries and conveyed a passion for the things of the Spirit, which live on in the hearts of many of the leaders to this day.

One could call the years 1965–1988 the "Leland Edwards Era" of missionary leadership. Leland, son of a great pioneer missionary, Arthur Edwards, grew up in Panama, where he served until late 1959. His great understanding of the Hispanic culture and grasp of the Spanish language made him extremely valuable in the direction of the missionary program, especially in the countries of Central and South America.

Leland Edwards learned from his parents, and from Dr. Mitzner, who was a "second father" to him, the importance of prayer and of following the Spirit's guidance. He also understood the need for following policy. Thus, during his tenure, definite policies were for missionary conduct were established. Edwards attended cross-cultural conferences, interdenominational missionary conventions, and other missions-related meetings with regularity. His wife, Barbara, gave valuable assistance, and he worked hand in glove with Dr. McPherson.[29]

After nearly a quarter century of headquarters ministry and about sixty years of world missions service, Leland and Barbara retired. There is no way to measure the love and esteem their tenure of service begot in the hearts of our missionaries. However, when the fruit of their labors is examined, there is much for which to give God glory and the Edwards our thanks.

From the time Leland Edwards became director of missions in 1965 until his retirement, the number of overseas churches and meeting places grew from 1,527 to 17,627 congregations. In 1965 the Foursquare Gospel was being proclaimed in twenty-seven countries; in 1988 there were over one million members and adherents in sixty-two countries outside the United States and Canada.

In 1988, together with the selection of Dr. John R. Holland as ICFG president, a new director of Foursquare Missions International was appointed. Prior to this appointment Dr. Roy H. Hicks Jr. and his lovely wife, Kay, supervised the Northwest District as well as pastored the large Faith Center Foursquare Church in Eugene, Oregon. He was a leader with high intelligence, sensitivity to the Holy Spirit, and a record for achievement. The future of Foursquare Missions was in good hands.

Dr. Hicks also enlisted many excellent and experienced members to assist him at the headquarters level in overseeing Foursquare missions ministries abroad. They include: Richard F. Schmidt, a former aircraft industry executive (also a former chairman of the board of regents of L.I.F.E. Bible College and member of the ICFG board of directors); Don McGregor, who served as regional field representative (also a former pastor, executive director of L.I.F.E. Bible College, and missionary to the Philippines); John Amstutz, who has served as missionary to Jamaica and a faculty member of L.I.F.E. Bible College; Lee Schnabel, a former missionary to Central America and an accomplished linguist; David Metsker, former missionary to Nigeria and director of L.I.F.E. Theological Seminary in Lagos, Nigeria; Gary Cooper, former captain with the Los Angeles Police Department, pastor, and missionary to Hong Kong; and Margie Waldo, who represented Foursquare Missions International to Europe. (Roy Hicks Jr. died in 1994.)

Foursquare Missions International was directed by proven leaders and staffed by personnel with the finest credentials and experience. Will F.M.I. rightly interpret the Spirit's leading for these times? Will they respond to the challenge of a world just waiting to be evangelized? There is every reason to believe that they will!

Chapter 7

THE SEPARATED BRANCHES OF THE VINE

1932–1984

NO MATTER HOW healthy a vine may be, in periods of rapid growth there is activity and traffic and some branches will get broken and separated from the main trunk. The same observation holds true for ecclesiastical vines and branches. There is no church organization that has not experienced the secession of some branch congregations or groups of churches. Over these many years the International Church of the Foursquare Gospel has, in comparison to its growth, had very few such experiences.

Even in apostolic times there were occasions when sincere, godly workers found it necessary to go separate ways. Beginning their second missionary journey, Paul and Barnabas were unable to agree as to the inclusion of John Mark in their party. So unmovable in their convictions were both apostles that they went different directions with newly selected companions.[1]

The Jerusalem church could not reach an agreement on the ceremonial law, circumcision, or the Hellenistic culture. An ecumenical council was called to settle the matters of disagreement. Under the guidance of the Holy Spirit agreement was reached and New Testament principles of conduct were established. However, a Judaizing party continued to oppose Paul and to content for legalistic practices. And today, sincere Christians still may disagree over patterns of individual conduct or church government without ceasing to love one another.

Rev. John R. Richey and Open Bible Standard Churches—1932

Because of the loose affiliation that existed in the early development of Foursquare churches, it was not unusual for single separations of a church or mission station to take place now and then. However, a major separation of a group of churches from ICFG occurred in 1932, just five years following the church's incorporation. In August of that year a group of thirty-two pastors in the states of Iowa and Minnesota, under the supervision of Rev. John R. Richey, voted to withdraw. According to a Des Moines, Iowa, newspaper, "'Certain widespread publicity' and policies of the International Church's leadership were given by the Rev. Mr. Richey as reasons for the withdrawal."[2]

Several reasons were given for the separation. Among the primary causes for disagreement were: (1) a proposed bylaw change requiring all Foursquare church properties acquired after January 1934 to be held centrally by the ICFG; and (2) strong central government and the life-tenure of Mrs. McPherson as president.[3] Concern was also raised over the personal decision of Mrs. McPherson to marry Mr. David Hutton, a matter that she herself later considered to be one of the worst mistakes of her life.[4]

Certain congregations in Iowa and Minnesota remained as part of ICFG, and several who initially withdrew later returned. Individuals on both sides of the division appeared to act in good conscience and friendships remained unbroken.[5]

With references to these issues, since any minister's personal life cannot be separated from the affairs of their ministry, Mrs. McPherson's decision greatly impacted the church that she founded. As to the issue of strong central government with life-tenure, when compared with some Pentecostal groups, the history of Foursquare unity would show it to have been a blessing.

Rev. John Richey and the pastors who withdrew formed the Open Bible Standard Bible Churches, with their headquarters located in Des Moines. These ministers were some of the finest products of L.I.F.E. Bible College. Because of their unquestionable sincerity and godliness, their church prospered.

OBSC historian, R. Bryant Mitchell, comments on the separation:

> Looking back at this event from the perspective of half a century, it should be said that the action of the Iowa group was a matter of conscience. Likewise, for their close friends and co-laborers who chose to remain with the parent group, it was also a matter of conscience. In the intervening years, both groups have prospered. There has been a spirit of mutual respect and brotherly love manifested by the leadership of the two organizations.[6]

In review, one could think of ways the separation might have been avoided. Surveying church history, it is not too difficult to imagine steps that could have been taken to greatly reduce the number of different denominations. Yet one has to believe that the variety of modes of worship and approaches to ministry appears to have given the gospel a far wider appeal than it would have had, wrapped in a single denominational garment.

Division is not ideal, but God sometimes uses our human weaknesses to accomplish a far greater work. It is altogether possible that separated, the ICFG and the OBSC, though fraternal and cooperative, have accomplished far more than had they remained under a single covering.

Is it not possible that the creation of the National Association of Evangelicals (NAE) and the Pentecostal Fellowship of North America (PFNA) has provided all evangelical and Pentecostal Christians a unity in diversity that enables Bible-believing Christians to serve God with a united front?

Could it not be that the two teams of Paul with Silas and Barnabas with John Mark accomplished more than the one team might have ever dreamed? Can there not exist true ecumenicity without denominational union that reduces Bible doctrine to the lowest common denominator? Between the ICFG and the OBSC there is love, respect, and central purpose on which structural unity could never improve. If we are not denominational "brothers," then we are certainly "first cousins," and always "brothers" in Christ!

Riverside, California—1934

Another separation of a branch had great historical importance for the ICFG. To understand what took place, one must return to the first graduating class of the Foursquare Bible Institute (L.I.F.E.).

The first class consisted of two men and fourteen women. Among these students of the spring 1925 class was a married couple, Mr. and Mrs. Delmar V. Alderman, who possessed outstanding promise for the ministry. They were the first graduates to be ordained to Foursquare ministry. Mrs. Alderman was the preacher; her husband was a capable teacher and business manager.

The Aldermans accepted appointment to pastor a large church in Riverside, California, that had been pioneered by the world-renowned evangelist Dr. A. G. Garr of Charlotte, North

Carolina. The church prospered under their ministry, and by 1929 property had been acquired and a beautiful new sanctuary and Christian education building had been erected. On Sundays more than six hundred people filled the pews.

Upon the resignation of John Goben as general supervisor of Foursquare churches in 1929, Mrs. McPherson asked Rev. Alderman to accept the position at Foursquare headquarters. He accepted, but Mrs. Alderman continued to pastor the Riverside, California, church. One year later, however, Rev. Alderman asked for a one-year leave of absence from the corporate office to return to Riverside to strengthen the internal organization of that local congregation. In 1931 the Aldermans reluctantly resigned the pastorate, at Sister McPherson's request, in order to give full-time to the work of supervision. The vacancy in the Riverside church was filled by Rev. and Mrs. William Wildman.[7]

Problems arose between ICFG and the Alderman family. Several things had become a problem for them: the reasons and circumstances surrounding the withdrawal of the Iowa churches under their close friend John Richey; the change in the way local church properties were centrally held; and a call from the majority of the Riverside congregation who had never given them up and could not accept Rev. and Mrs. William Wildman as their replacements. The Aldermans withdrew from the ICFG in early 1934.

As general supervisor, Rev. Alderman had agreed with the new bylaws proposal to hold all branch properties under the corporate title. The Riverside, California, property was transferred by the local trustees to the International Church of the Foursquare Gospel. But when he withdrew from the denomination, Rev. Alderman improperly retained the deed. Returning to Riverside while the Wildmans were on vacation, and with the deed in their possession, the Aldermans (still greatly loved by the people) took charge as pastors. Rev. and Mrs. Wildman returned home to find the church closed to them.

There were still between eighty to one hundred people of the Riverside, California, congregation who remained intensely loyal to the ICFG, its founder, and its message. Together with Rev. and Mrs. Wildman, local Foursquare laymen such as the Burts, Hoovers, Whites, Harrises, Bill Cantor, Daytons, Harts, Willises, Mrs. Carmain, and others requested that the Riverside Foursquare Church continue in a rented facility. They expressed their will to stay with a denomination that they felt God was blessing; for in national evangelistic tours by Mrs. McPherson in 1933 and 1934, new churches had been planted in twenty-one states across the United States.[8] In January 1935 the Wildmans accepted the pastorate of the Denver, Colorado, Foursquare Church. Dr. and Mrs. Nathaniel Van Cleave were sent to pastor the Riverside congregation.

Since the original Riverside property had been transferred to the ICFG, a lawsuit was brought against the Aldermans and their group to recover the property. The case rested on the fact that the deed gave legal title to the denomination and that there existed a solid following of Foursquare people who desired to perpetuate the church. Following a year of deliberation, the judge (though in sympathy with the Alderman group) decided in favor of the ICFG, declaring that the law was clearly on the side of the denomination.

The media, however, had represented the case as an example of a foreign corporation wresting property from a local constituency. Thus, though the Foursquare group took possession of the original property, a bias had been formed. The Van Cleaves were placed at a disadvantage in building up the congregation or reaching the community. After one year Rev. and Mrs. Van Cleave resigned to assume the pastorate of the Decatur,

Illinois, Foursquare Church. They were replaced by Rev. and Mrs. Howard P. Courtney Sr., who did an outstanding work. The Courtneys stayed more than three years, until they were appointed as supervisors of the Great Lakes District.

The Riverside litigation became a landmark case. It established the fact in precedence that a church denomination with central government holds property for the use of its member congregations. It cannot be taken away by a dissident group. This would become of great importance in the 1970s, when one of the Phoenix, Arizona, church groups withdrew and sued the ICFG to recover property that had been given to The Foursquare Church. The case was decided in favor of the ICFG.

Such a landmark precedent is not, however, the only result that came from the recovery of the Riverside property. A Foursquare church has remained in that city until the present, with others being started in the surrounding areas.

One of these is the Arlington, California, Foursquare Church, pioneered near the end of the Courtneys' ministry in Riverside. It was first pastored by Rev. Mary Johnson. Later, under the ministry of Rev. and Mrs. Barney Northcote, the Arlington congregation became larger than the original Riverside church and is today one of the leading churches in the Southwest District.

The church that seceded under the Aldermans also prospered and remains one of the stronger churches in the Riverside area. It is affiliated with a non-Pentecostal organization.

Another great blessing arising from that difficulty must be shared. One of the loyal Foursquare members that remained steadfast during this time was Mrs. Carmain, the mother of Mrs. Harold Jefferies and Rev. Jack Carmain. Together with her husband she operated an independent general store on Magnolia Street in Riverside. Though her husband was not a professing Christian at that time, Mrs. Carmain loved to assist needy people by providing groceries and clothing from their store.

In the late 1930s a family moved into a humble place near the Carmain store. Noticing that the man of the family was lame and that the children were poorly dressed, Mrs. Carmain took them food. One day she invited them to attend the church, which was still being pastored by Rev. and Mrs. Courtney. She was informed that while the family were Christians, they were reluctant to attend church because they, especially the children, lacked clothing and shoes. Mrs. Carmain saw that the need was filled, and on the next Sunday the entire family attended the Foursquare church.

These newfound friends were named John and Mary Thrasher. They united with the church and became very active, faithful workers. Mary would assist Mrs. Carmain and Mrs. Courtney in witnessing and visitation. A pair of shoes had won a family!

But that's not the end of the story.

In 1939 Rev. and Mrs. Howard P. Courtney Sr. became supervisors of the Great Lakes District. They set up residence in Urbana, Illinois. On one of their winter itineraries among the churches in the area, they stopped by the district office only long enough to pick up their mail. They then resumed their journey. But because of a snowstorm they had to stop for the night in the city of Elgin, Illinois. There they found time to read their mail.

To their surprise, one of the letters was from the Thrashers, who had moved to Newcastle, Indiana. In the letter they were pleading that a Foursquare church be started in that city, and they promised to go door to door inviting people.

In 1943 a tent meeting was held in Newcastle. The Thrashers were among the most active in starting the pioneer work, faithfully supporting Rev. and Mrs. H. L. Myers, the church's first pastors. In 1949 Rev. and Mrs. Lindsay Flowers, originally from

Newcastle, were appointed as pastors. Under their shepherding, the congregation became one of the leading churches of the Great Lakes District and remains so until this day.

Because of a pair of shoes, not only was a family won, but also the family was instrumental in the founding of a great church. How important it proved to maintain a Foursquare presence in Riverside, California!

Dr. and Mrs. Sidney Correll—1940

Among the first graduating class of L.I.F.E. Bible College in 1925 was a talented young lady evangelist who helped pioneer the Foursquare church in Pasadena, California. Helen Elliot (Correll) was a classmate of Eva Alderman and Louise Richey.

Soon after graduation, Helen married Sidney Correll. Together they pioneered the church in Fullerton, California. The Corrells also pioneered at least seven congregations in California, Colorado, Iowa, Wisconsin, and Illinois. Dr. Sidney Correll, for nine years the supervisor of the Great Lakes District, distinguished himself as a champion of Foursquare missions and visited many of the fields.

In 1940 the Corrells withdrew from the ICFG.[9] Reasons for the separation were never made public; however, some who were close to Sidney and Helen discerned several motives.

First of all, Dr. Giles Knight was the general supervisor at that time. While he had rendered an invaluable service to our founder, to Angelus Temple, and to the denomination as a whole, certain of the leadership were frustrated by Knight's administrative style. Sidney Correll was one of them. Rev. Correll had many innovative ideas about foreign missions, which at one time seemed revolutionary or, perhaps, ahead of the time. Dr. Knight, who was also director of missions at that time, was not responsive.

Sidney Correll had also moved the Great Lakes District office from Kenosha, Wisconsin, to Cleveland, Ohio, in order to be nearer the center of the district's area of responsibility. When the large church in Dayton, Ohio, needed a pastor, Rev. Correll again moved the office to Dayton and began shepherding the congregation.

In 1938 Dr. Knight initiated a rule that district supervisors could not pastor a church while holding their office. It was understandable, for the work of supervision requires devoting full time to the district office and visiting the churches on Sundays. Pastoring was a full-time job in itself. Sidney Correll, however, might have been an exception. With the ultimatum to give up one or the other and feeling that the rule's enforcement was aimed at him, Rev. Correll chose to continue pastoring the Dayton church, where they were greatly loved by the people. He relinquished the district to Dr. Howard Courtney Sr. in the spring of 1939. From that time on, it appeared that a degree of alienation existed. It might be mentioned that the rule also applied to Dr. Harold Jefferies of Portland, Oregon, who resigned his supervisory role in the Northwest District to Dr. Clarence Hall.

When the congregation in Dayton had found an ideal site for a beautiful new church facility, to avoid an inflated price, they purchased the property in the name of one of the church council members. Dr. Knight insisted the new property be placed in the name of the ICFG, the rule for all Foursquare properties. The council member in whose name the property was being held refused to comply. Apparently the feeling that Rev. Correll was being uncooperative and charged with the responsibility of enforcing the bylaws, Dr. Knight issued a dated ultimatum. The Corrells withdrew from the ICFG in 1940, as did the Dayton congregation.

Looking back, one can see how patience on the part of both leaders might have preserved unity. In any case, following the separation, Dr. Correll founded a nondenominational parachurch missionary organization called "United World Mission." A number of Foursquare churches joined him in the effort. Some returned later to the Foursquare family, reducing the loss to not more than five or six churches (mostly in Ohio). Notwithstanding, by 1949 there were more Foursquare churches in Ohio than in any other state outside of California.

The United World Mission continues to the present doing an effective missionary work. The Corrells have loved and respected the ICFG, and the feeling is mutual. At the time of Sidney's death in September 1991, the Corrells resided in Roanoke, Virginia, and often attended Foursquare events. Helen continues to show those lovely and loving qualities that delineate the true Christian woman. Ministers who received their start in ministry of the Corrells have fond memories.

It is unfortunate that personal feelings, as well as emotional situations, often bring irreversible separations. But how wonderful it is that God heals wounds and prevails over human errors!

The Door—1983

One other major separation of branches happened in Arizona. The relational straw that "broke the camel's back" of fellowship with a number of pastors from that area was precipitated in a confrontation during the 1983 International Foursquare Convention in Glorieta, New Mexico. To understand the evolving alienation, however, it is necessary to begin the story in 1969.

During the 1960s the "hippie" counter-culture started among the youth in the San Francisco area, impacting the whole

American society. Tens of thousands, in a spirit of antiestablishment, dropped out of the conventional society and relocated in wilderness areas or inner-city communes. One favorite area was the mountainous desert around the city of Prescott, Arizona.

In 1969 Rev. and Mrs. Wayman Mitchell asked for and received appointment to the Prescott, Arizona, Foursquare Church. Rev. Mitchell had grown up in the Prescott area and felt a concerned interest in the counter-culture youth of the area. He began winning many to Christ. By 1972 the church was almost filled with young people in overalls and faded jeans.

Because Rev. Mitchell constantly urged personal witnessing, the church was soon filled to overflowing. The more mature workers among the converts began to look beyond Prescott to other harvest fields. Coming from an antiestablishment mindset, the workers preferred to call their branches "The Door." Before long, "Doors" were springing up all over Arizona, even expanding into New Mexico, Colorado, and a couple of countries overseas.

There was much to admire and to learn from "The Door." What marvelous results would be accomplished if all our churches would embrace the same zeal for outreach and witness. Unfortunately, however, Rev. Mitchell had certain negative experiences during his Bible college training and, therefore, discouraged and even criticized formal Bible college education. Consequently the young men he disciple in Prescott received no Foursquare Bible college training but began to pioneer new churches. They received a regional district license rather than full ordination.

In addition, only a certain style of primitive and militant evangelism was considered acceptable by the group. Anyone participating in an alternative or a more reserved approach to ministry was scorned. When the group attended conferences and conventions, they generally sat together, avoiding fellowship with the other ministers. At times, they would rise and "walk out on" a conference session, should the message not conform to their approved style.

It must be admitted that some visiting ministers and leaders, unaware of the Prescott phenomenon, did unwittingly make occasional statements that appeared to be demeaning toward the unordained men and their unconventional dress. Therefore the "Arizona group" felt forced to take a defensive posture. Yet, to be equally fair to the facts, Rev. Wayman Mitchell did nothing to mend the fences and progressively encouraged his group in the separation of their churches. Though he was the state superintendent of all the Foursquare churches in Arizona, he would make organizational charts or maps of Arizona that excluded all other congregations. Many prophesied that Rev. Mitchell was preparing to start another organization. And as time passed, the "other" Foursquare congregations in Arizona, New Mexico, and Colorado began to resent the Prescott movement, which they felt had pointedly opposed or rejected them. One very antagonized Foursquare congregation withdrew because they felt the ICFG officials were being too tolerant.

During the executive council meeting at the 1983 convention in Glorieta, New Mexico, a large representation of Foursquare pastors rose to object to the tactics, methods, and attitudes of the Prescott group. Rev. Mitchell made no attempt to answer the questions being raised. It was clear that he interpreted the questioning to be a sign of prejudiced disfavor. He left the convention with his followers. The board of directors was asked to seek a solution during the ensuing year and report back to the convention body.

After much prayer, hoping to explore every possible ground on which to establish understanding and continue fellowship, the board of directors invited Rev. Wayman Mitchell to attend a special meeting. The meeting was held, but no solution to the problem was found. Rev Mitchell, within a few weeks, commenced withdrawing the churches he had pioneered.

When the separation was final, no properties or assets had been lost by the organization. However, some very fine workers and congregations were now working under another banner and in other fields. The "Doors" continued to minister successfully to "difficult-to-reach" cultures. The thirty-five Foursquare churches in Arizona are, in many ways, stronger than ever. Though it was a very painful experience, the elimination of the tension brought healing. Several fine independent Arizona churches have since united with the ICFG. Some of those who had originally separated themselves from the ICFG to follow Rev. Mitchell have now returned to the denomination with Christlike attitudes and a precious spirit of repentance and forgiveness.

It needs to be said that throughout this troublesome time, which included the tenures of Southwest District supervisors Nathaniel Van Cleave and John Holland; general supervisors Howard P. Courtney Sr., Merrill Nicholls, and Roy Hicks Sr.; as well as ICFG president Rolf K. McPherson and many Foursquare pastors, the fullest respect and every reasonable consideration, including financial support for new churches, were given to the Arizona group.

Wayman Mitchell's vision and attitude were so individualistic, it would seem difficult for him to fit his group into any organizational mold aside from their own. With few exceptions, the workers had come from the counter-culture movement and perhaps had given up any hope of cooperation with the society that surrounded them. When they became Christians, they gave up their sinful ways; many were delivered from drugs and the rock culture. But they did not shed their aversion to the establishment. To them the established culture belonged to the society from which they had rebelled. When conflicting attitudes clashed in the executive council, any remedy for the affliction vanished.

The leadership of the ICFG continues to hold a great love for these dear brothers and sisters in the Lord and feels no malice toward Rev. Mitchell or any of those who separated from the denomination.

One blessing of the New Jerusalem will be that all believers will know one another as they are known. There will never be misinterpretation of motives, for crystal-clear truth and divine love fully shed abroad will make it possible for all to exist together in brotherhood. There will be no dissension. All have work assignments and domain to rule, but nothing will ever separate them into diverse groups.

Chapter 8

THE VINE ADAPTS TO STRESS

1939–1948

After the death of Moses the servant of the Lord, it came to pass that the Lord spoke to Joshua the son of Nun, Moses' assistant, saying: "Moses My servant is dead. Now therefore, arise, go over this Jordan, you and all this people, to the land which I am giving to them—the children of Israel. Every place that the sole of your foot will tread upon I have given you, as I said to Moses.

—Joshua 1:1–3, NKJV

Every branch that bears fruit He prunes, that it may bear more fruit.

—John 15:2, NKJV

Every long, enduring vine must at some time adapt to new stresses and to a new husbandman. (See John 15:1.)

By the year 1939, there were more than twelve hundred credentialed Foursquare ministers. From its conception L.I.F.E. Bible College graduated an average of eighty-five new workers each year for pastoral, evangelistic, missionary, or support ministries. The Foursquare Church was moving steadily forward.

There were 355 Foursquare churches located in thirty-three

states and four provinces in Canada. Thirty-five missionaries were preaching and teaching the Foursquare Gospel message in nine foreign countries, counting 127 mission stations. A series of "Holy Ghost rallies" and conventions during the 1930s had brought the spiritual level of Angelus Temple and its branches near to the initial revival intensity. To this time, very few circumstances or other barriers had challenged the progress of the Foursquare movement.

The Commitment of Leadership to Faithful Men and Women

The sprouting of Foursquare branches across North America was due in large measure to the successful revival campaigns of Aimee Semple McPherson, but nurturing those branches into maturity was the work of dedicated and capable district leaders.

In 1939 the Foursquare churches in California were under the supervision of Myron Sackett, originally from Iowa. Divisional superintendents included such strong pastors as Earl Dorrance (who late became a member of the denomination's board of directors, then a supervisor of the Southern California District); Charles Gaines (later supervisor of the Gulf States District); Melvin Todd; Howard Rusthoi (assistant pastor of Angelus Temple); Ada Teeple; William Nickerson; Wesley Norgaard; and Ethel Singleton.

Great Lakes District supervisor and church planter Sidney Correll led state superintendents such as Herman Walters, Gerald Boyer, Harry Caswell, Harold Myers, Harold Hunter, and Paul Royer, who later served on the faculty of L.I.F.E. Bible College. When Sidney Correll resigned in the middle of 1939, the district leadership was passed to Rev. Howard P. Courtney Sr., who later became general supervisor of the International Church of the Foursquare Gospel.

Frank Cummings, a strong leader and evangelist, supervised the Midwest District. State superintendents under his care were Louise Webster, Ellsworth Johnson, James Lowen, Warren Koon (later Eastern District supervisor), Guy Peacock, Otto Risser, and Fred Beard (later Midwest District supervisor).

To the Northwest, Harold Jefferies (thirty-one years as pastor of the Portland, Oregon, Foursquare Church) served as supervisor, with Elvin Swanson, Ray Wren, and B. A. McKeown (who pastored the Kingsway Foursquare Church in Vancouver, British Columbia, as well as several other large churches) serving as state superintendents.

Most of the above leaders had been saved, filled with the Holy Spirit, and called to the ministry during the founding revival at Angelus Temple. Growth under their inspired leadership was consistent with the original calling and purpose that the founder had envisioned.

The Foursquare Church Responds to World War II

In September 1939 Germany invaded Poland, launching a "global conflict lasting from 1939 to 1945 and comprising in the totality of its manifold military engagements and related political, diplomatic, and economic struggles, the most stupendous complex of events in the history of mankind."[1]

World War II affected nearly seventy countries. American deaths exceed 100,000. The financial cost of the war for the leading participants is estimated to have been in excess of $1 trillion. America's bill exceeded $317 billion. The war did not end until five days following atomic bomb drops over Hiroshima and Nagasaki, Japan. It was an event that left an ominous cloud of annihilation threatening all mankind.

Japan's attack on Pearl Harbor December 7, 1941, extended

the war to the Pacific area and brought the United States into active combat. Following the fall of France, Belgium, and the Netherlands, the United States began to support Great Britain and the Allies with food and arms. This support was financed through the sale of war bonds.

Aimee Semple McPherson and the Foursquare churches in Southern California responded wholeheartedly to the government's appeal for Americans to buy bonds. Read this report, published in the *Foursquare Crusader* magazine of August 1942:

> Aimee Semple McPherson has done it again! This was the unanimous verdict of the great throng of twenty thousand singing, shouting, enthusiastic people that jammed the entire south end of Pershing Square before Victory House the afternoon of June 20th, in Foursquaredom's "all out" defense bond and stamp effort for the U.S. Treasury Department.
>
> In introducing the pastor-founder of Angelus Temple, Mr. George Russell, manager of Victory House, referred to her as "the nation's most outstanding religious leader and the most radiant personality before the American public today."

That day Aimee Semple McPherson asked twenty thousand people to join her in prayer for the bond sale, and a new one-day record sale was the result. A commendation from the Treasury Department read:

> On behalf of the United States Treasury Department, please accept our deep appreciation for the wonderful program and Bond and Stamp effort you and your church and its members presented here on Saturday, July 20, at Victory House. It was outstanding in every respect and was appreciated by the vast audience. I am happy to report to you that you and your co-workers broke all existing records in the sale of War Saving Stamps and Bonds the day of your program.[2]

This is only one example of the founder's cooperation with all efforts for the betterment of our nation, city, and community.

When the conflict began in Europe, many Pentecostals, including Foursquare people, were opposed to American involvement. Some even opposed active military service. However, after the bomb attack on Pearl Harbor, Foursquare people became fully sympathetic with America's participation in a war to end Adolf Hitler's satanic-inspired scheme of world domination.

The war brought many severe limitations and inconveniences to the nation's style of living. Many foods were unavailable, with many essential commodities rationed. Homes were strained as youth were drafted into military service. Transportation was restricted as gasoline and tires were rationed. Ministers' visitation schedules were curtailed by limited gasoline stamps. Following Pearl Harbor, in California and similar coastal regions, blackouts were required due to fear of aerial attack. For a time, many night activities were canceled.

Church schedules were drastically changed. Prior to the war most Foursquare churches conducted at least three midweek services: Bible study (Tuesday nights), prayer and divine healing service (Wednesdays), and youth service (Fridays). Some even added Monday and Saturday evening street meetings. Revivals lasting two to four weeks were commonplace.

During the war, limited gasoline supply caused churches to limit services to only Wednesday nights. Most revival campaigns were reduced to one week duration. Whereas before the war the best-attended services were the Sunday night evangelistic meetings, now, because of blackouts and rationing, Sunday mornings became the most popular services. And since that time, the old prewar schedules have seldom returned. Local church revival campaigns have now given way to city-wide united crusades, with evangelists becoming scarce.

To the founder of the Foursquare Church, however, the war became a challenge. In the *Foursquare Crusader* of July 1942, Aimee Semple McPherson chronicled her plan and schedule:

> Despite the fact that many organized ventures have ceased expansion for the "duration" (war), the International Church of the Foursquare Gospel plans no let up in letting people know that Jesus saves, that He heals, and that He is coming back.
>
> Aimee Semple McPherson...has herself launched into a more vigorous campaign for Christ. With lightning speed she has conducted a nationwide coverage. Several months ago it was New Orleans; then Nashville, Tenn.; Joplin and Webb City, Mo.; then Springfield, Ohio; Centralia and Chehalis, Washington; and Portland, Oregon; then the opening of a new and great work in Fresno, Calif. At all these places it was new churches being added to the ranks.[3]

The Foursquare Gospel organization was determined to press forward with the fulfillment of the founder's vision of reaching the world with the full gospel message. The theme and purpose of the 1943 *Foursquare Convention Yearbook* stated:

> Desiring to cooperate with our Government to the fullest extent in the present all-out war emergency, and looking forward to a larger opportunity to spread God's Word through greater Foursquare channels after the United Nations have achieved a just peace; Aimee Semple McPherson, president and founder of the International Church of the Foursquare Gospel, called all the Foursquare ministers and church leaders across the continent in our 412 churches and in foreign fields, missionaries representing 250 foreign mission

> stations to a ten-day International Ministerial War Council and Post-War Planning Conference June 16–25 inclusive.
>
> Every minister, evangelist and delegate who could be reached to express and opinion, agreed that the...War Council and Post-War Planning Conference was the most spiritually profitable assemblage ever called by Aimee Semple McPherson.
>
> The spiritual crescendo was supplied by Sister McPherson, in her timely illustrated sermon: "America's Post-War Mission to Millions."[4]

Throughout much of the war period, the *Foursquare Magazine* carried reports from and about our men in military service. A number of Foursquare families lost sons in the conflict. A number of Foursquare ministers offered themselves for the chaplaincy. These included Capt. Howard Rusthoi and Capt. Clifford Musgrove, who served on the European front. Both of these men, from Foursquare families very active in the early days of the movement, engaged in successful evangelistic crusades after the war, followed by pastorates of large churches. Rev. and Mrs. Rusthoi assisted Dr. McPherson at Angelus Temple in the late 1940s and early 1950s.

Chaplain (Lieutenant) Clarence Potter had served for several years as youth leader of the Fullerton, California, Foursquare Church. From the front, he wrote:

> Our services here are in barn lofts, wrecked buildings, school houses, taverns, old forts, and what have you. They are often called at a moment's notice. The men are responding readily to the services in spite of the rain, snow, ice and blackouts. I have seen about fifty men on their knees at one time praying the sinner's prayer.[5]

A poignant letter, written by Chaplain Musgrove, was published in the same issue:

> It really has been the prayers of you folks at home that have kept us. Christmas Day we were in the field a good share of the day holding services and the rest of the time we were dodging shells. These days are hell on earth. Many times that day, we held the hand of a dying boy praying for him. Many of them died in my arms…over here I have learned what simplicity really is. The world is hungry for Christ, not for sermons. I received the memorial copy of the *Foursquare Magazine* today…it brought tears.[6]

Capt. Alexander B. Cowie and his family had emigrated from Scotland to the United States in 1920. The family had settled in South Los Angeles where they became charter members of the Goodyear Foursquare Church (now known as the Florence Avenue Foursquare Church, then located in South Los Angeles). After graduation from L.I.F.E. Bible College, Alexander served as an Air Force chaplain in both World War II and in the Korean conflict. Between the wars he pastored the Van Nuys, California, Foursquare Church, building a new sanctuary that still stands as part of the complex of the world-renowned "The Church On The Way," pastored by Dr. Jack Hayford.

In a letter from the battle zone, Capt. Cowie wrote about the dangers our chaplains faced:

> I am the island stockade chaplain. There are many opportunities to lead men to Christ. Just now as I am writing you, there is a battle going on just about three hundred yards from us and the shrapnel is flying in all directions, but you are always "safe" when Christ is near. I have been helping the Red Cross. The hospital casualties are much work too, I testify to all of them, and pray with many and God always blesses.[7]

Some of our Foursquare servicemen made great sacrifices. Some performed important duties outside of the combat areas. One unusual service was rendered by one of the Foursquare youth leaders, Andrew Sawchuck. His testimony appeared in the *Foursquare Magazine*:

> Andrew Sawchuck, former Crusader captain of the East Los Angeles Crusaders, was one of the twenty-seven United States Naval Officers and men who formed part of the highly secret corps of communications and interpreter experts at the Yalta Conference (a conference between President Roosevelt, Prime Minister Churchill and Joseph Stalin in Feb. 1945).
>
> He was awarded a letter of commendation for his work with the American staff of interpreters and communications men who served at the conference.[8]

After the war Mr. Sawchuck became an insurance executive. He continues to be a lay leader in the Florence Avenue Foursquare Church in Santa Fe Springs, California. For several terms he also served the denomination as a member of the board of regents, L.I.F.E. Bible College.

Throughout the war Foursquare leadership demonstrated increasing concern for our men who were engaged in the conflict, as well as for their families. *Foursquare Magazine* editor Rev. Raymond Becker called attention to a newly organized ministry to servicemen.

> "Something new has been added" to the extensive and rapidly growing list of activities and enterprises of the International Church of the Foursquare Gospel. This "something" is a service bulletin, to be published periodically, designed and planned to appeal exclusively to men and women in the armed forces of our country. Realizing the urgent necessity for an endeavor of this nature, Dr. Rolf McPherson has

> created a special Servicemen's Department under the supervision of Dr. Frank Cummings to take care of this need.[9]

The war impacted Foursquare doctrine, especially the doctrine of the second coming of Jesus Christ and the "fourth corner" of the Foursquare Gospel. As in all times of global conflict, students of prophecy were alerted to the "signs of the times." Some teachers speculated about Benito Mussolini, Adolf Hitler, or Joseph Stalin being the possible Antichrist. One pastor wrote a booklet identifying Mussolini as the "man of sin" and afterward was embarrassed, saying, "I'd give a thousand dollars if I could recall all those booklets."

Another pastor, perhaps overly eager to find pertinent signs, announced that he would preach on the latest fulfillment of prophecy, "tire rationing," taking as his proof text Isaiah 3:18, "In that day the Lord will take away... their round tires." He was not a little embarrassed when one of his members, a Bible college student, pointed out that the "prophetic text" applied to the wealthy women's tiaras or necklaces, not automobile tires. While there is scriptural warrant for being alert to signs of the last days and to the imminence (any moment) of Christ's return, careless treatment of the prophetic word is like "crying wolf" too often, eventually leading to disinterest in a precious doctrine.

The war itself did not reach the continental United States, but many missionaries experienced its ravages. The following report was received from our missionaries in Hong Kong:

> With joy we received a Radiogram RCA from Edwin Lee, our missionary at Hong Kong, telling of his safety and how God wondrously aided him in saving his work and moving same into the interior of China. Responding at once the International Church office cabled money to Brother and Sister Lee. Prayer was solicited for their continued safety.[10]

When it became clear that Adolf Hitler, whose armies seemed invincible, planned to conquer the world, American Christians began to pray in earnest for the victory of our Allies. The thought of worldwide Nazi dictatorship made the British and Americans shudder. It appeared that only God could turn the tide.

Clearly, divine intervention saved the free world. Hitler's disciplined and well-equipped armies quickly occupied Poland. Turning westward, they then penetrated the supposedly impregnable Maginot Line as if it were cardboard. France, Belgium, and Holland were conquered; nothing but the English Channel stood between the German war machine and the poorly prepared British Isles. However, for some reason, Hitler delayed, pursuing other objectives. He underestimated the endurance of the British and the resolute courage of Winston Churchill. He supposed he could bring the British to their knees with the bombing attacks of the Luftwaffe. Before the Nazi army could reorganize to cross the channel, England, with help from America in the form of food, planes, and arms, was bombing Germany.

Lusting for conquest, Hitler decided to attack Russia, hoping to subdue the USSR within a few weeks or months at the least. Then he could once again concentrate on Britain. The worst weather in years slowed the Wehrmacht so that the winter snows that had been the downfall of Napoleon became the pitfall of Hitler. By the time the snows of winter and the thaw of spring had ended, Russia was prepared. With American supplies, they turned back the Wehrmacht of Germany.

Hitler solicited the help of the emperor of Japan, urging that nation to attack the United States. The attack on Pearl Harbor brought America into the conflict. The U.S. Navy recovered from the tragedy and engaged Japan in the Pacific. The

American armies joined the European Allies. On June 6, 1944, the American and British troops, under General Dwight D. Eisenhower, crossed the English Channel and began the penetration that brought Hitler to his end.

Germany surrendered on May 8, 1945. The Japanese conflict continued until August 14, 1945, when the emperor of Japan surrendered to General Douglas MacArthur. Divine providence had prevailed, inspiring and responding to believing prayer.

The Baton Is Passed

Before the war ended, however, the Foursquare movement lost its brilliant founder and president, Aimee Semple McPherson. She had been ill for some time with a fever contracted while on vacation in Mexico. In the summer of 1944, feeling capable of doing evangelistic work she so relished, Mrs. McPherson scheduled a September crusade in Oakland, California, to coincide with the opening of a new church. Though often running a temperature of 103 or 104 and finding it difficult to rest, Mrs. McPherson still looked forward to conducting meetings in the Civic Auditorium. For the opening sermon she chose to speak on the Foursquare Gospel. This was the same auditorium where twenty-three years earlier the Lord first inspired the name for the message that she would send around the world.

The events of her death are recorded in the widely circulated *Dictionary of Pentecostal and Charismatic Movements*.

> She [Mrs. McPherson] preached a sermon on the evening September 26. That night she went to bed and was found the following day, dead from what was described as "shock and respiratory failure" following an apparently accidental overdose of a medical prescription. She was buried in Forest

> Lawn Cemetery in Glendale, California, in one of the largest funerals ever held in Los Angeles.
>
> The impact of the life and ministry of Aimee Semple McPherson is a significant one by all accounts. She was a colorful, sometimes controversial, figure. But she was also an extremely gifted communicator and organizer, a competent musician, a prolific writer, in many ways a servant of the people, especially the poor; and an instiller of vision who challenged her followers to trust in Jesus Christ, "the same yesterday, today, and forever" (Heb. 13:8), a theme prominently displayed in many Foursquare churches today. She was undoubtedly the most prominent woman leader Pentecostalism has produced to date.[11]

The loss seemed irremediable. How could an organization replace such a talented and charismatic founder and leader? The answer is, "She was never replaced." The time had come for a large step in the maturation of the Foursquare movement. It was needful for the people to cease depending for progress upon a world-renowned leader, and for everyone to become personally involved.

Many Foursquare members wondered what would happen to the church. Outside the Foursquare ranks, critics predicted that the "Foursquare vine" would shrivel and die. However, knowledgeable people took confidence in the fact that the vine had been planted in the soil of Christ-centered revival. The edifice named "Church of the Foursquare Gospel" had been build solidly upon the Rock, Christ Jesus. And what is built on Christ, the living Word, as He has set forth in the written Word, will not fall when the storms come (Matt. 7:24–25).

Actually, God had guided Aimee Semple McPherson in the preparation of a strong, capable, and loyal leader and successor. She had appointed her son, Rolf Kennedy McPherson, to the board of directors and to the position of executive secretary in

January of 1940. Rolf Kennedy McPherson, who had been born on March 23, 1913, in the city of Providence, Rhode Island, had expected to assist his mother in the broadcasting of the gospel over KFSG and in management after graduating from the Southern California Radio Institute in 1933. He was also called to preach the gospel and attended L.I.F.E. Bible College, after which he did evangelistic work and assisted his mother in the services at Angelus Temple. He was ordained in to Foursquare ministry in 1940.

In the spring of 1944, upon the resignation of Dr. Giles Knight, Rolf was appointed to the positions of vice president and secretary-treasurer of the International Church of the Foursquare Gospel. To assist him, Mrs. McPherson (upon the request of her son) moved Dr. Howard P. Courtney Sr. from the office of Great Lakes District supervisor to the positions of general supervisor and director of foreign missions for the entire denomination.

Howard Perry Courtney was born in Oklahoma in 1911. While he was a boy, the family moved to California, where Howard sold newspapers on the street corners of Santa Monica. He was converted in 1925 under the ministry of Rev. Anna D. Britton and enrolled in L.I.F.E. Bible College in 1929. With his unbounded enthusiasm and strong voice developed as a newsboy, Howard began to preach at the age of sixteen. After graduation from L.I.F.E., he married Vaneda Harper, who had come to L.I.F.E. from Champaign-Urbana, Illinois, where she had attended the University of Illinois. Graduating in 1932, the Courtneys went to the Great Lakes area, where they pastored in Racine, Wisconsin, and Terre Haute, Indiana.

Recognizing Howard as a powerful, Spirit-filled preacher and Vaneda as a highly competent executive secretary, Dr. Harold Jefferies, then Northwest District supervisor and pastor of the Portland, Oregon, Foursquare Church, invited the Courtneys in

1934 to serve as assistant pastors and assistant supervisors of his district. Later, in 1940, because of their unusual leadership and experience, Mrs. McPherson appointed them as supervisors of the Great Lakes District.

Now, in 1944, with the board of directors composed of Rolf McPherson, Howard Courtney Sr., Earl Dorrance (California supervisor), and W. B. Teaford (dean of L.I.F.E. Bible College), all of whom were saved and trained under her ministry, Mrs. McPherson could concentrate wholly on the ministry of the gospel. Unknown to her, she was also being guided by the Lord in preparation of the Foursquare movement for her near but unexpected passing.

An excerpt from the preface to the 1945 yearbook, written by Rolf K. McPherson, reveals how well he was ready to take the helm of the Foursquare ship:

> The Word informs us that as Foursquare ministers and laymen we should have a burden for souls, and if we lack that burden we should pray until we receive it! Of course, God could deal with souls Himself, but in His infinite wisdom, He has chosen rather to work through human instrumentality. If we fail to get sinners into our churches and to preach Christ to them; if we fail to go "into the highways and hedges" of the mission fields—home and foreign—and to tell the lost of Jesus Christ, then we are failing God completely.
>
> In the post-war progress and the future of the church we simply cannot afford to lose step and fall behind. There will be a greater need than ever before for the Gospel of the "Prince of Peace," and the fundamental church alone can fill this need.
>
> I am thankful to God that the Foursquare Organization has officers, pastors, evangelists, missionaries and members who have a definite vision for the future of the work. Concrete plans are being made, some of which we are even

> now able to put into operation, that will make our watchword, "Around the World with the Foursquare Gospel."

Few people have been faced so suddenly with a challenge as great as that which Rolf McPherson faced at the passing of his mother. There was the challenge of the pastorate of Angelus Temple, the presidency of the Bible college, the presidency and leadership of the International Church of the Foursquare Gospel, and the editorship of the *Foursquare Magazine*.

Dr. Rolf K. McPherson, upon whom the board of directors had conferred a Doctor of Divinity, accepted the final responsibility for these various operations, with the counsel and assistance of many outstanding ministers. He always gave God the credit for wisdom in the selection of helpers to fill the many offices of the International Church of the Foursquare Gospel. He testifies that the Lord promised him, "I built this work, and I will keep it going."

In the operation of Angelus Temple and the International Church of the Foursquare Gospel, Dr. McPherson was assisted by Dr. Howard P. Courtney Sr., who had oversight of nearly four hundred churches. Dr. Frank Cummings, former Midwest District supervisor, was brought to headquarters to help in the business of the church and to direct the McPherson Memorial Project. Early ministers sharing in the twenty-one preaching services a week in Angelus Temple were his wife, Lorna Dee McPherson, and Thompson Eade, Chaplain Howard Rusthoi, Raymond Becker, Kelso Glover, Sister Hal Smith, and H. Wesley Cooksey.

The Bible college leadership was entrusted to Dean Watson B. Teaford and D. F. Myers. Dr. Howard Courtney Sr. and Harold Chalfant worked with the foreign missions department; the KFSG radio ministry was directed by Jack Carmain, Charles Walkem, and Earle Williams; and Evelyn McGowan and Raymond Becker produced the magazine. Youth ministry was entrusted to Harold Chalfant, Earle Williams, and Charles Hollis, and in Sunday school promotion: Harold Chalfant, Bert Bruffet, and Evelyn McGowan.

Of all the talented and faithful people who have given important assistance to Dr. McPherson, on none has he depended more over a longer period of time than Dr. Leita Mae Steward, secretary to both Dr. McPherson and the corporate board.

Leita Mae Steward was born in Durango, Colorado. In 1928 her family moved to California where, urged by her grandmother, Cora Whittlesey, they attended Angelus Temple. There, Leita Mae accepted Christ.

After four years of training in the Ventura, California, Foursquare Church, the Steward family settled in the Randsburg, California, desert community. Out of a zeal for Christian service, they pioneered a new church for Johannesburg, California. It was there God challenged Leita Mae to completely surrender her life. One week later, Dr. Harold Chalfant drove to her home to ask her to become the Desert District Crusader commander. Later, while serving in this capacity in Victorville, California, she attended a summer camp at Camp Radford and was called to full-time ministry.

In the spring of 1942 Leita Mae enrolled in L.I.F.E. Bible College, graduating in 1945. While a student, she worked as secretary to Dr. Giles Knight, then vice president of the denomination. Later, she served for a short time in the accounting department at Foursquare headquarters.

Not long after the retirement of Dr. Knight, she was asked by Dr. Rolf K. McPherson to serve as his secretary and office manager, positions she has faithfully and efficiently filled for the duration of his presidency. In addition to her service at headquarters, Leita Mae has taught a large Sunday school class in

Angelus Temple for many years and has been instrumental in acquiring and operating the "House on the Hill" with its multifaceted ministries.[12]

Though he had such excellent assistance, it was at "Doctor's" desk where the "buck" stopped. But he was fit for the challenge:

> The last few months of her earthly existence, Sister McPherson experienced much joy and comfort in the knowledge that her son was shouldering the full responsibilities of Angelus Temple and the worldwide Foursquare organization. She had expressed a desire on many occasions that he should be her successor, God willing; for he had stood faithfully and loyally behind her at all times, under all circumstances and conditions. She stated that she had unbounded confidence in his ability to carry out her vision and to keep the church intact and united in the effort of world evangelism.
>
> How efficiently and successfully he is accomplishing this task is proven conclusively by the results not being achieved through his humble and sincere leadership and ministry—both in the pulpit and behind the administrative desk.[13]

The change of a generation in leadership did not slow the progress of the denomination. By 1949 the number of churches had increased from 355 to 521, and two states were added, from thirty-three to thirty-five. Almost unnoticed was the improvement in churches from rented store fronts and tabernacles to more adequate facilities. In the decade of the 1940s, which saw the bloodiest war in history as well as the loss of our founder and leader, the finances, including income for foreign missions, more than doubled.

There were other organizational features and benefits implemented by Dr. McPherson, with the able assistance of Dr. and Mrs. Howard P. Courtney Sr.

In 1948 the Foursquare Church joined with the Assemblies of

God, the Church of God (Cleveland, Tennessee), the Open Bible Standard Church in Des Moines, Iowa, and the Pentecostal Holiness Church to form the "Pentecostal Fellowship of North America." The purpose of the PFNA was to promote interchurch Pentecostal fellowship and united action. That fellowship's first committee was composed of J. Roswell Flower (AG), E. J. Fulton (OBSC), Herman D. Mitzner (ICFG), and H. L. Chesser (CG). Dr. Courtney was a member of the organizing committee, and he and Dr. McPherson served on the board of administration from the beginning until the mid-1970s. Dr. Merrill Nicholls followed Dr. Courtney as the chairman of the board of administration and was serving in this position at the time of his death. Today, most Pentecostal organizations that are evangelical and Trinitarian have joined the fellowship.

Kindred to the PFNA has been the World Pentecostal Conference, which was organized in its present form in 1947. For most of the WPC's existence, Dr. Howard P. Courtney Sr. has served as a member of the advisory committee. The World Pentecostal Conference has convened once every three years in some key city of the world providing unity and fellowship for the fastest-growing sector of the Christian faith. Conferences have been conducted in Zurich, 1947; Paris, 1949; London, 1952; Stockholm, 1955; Toronto, 1958; Jerusalem, 1961 (over which Dr. Courtney served as chairman); Helsinki, 1964; Rio de Janeiro, 1967; Dallas, 1970; Seoul, 1973; London, 1976; Vancouver, British Columbia, 1979; Nairobi, 1982; Zurich, 1985; and Singapore, 1989.[14] In 1992 the 16th World Pentecostal Conference was held in Oslo, Norway.

The International Church of the Foursquare Gospel has never been a separatist organization. On its cornerstone, Angelus Temple dedicates its members to "interdenominational and worldwide evangelism." The speakers at the opening

International Foursquare Convention were chosen from a variety of denominations. Thus, it was only natural that the church become a part of the National Association of Evangelicals in 1952 and be extremely active in that fellowship's commissions. Regular donations are given to the NAE, and the NAE Annual Convention is high on the agenda of a number of our ministers and leaders.

A great boon for Foursquare churches, especially in California, was an arrangement rarely extended to churches, made with the Bank of America NT&SA, whereby churches are able to obtain loans for property purchases and church construction. Because of the establishment of a "AAA" credit rating, the recommendation of the Bank of America, and companies with whom ICFG was doing business, the national church office was able to secure similar arrangements with many banks in other states.

A department was established within the national church office to manage the mortgage collections and loan payments. Operations have proven so efficient and helpful to the board that, at this writing, the denomination has never had a foreclosure on a Foursquare church property. There was also established the Foursquare Loan Fund to assist in church construction and improvement when other financing was not prudent or available. As this fund has grown, it is able to carry a larger share of the overall financing through small loans.

For the year 1990, the ratio of debt to property valuation in the International Church of the Foursquare Gospel was 18 percent, equivalent to owing $18,000 on a $100,000-property. ICFG's financial soundness is an amazement to financial institutions.

To those pastors and churches who have participated in the plan, the Foursquare Retirement Fund has proven an added blessing. Begun in the late 1940s, the retirement fund is in force when the local church agrees to send to the national church office a certain amount that is equal to a percentage of the pastor's salary. As an IRS qualified plan, it has provided certain tax advantages. In the case of pastoral changes, the local churches are encouraged to implement the plan for the incoming pastor. Over the past decade, the Foursquare Retirement Fund has provided nearly $300,000 to retirees. But the tragedy is that the participating churches have been too few.

A Benevolence Fund was begun in 1941 to help Foursquare ministers in cases of hardship, sickness, or death. The fund is maintained by a percentage of the annual minister's credential fee. To receive consideration, ministers must keep the credentials current. Assistance, based on need, is given in cases of unreimbursed medical costs of death. At this writing there are more than four thousand Foursquare ministers who carry credentials.

An additional source of assistance for churches is the McPherson Memorial Extension Fund, started in the middle 1930s. It was originally intended for the expense of Mrs. McPherson's outside revival campaigns. Following her passing, the fund, which is derived from a percent of tithes paid by the churches, was used for the first building costs of new churches. However, in more recent years, the funds have been used to help churches in a variety of local church property and facility development. The denomination's board of directors allots the funds in response to the recommendation by the district supervisors.

Dr. McPherson was the catalyst for acquiring a headquarters building for the denomination. For many years the offices were located in the L.I.F.E. Bible College building and original Angelus Temple parsonage. However, in the late 1950s, the buildings had become overcrowded. At the same time, the California Federal Savings was desirous of constructing an eight-story bank building near Angelus Temple. The bank officials approached Dr. McPherson about purchasing property the church was acquiring for parking adjacent to Glendale Boulevard. A plan was proposed by which the ICFG would be given an option to repurchase the building upon completion. Even if the repurchase was impossible, spaces would be available in the new building for the headquarters offices of ICFG. Three levels of parking spaces would be available for Sunday and weekday evening church services.

The building was erected, and Foursquare headquarters occupied the second floor. When the time came to exercise the purchase option, it was decided to continue renting, in order to conserve corporate reserves. However, ten years later, the bank again offered the building at the original cost, and the board of directors, chaired by Dr. McPherson, accepted their offer. Through careful planning, the building was purchased with the help of departmental loans. Where the building had barely broken even, good management turned this about, and the loans were paid off well ahead of schedule.

As of this writing the International Church of the Foursquare Gospel occupies most of three floors of the building, and the remainder of the space is leased to cover the cost of maintenance. Recently the City of Los Angeles mandated a major safety retro-fit for high-rise buildings. This included fire sprinklers and was completed just in time to quench a fire, set by vandals, which would have destroyed several floors of the building. While the work was costly, it more than paid for itself by this one experience.

There is much more to be added to the advancement of the Foursquare Church under the leadership of Rolf Kennedy McPherson. Actually, it will take most of the rest of this book to tell that story.

Chapter 9

THE VINE BEARS MORE FRUIT

1948–1958: Postwar Expansion

JESUS KNEW THAT after a period of cultivation and fertilization, a vine bears new fruit:

> Every branch that bears fruit he prunes, that it may bear more fruit...I am the vine, you are the branches. He who abides in me, and I in him, bears much fruit; for without me you can do nothing.
>
> —JOHN 15:2, 5, NIV

After the trials of the Great Depression and World War II, and in spite of a major change in the leadership of the denomination, the Foursquare Gospel "vine" enjoyed new growth and expansion. In 1948 there were 437 churches; by 1958 that number had grown to more than 700 congregations. It is accurate to say that immediately following the loss of ICFG's charismatic founder, there was some decline. However, beginning in the mid-1950s, steady growth ensued.

In January 1948, the International Church of the Foursquare Gospel celebrated its twenty-fifth anniversary with a "Jubilee Convention," held at Angelus Temple. It was the greatest

Foursquare convention yet conducted, with the five-thousand-seat auditorium filled to capacity.

Harold Chalfant, international director of youth and Christian education, served as the convention chairman. He reported:

> During the passing of the years the first three districts (outside of California) have enlarged themselves until now we have seven active districts: Eastern, Great Lakes, Gulf States, Midwest, Northwest, Southern California and the Western.
>
> The departments of Youth and Christian Education over the years have made tremendous strides, and this convention introduced a number of new plans for enlarging their scope and ministry. The new Boom Barrel project of "Invading the Orient for Christ" met with widespread enthusiasm.
>
> The Foreign Missionary Department alone has 205 stations under its jurisdiction... Dr. Rolf McPherson presented an overall report the new FM station KKLA, the new dormitory being erected for L.I.F.E. Bible College, properties acquired, but greater than these, he brought to our attention the wave of spiritual increases that has honeycombed entire Foursquaredom...
>
> One thing can be said of the largest convention ever held by this organization, the twenty-fifth Jubilee Convention—it was surely a JUBILEE.[1]

Rev. Chalfant went on to mention the growth of districts from three to seven. Actually, the "three" excluded the California District and the Canadian District (which was at first a part of the Northwest District). In 1939 the huge Midwest District, supervised by Frank Cummings, extended from Arizona to Florida, far too wide for any supervisor to cover, even though the southern states then had only one or two Foursquare churches. Growth in the late 1930s demanded and made possible the creation of the Gulf State District, overseen by Rev. and Mrs. Charles Gaines.

An Eastern District, separate from the Great Lakes, was created in 1944. At that time Dr. and Mrs. Howard P. Courtney Sr. were called to Los Angeles to assume the responsibility as general supervisor. Appointed as supervisors to the new district were Rev. and Mrs. Warren Koon. Dr. Courtney served as general supervisor and director of foreign missions until 1949, when he became co-pastor with Dr. McPherson at Angelus Temple. Dr. Herman Mitzner was then appointed as general supervisor and director of missions.

In 1953 the positions of general supervisor and director of missions were separated, with Dr. Courtney returning as general supervisor and Dr. Mitzner remaining in the office of director of foreign missions. Filling the vacancy at Angelus Temple was Dr. Watson B. Teaford, who had been dean of L.I.F.E. Bible College. Dr. Clarence Hall resigned his position as Northwest District supervisor to become dean of L.I.F.E.

Creation of New Districts

By 1946 the California District had grown to 178 churches, spanning California and Nevada. A new district was created with a southern boundary that extended across California from just south of San Luis Obispo, Bakersfield, and Johannesburg, and included portions of Nevada. This new district contained forty-eight churches and was assigned to Dr. and Mrs. Frank Cummings. It is important to note that throughout Foursquare history the qualifications of a man for district supervision have always included those of his wife, who has worked closely with her husband in that particular ministry.

The purpose of structuring the Foursquare movement into districts was threefold. The district was to provide a leader, free from pastoral responsibility, who could provide reasonable, nearby representation to the churches from corporate headquarters. A district would also permit the different regions of the nation to develop in conformity with the culture of their given area. And, such a structure would enable groups of churches to sponsor within reasonable distances a family spirit for camps, rallies, conventions, conferences, and various other projects.

Obviously, if the district area was too large, these purposes were weakened. Therefore, most of the districts also developed state or divisional groupings to more efficiently fulfill these aims. The divisions were superintended by ministers who usually pastored the largest church in the area. Consequently, they had limited time to give to the other congregations under their care. The ideal condition was the making of the largest number of districts that could be financially supported.

A significant strengthening of the Great Lakes District was brought about by two circumstances. First, there was the union with ICFG of the large revival center in Moline, Illinois, widely known as the Moline Gospel Temple. Its pastors of many years, Dr. and Mrs. A. W. Kortkamp, requested of Dr. McPherson that a capable Foursquare minister be sent to that church to act as associate pastor, with the idea of union after a year.

Nathaniel and Lois Van Cleave, on furlough from missionary service to Puerto Rico, were sent. One year later, in June 1949, the members of Moline Gospel Temple voted to become a Foursquare congregation. Charles and Ruth Hollis, who had been serving as youth ministers at Angelus Temple, were sent to fill the pastorate. The Kortkamps remained as pastors emeritus until Rev. Kortkamps death; Rev. and Mrs. Hollis have remained as pastors of that marvelous church to the present, a tenure of forty-two years.

The second circumstance was the phenomenal growth of the Decatur, Illinois, Foursquare Church under the ministry of Rev. and Mrs. Kenneth Erickson. During the decade between 1950 and 1960, the Decatur church grew to proportions virtually equaling the Moline Gospel Temple. For many years, the Foursquare churches in Decatur and Moline, Illinois, joined Portland, Oregon, as being the three largest Foursquare churches, outside of Angelus Temple.

During the decades of the 1970s and 1980s, they were joined by large churches in Gresham, Oregon; Eugene, Oregon; Beaverton, Oregon; Kirkland, Washington; Newcastle, Indiana; Van Nuys, California; Manhattan Beach, California; Santa Fe Springs, California; and Fresno, California.

With postwar prosperity and growth, several new districts became a possibility. By 1954 the Southern California District, supervised by Dr. and Mrs. Earl Dorrance, had grown to include more than two hundred churches. Though the area was not large, the number of churches became more than one supervisor could adequately oversee.

At the 1956 international Foursquare convention held at Moline, Illinois, Dr. McPherson, with suggestion from Dr. Courtney, appointed Dr. and Mrs. N. M. Van Cleave to a new district formed out of the Southern California District. The boundary in Los Angeles County was Lakewood/Rosemead Boulevard, from Long Beach to the mountains. The area included Orange, Riverside, San Bernardino, San Diego, and Imperial counties, plus the entire state of Arizona, which had been apportioned from the Midwest District. It was called the Southwest District.

Until that time, the Gulf States District had extended from El Paso, Texas, east to North Carolina. A new district was also created by taking all the states east of Louisiana to the Atlantic

Ocean and north to the Virginias and Kentucky. This new region was called the Southeast District. The remaining Gulf States churches, including New Mexico, Texas, Oklahoma, Arkansas, and Louisiana, were renamed the South Central District.

Rev. and Mrs. A. B. Teffeteller were appointed as Southeast District supervisors. The number of churches in the Southeastern United States was not large (less than fifty), but the area covered ten states: Mississippi, Alabama, Georgia, Florida, North and South Carolina, Virginia and West Virginia, Tennessee, and Kentucky.

Foursquare growth in the Southeast was slow. Perhaps some of this was due to the thriving of the Church of God of Cleveland, Tennessee, probably the oldest Pentecostal organization in America. With a wonderful testimony in that area of the nation since before the turn of the century, the Church of God has had wonderful fellowship with the Foursquare Church in spite of a significant doctrinal difference in respect to sanctification as a crisis experience, and other items of worship. However, the Southeast District has now begun to experience considerable growth.

Revival Fires Fanned

Postwar revival began to manifest in the ICFG during the early 1950s. At the 1951 convention the largest number of converts won in ICFG history were reported—30,820 in one year. In 1951 and 1952, gospel teams were sent to foreign fields, producing phenomenal results. Missionary offerings in 1952 far exceeded any previous year, and the 1953 convention reported 46,812 converts. Each year the harvest of new believers became larger.

In 1954, due in large measure to the number of missionaries sent out during this postwar period, the total of converts was 228,435—four times the number in any previous year. In the

United States there were 5,352 persons baptized in water and 7,300 persons baptized in the Holy Spirit according to Acts 2:4.

The 1952 International Foursquare Convention schedule was planned with the prayer-begotten purposes of stimulating renewed dedication to postwar revival. The president, Dr. McPherson, wrote:

> There is a mighty spiritual awakening taking place throughout the land. Soul-saving and body-healing revivals are the order of the day...
>
> This is the time for all of us, every pastor, evangelist and Gospel worker to awaken form our lethargy and get under the showers of blessing...
>
> 1. Primarily we will see the terrible condition of the lost...
> 2. Then we will see Jesus in a truer light, and we will want others to see Him;...
> 3. We will see the abundant harvest, "The harvest is plenteous," said Jesus, "but the laborers are few." Awake to the work!...
> 4. We will see signs and miracles wrought in our ministry...
> 5. Many of us do see these manifestations, but it takes absolute faith in Jesus Christ, "the same yesterday, and today, and forever,"...
> 6. WE will see the coming King. But until He does return we are to "occupy," with an eye alert to any and all opportunities to win the lost, to lift up the crucified Christ, and to labor in whatever harvest field God might place us.[2]

The Foursquare Church was interested in soul-winning and the growth of the body of Christ in all its ramifications. Its founder's spirit is etched on the cornerstone of Angelus Temple,

"DEDICATED UNTO THE CAUSE OF INTERDENOMINATIONAL AND WORLDWIDE EVANGELISM."

At the founding meeting of the Pentecostal Fellowship of North America, ICFG representative Herman D. Mitzner was one of the signatories. And through the years ICFG has been an active member and participant in the PFNA, as well as in the Pentecostal World Conference.

The ICFG's fellowship was extended not only to other Pentecostals but also to other Bible-believing associations. At its 1952 Convention The Foursquare Church voted to join the National Association of Evangelicals.

> The ministers felt that an application for membership in the National Association of Evangelicals should again be submitted. It was also voted to participate, upon acceptance, by asking every member of Foursquaredom to give an offering during the month of July of not less than three cents and, if possible, as high as five cents. This would enable the organization to join the NAE in its great world effort by showing a united front with evangelical churches of our country. Dr. Henry E. Hedrick, regional director (of NAE), presented the program with its great challenge. Individual ministers can receive additional benefits by joining the NAE and carrying their membership card.[3]

United Foursquare Women and Council of Foursquare Men

In the 1950s, two strong service organizations were organized within ICFG: The Council of Foursquare Men (CFM) and the United Foursquare Women (UFW). Their purpose was to provide laymen and laywomen opportunity in united action to help their church organization accomplish its mission.

The first step toward a men's fellowship was made in 1952.

At that year's convention the delegates voted their approval of a men's group to be called "Foursquare Fellowship Forum." However, when the group organized in 1955 they adopted the name "Council of Foursquare Men." Active organizers of the CFM were Karl Williams and Charles Carpenter.

In addition to fellowship realized in a number of the larger churches, men's camps experienced excellent success. The CFM camps at Camp Cedar Crest attracted capacity attendance. But perhaps the principal achievement of the CFM was the CFM Press—a printing ministry which produced literature for foreign mission field evangelism

The CFM ceased to exist in 1984. The demise was largely due to the effectiveness of local men's ministries in which many Foursquare men were active. The press, however, has survived and as Foursquare Missions Press, provides multiplied thousands of pieces of gospel literature annually. Under the leadership of Karl Williams, scores of people from various churches give their time, labor, and donations to sustain the enterprise and "man" the presses.

The idea for a worldwide women's organization came from two supervisors' wives, Lois Van Cleave and Edythe Dorrance. Permission was first sought from Dr. Rolf K. McPherson, who then referred the proposal to the 1955 convention floor. The convention approved the resolution, making the UFW a women's group UNITED for action.

Mrs. Billie Card, wife of a Costa Mesa, California, architect, was the first president of the UFW. She was followed in office by Leona Williams, Katie Loggins, and Shirley West. The UFW built two central buildings for housing their international offices and storing various articles for selection by missionaries en route to and from the field, or for shipment overseas as the need arises.

The first building was located in Santa Ana, California. When a civic center project displaced the first UFW "Alabaster House," a second one was built in Norwalk, California.

The United Foursquare Women has thrived until this writing, but there has been some thought that in more recent times the laywomen, for whose participation the UFW was conceived, have been overlooked in leadership. Whether this is true or not remains to be examined, and if so, some modification will be effected.

Mount Vernon Bible College Established

A large postwar advancement was the establishment of a Foursquare Bible college located east of the Mississippi River. Though the proposal was adopted by the 1956 convention body, the specific purchase of property was approved at the 1957 convention:

> The Convention body accepted the proposal of the Bible School Expansion Committee to purchase a 343-acre Bible School site in Mt. Vernon, Ohio, for Bible School students east of the Mississippi, who find it difficult to come to the West Coast for school. Authorization was further given to put into condition the existing four story building and to construct additional facilities to take care of the needs in order that the school may be opened in September of this year. Over $100,000 is needed this year to open, then $60,000 will be needed later to complete the purchase price. Dr. Orlando Shields, who has been assisting Dr. Clarence Hall in LIFE Bible College in Los Angeles, has accepted the appointment as the Dean of the new college.[4]

Much more has been written about Mt. Vernon Bible College in chapter 3. The drive for an eastern college was spearheaded by Vincent Bird, Warren Koon, and A. B. Teffeteller, supervisors of the three districts east of the Mississippi.

Further Expansion

Another project proposed by Dr. Howard Courtney Sr. and passed by the 1955 convention body was the church sponsoring plan. Those churches adopting the plan would, alone or in concert with other churches, pioneer a church in another part of the city in which they were located. They were also free to choose a nearby town or community and through personal support and finances, maintain and encourage the pioneer church until it could stand alone. Often, a new work would begin as a Sunday school or a home Bible study. The church in Lubbock, Texas, pastored by Rev. Fred Dawson Sr., implemented the plan, which resulted in five churches being planted in the greater Lubbock area.

The following year Dr. Courtney commented:

> It is with gratitude and thanksgiving that we announce the gaining of forty-four new Foursquare Churches in the United States and Canada in 1955. This is the greatest year of progress in the history of the organization, and it is especially gratifying to see this enlargement occur during the first year of the church sponsoring plan adopted at the 1955 Convention. Reports are coming in monthly of established churches that have caught the vision.[5]

A considerable number of churches implemented the church sponsoring plan, resulting in new works being opened. In some cases, however, the pioneering work was not completely carried out, resulting in the new works being closed at a later date. Others were left struggling. The keys to success for the praiseworthy plan were careful planning, thorough area research, and capable pioneer pastors.

In the mid-1950s, faithful ministry was encouraged and awarded. On the home missions night of the 1956 convention, gold lapel pins were awarded to all ministers who had served ICFG for twenty-five uninterrupted years. One hundred thirty-three ministers qualified and during the service were recognized. The award ceremony has continued to be an integral part of the annual Foursquare conventions. In 1979 the awarding of a fifty-year pin was begun, but the number of recipients awarded annually is understandably smaller.

At the 1956 international Foursquare convention, held in Los Angeles, California, the L.I.F.E. Bible College Alumni Association was reorganized in toto. A committee, composed of Drs. Clarence Hall, Guy P. Duffield, Nathaniel Van Cleave, and Chester Allen, proposed an alumni association that would meet regularly to form plans for assisting Bible school students through scholarships, annual support for the school, solicitation of endowments, and maintenance of the college campus. The new association would regularly elect officers and provide active support. An annual lectureship was strongly urged. The first elected alumni president was Nathaniel Van Cleave, with Guy P. Duffield being asked to deliver the first annual lectureship on the subject "Pentecostal Preaching."

DISTRICT LICENSING

During the decade of the 1950s, a special ministerial credential known as a "district license" was issued. The original intent was to recognize the temporary right of a person appointed by the district supervisor to minister. They would be able to act as pastor of a church where a regular ordained or licensed minister was unavailable. This exigency was necessary in cases where the church was very small and could not obtain an ordained minister. The credential was not conceived as permanent; it had to be renewed annually. It was sometimes given when the pastor of a new church had not yet qualified for regular license or ordination.

Later, however, the district license began to be issued to young workers who had pioneered churches on their own initiative. This practice became common in the 1970s and 1980s, until more than half of the new churches added to the denomination are at this writing pastored by workers with a district license. In order to receive such a license, a short correspondence course in Foursquare Church polity from L.I.F.E. Bible College must be completed.

Such a development in the recognition of new workers caused Bible college and seminary students to ask, "Why study for years to qualify for Foursquare ordination?" That question needs to be answered. It should be noted that many of those who have district licenses have extensive education from other sources.

For years, because of the Foursquare founder's strong belief in adequate, formal Bible training as proper qualification for ordination, graduation from L.I.F.E. or an equivalent school was required. Moreover, in the early days of various Pentecostal movements, few of the pastors and evangelists possessed formal education beyond high school. Yet, full gospel churches sprang up across the nation.

It must also be mentioned that many abuses, failures, and false doctrines in Pentecost could be attributed to inadequate training and ignorance of the Word. To the founder of the International Church of the Foursquare Gospel, at least two years' intensive Bible training seemed a minimal standard for pastors, evangelists, and missionaries.

Now, exceptions are being made. Is there a need to return to the original standard? Should the issue remain ill-defined? Or should there be further liberalization of ICFG's ministerial credential standards? One must believe that the blessed Holy Spirit and knowledgeable leadership will guide The Foursquare Church in the right direction.

Chapter 10

THE VINE GROWS MORE SLOWLY

1958–1971

THE PHENOMENON OF slowed growth is not at all unusual. It will happen when the life of an organism is delayed by changes in soil, climate, or cultivation. Jesus said:

> He cuts off every branch in me that bears no fruit, while every branch that does bear fruit he prunes so that it will be even more fruitful... Remain in me, and I will remain in you. No branch can bear fruit of itself; it must remain in the vine. Neither can you bear fruit unless you remain in me.
>
> —JOHN 15:2, 4, NIV

During the years between 1958 and 1971, the growth rate of the International Church of the Foursquare Gospel slackened. In 1960 there were approximately 750 churches throughout the United States; in 1970 the ICFG counted 800—an average of five new congregations each year. A greater number of churches had been started, but almost as many churches were closed. During this season, however, roots were being deepened and church facilities were relocated and improved. Such changes made possible efficient use of manpower and resources.

Statistics of Foursquare Missions International reveal the same story. In 1960 there were 106 missionaries serving twenty-three countries; by 1970 the number had risen to 125 missionaries working in twenty-five countries. In that decade only two new countries were reached by the Foursquare Church; Papua New Guinea—opening the possibility to liberate Stone Age people with the gospel—and Nigeria, which later became a gateway to many other African countries. And if missionaries who had been "borrowed" from other church groups (as in Papua New Guinea) were deducted, the number of missionaries sent and supported by the ICFG would have diminished by one during that decade.

Churches and pastoral training took place within countries, producing strong national ministry. The benefit of this has in later years made it possible to turn over entire mission fields to national boards, freeing missionaries to become counselors or move on to new endeavors.

Again, it must be stated that a number of new missionaries were sent, but in many cases it was a changing of the guard. Many of the pioneer missionaries retired and were replaced with others who had to be trained to take their places. Missionary offerings during that period of time increased significantly, but income did little more than keep pace with the increasing costs of sending and maintaining personnel.

At home in the USA there were congregations that grew significantly. But many churches felt comfortable with "holding their own." New converts were reported and memberships increased, but the churches groped for a way to close the rear exit to their sanctuaries. A typical church report for one year read one hundred saved, five baptized in water, and four people filled with the Holy Spirit.

Often skillfully organized programs and activities substituted for united prayer and a revival spirit. One person said, "We used to stand on the promises. Now we just sit on the premises." In many cases church life that once meant involvement and mutual participation had become a mere spectator sport. Historians for the Assemblies of God and other Pentecostal organizations chronicle similar periods of readjustment and deceleration of progress.[1]

How can the postwar change and deceleration be explained? The problem was cultural, economic, and spiritual.

Cultural Factors

After successive conflicts in Europe, the Pacific, Korea, and Vietnam, veterans returned home with an urge to change the world. Thousands who went to war from the farms opted for the city life where lucrative employment awaited. The widespread new affluence and urban living brought cultural change. Veterans with educational benefits from the "G.I. Bill" filled the colleges and universities. The lure of the "world," intensified by a television set in every home, changed the meaning of "worldly pleasure."

Pentecostal youth, who in the prewar period would have gone to Bible college, enrolled in universities and state colleges. Whereas before the war a high school diploma was adequate, in the postwar era with the new technologies, a B.A. degree from a university was a minimum requirement for desirable employment.

By the 1960s, with higher incomes, better education, and enhanced cultural awareness, Pentecostal pastors felt the need to pattern after the "old line" churches that seemed to be better prepared to appeal to the new culture. Many urban Foursquare churches adopted new liturgies, tighter organization, and more culturally consistent programming. In some cases, pastors and members were so fearful of being thought of as a "cult" that the name "Foursquare," which didn't seem to have for the unchurched an ecclesiastical ring, was relegated to fine print on the bottom of stationery and substituted by a "slogan" name. However, it must be said that, currently, "slogan names" are being used by churches of many denominations.

Economic Factors

While incomes increased considerably, so did inflation. Established churches fared well, but the cost of pioneering new congregations became prohibitive, especially in many urban areas. Zoning and building commissions established strict rules about where a church could locate or even meet temporarily. Church structures were barred from residential areas, unless they were zoned for or allowed church use. To provide for parking requirements, church properties had to be three to four acres in size. In large cities, especially in California, such properties in desirable areas could only be afforded by a large congregation.

District extension budgets were limited to only a few pioneering projects per year. Churches might start in a school, a lodge hall, a public auditorium, a tent, a large store building, etc. But the worker and family had to be supported for a lengthy period of time. Real estate payments often consumed a large portion of district funds that normally were planned for new extension work.

In the early 1940s, ICFG leadership established credit with a large California bank to obtain loans for church buildings within the state, but the churches were required to have suitable land free from debt in order to secure the loan. Additionally, the board of directors established a small fund derived from a loan from the missions reserve (long since repaid) and the investments of some Foursquare members wanting to help ministers finance their churches. Called the International Foursquare Loan Fund, "IFLF" for short, it provided small loans for secondary financing and for use in areas unable to borrow locally. The fund has grown considerably, and it is a hope that someday all financing can be done internally.

Thus, it may be said that the slowdown of church growth was due in part to greatly increased costs and newly imposed regulations governing public assembly. However, necessity became the mother of invention, and new means were devised to deal with new problems.

Spiritual Factors

Throughout history, all great revivals have subsided over a period of time. Foursquaredom had experienced several decades of Pentecostal revival. People were attracted to Foursquare churches because of the evidence of the Spirit's power and presence. There had been intensity of worship, a strong evangelistic spirit, and the transformation of lives. Throughout the years Angelus Temple sent out thousands of its best workers, and the revival spread across the country and around the world. In greater Los Angeles alone more than 150 Foursquare churches were established. But when Foursquare worship services (and classical Pentecostal services in general) became more formal, less spontaneous, and tentative about spiritual manifestations, their unique attraction to the spiritually hungry was lost.

One explanation for the spiritual "cooling" trend was a reaction to an increasing number of independent Pentecostal extremists whose heralded "signs and wonders" and unscriptural "new revelations" spawned an army of unattached admirers who traveled from church to church. These wanderers tended to "take over" anywhere they found a measure of spiritual freedom. The decade of the 1960s was a time of reorientation and re-study of Pentecostal truth.

The Foursquare movement learned from its founder to maintain a middle-of-the-road policy. It was not always popular to refuse to be swayed from side to side. Aimee Semple McPherson wrote:

> Formalism to the left of us, fanaticism to the right of us, the Foursquare Gospel is called to march straight down the middle of the King's highway. Don't turn to the right, don't run to the left. Lean neither toward frigidity and coldness, modernism and higher criticism, nor toward fanaticism which has run into a corner and ostracized itself from all thinking, sober-minded folk.
>
> The Lord has called me to walk in the middle of the road. At first it was a lonely road, but now thousands of people are climbing up the steep walls of this eternal pathway from both sides and joining the marching army. Hallelujah!

Two unexpected events were related to the "dry spell" in the history of the classical Pentecostal organizations. The first was called, "The New Order of the Latter Rain." This movement had its origin in 1947 in a Bible school in North Battleford, Saskatchewan, in Canada. Several men who had left the Pentecostal Assemblies of Canada joined with a teacher who had seceded from the Foursquare Church to form an independent Bible school. The principal leaders were George and Ern Hawtin.

In the newly organized school, emphasis was placed on prayer and fasting, as well as on spiritual gifts. In a brief period of time, an outpouring of the Holy Spirit, somewhat like that at Azusa Street in 1907, resulted. Leaders in several Pentecostal movements feel that the "latter rain" outpouring was initially a genuine moving of the Holy Spirit.

Unfortunately, some elements in the movement took some wrong turns. For them the entire emphasis turned to spiritual gifts, especially the gift of prophecy, which was imparted by the laying on of hands by leaders who called themselves "Latter Day Prophets." The pattern of 1 Corinthians, chapter 14, governing the exercise of vocal gifts, was completely ignored. Most regrettably, the movement engendered a spiritual pride at many locations, becoming very divisive. Anyone who wanted to experience the "latter rain" was required to "come out" of the "apostate" established Pentecostal churches, called Babylon.

The Assemblies of God lost several strong churches. The International Church of the Foursquare Gospel lost an excellent missionary. Because of the extremes of the so-called "Latter Rain" movement, the classical full gospel churches tended to shy away from anything that resembled that error. Several of the independent healing evangelists were influenced by the "new order," putting Pentecostal church leaders even more on the defensive. Bible college faculty warned students about extremes. All of these factors led to caution about manifestations, even about the genuine moving of the Holy Spirit.

Whatever the excesses of some, fairness requires the acknowledgment of the fact that today many fine churches in America exist which date their birthing to that error. They are churches that captured the blessing of a move of the Spirit while avoiding the attendant error.

Rise of the Charismatic Movement

A decade later there rose up a movement that some students of church history see as being related to the "latter rain." However, the results seem positively different. The parish priest Father Dennis Bennett, of St. Mark's Episcopal Church in Van Nuys, California, together with his wife, Rita, and a group of parishioners, was baptized with the Holy Spirit. When that outpouring (which was growing weekly) became known by other ministers of the church staff, strong opposition arose.

Rather than split the church, the Bennetts asked to be reassigned. They were appointed to the very small St. Luke's Church in Seattle, Washington, which later became a center of charismatic activity. Hundreds of ministers and laymen from various Protestant denominations traveled to Seattle in quest of the Spirit's fullness.

In some "old-line" denominational churches, the charismatic outpouring was aided by the activities of Jean Stone, member of the St. Mark's Episcopal Church. Under the minister of Father Bennett, she had received the Pentecostal outpouring in the initial prayer services. Jean was responsible for the stories of the outpouring at St. Mark's being published in *Time* and *Newsweek* magazines. In 1960 she formed the Blessed Trinity Society, which published a magazine called *Trinity*.

During the 1960s Jean Stone and Harald Bredesen—a Spirit-filled Lutheran pastor, traveled nationwide heralding the Spirit's outpouring among the historic Protestant churches. Difference of opinion exists as to who coined the term "Charismatic Renewal"—Harald Bredesen, Jean Stone, or Oral Roberts. But in any case, Harald Bredesen's influence was considerable—his being credited with impacting such people as Pat Boone (entertainer), John and Elizabeth Sherrill (noted writers), and Pat Robertson (founder of Christian Broadcasting Network), who was Bredesen's assistant just then coming into the Pentecostal experience.[2]

Others who figured in the early history of the Charismatic Renewal were David du Plessis, a South African Pentecostal leader who felt called to interpret this move of God to the historic denominations and later to the Vatican; David Wilkerson and John Sherrill, whose books (*The Cross and the Switchblade* and *They Speak With Other Tongues*, respectively) powerfully influenced a prayer group at Catholic Duquesne University in Pittsburgh, Pennsylvania, and later a group at Notre Dame, sparking the Catholic expression of the Charismatic Renewal.[3]

How did the Charismatic Renewal affect the growth of the Pentecostal denominations? In the early twentieth century beginnings of Pentecost, due to the liberal trend of the historic denominations, many flocked to full gospel churches. In fact, a large percentage of the earliest members of Pentecostal churches had been Baptists, Methodists, Lutherans, Presbyterians, Catholics, etc. They were not proselytized; their spiritual hunger drew them to meetings where the power of the Holy Spirit was present.

But as the power of the Holy Spirit began to "fall" upon the above-mentioned denominations, those who experienced the Spirit's infilling were encouraged to remain in the churches where they might have a great influence. Therefore, the traditional Pentecostal churches were gaining very few of those who had been baptized with the Spirit through the charismatic meetings. Furthermore, when the news of the charismatic outpouring and renewal spread across the world, the spiritually hungry were attracted to known charismatic centers. When those centers proliferated, they seemed to be where the action was. The Full Gospel Businessmen's groups and the independent evangelists of radio and television identified with the "newer" Pentecost.

As it was in the early beginnings of the Pentecostal movement, some groups went to unscriptural extremes. Leaders of the classical Pentecostal denominations who had worked through the extremist trends previously began to take a dim view of the charismatics. And when negative reaction prevailed, positive advance slowed. Consequently, many of the established full gospel churches became afraid of the charismatics and hesitated to encourage freedom of worship.

In the midst of this, however, church historian Vinson Synan credits the Foursquare Church as being more open to the charismatics than some of the other Pentecostal groups. He writes:

> Of all the classical Pentecostal denominations, the Foursquare Church has been the most affected by the charismatic renewal. To many outsiders, the worship services of the church are such that charismatics from mainline denominations feel immediately at home.[4]

The Foursquare "openness," observed by Synan, did not fully flower until the 1970s, when Jack Hayford, Roy Hicks Sr., Roy Hicks Jr., Jerry Cook, and others of Foursquare churches in the northwest United States became involved with charismatic centers. Such involvement will be covered in the next chapter.

In earlier days, when churches sensed a spiritual cooling, an evangelist would be invited who with a series of revival meetings—some lasting several weeks—would challenge the church to renewed consecration and service. In most congregations, two such "revivals" a year kept the church "on fire for God." In the postwar period, however, the evangelists who ministered to the local churches had practically disappeared.

During wartime the number of midweek services was reduced from a minimum of three meetings to only one. When the new mortgages forced both husband and wife to work, attendance at even one midweek service declined. People would not consistently attend nightly revival services. The evangelists often became pastors.

Simultaneously, Sunday night TV specials became the rage, and the Sunday night evangelistic service, which had at one time been the Pentecostal church's best attended service, lost its popularity to Sunday mornings. Such cultural changes did little to promote deeper spiritual life. All this called for a reassessment of priorities.

Para-Church Organizations

One additional contributor to decline in church attendance was the proliferation of para-church organizations. Groups such as Youth for Christ, the Full Gospel Businessmen's Fellowship, and any number of missionary societies and television ministries were based on real needs, performing what seemed to be a useful service. But they also drained finances and talented workers from established churches.

All specialized ministries, if they would have remained an arm of the church, could have been a great blessing to the kingdom of God. And many did. But others virtually ignored the established church, yet obtained their support from church members. They were accountable to no one. At their best, they became a challenge to the church to do a wider work.

There appears to be a tendency in the worldwide church that has experienced great revival to concentrate all activity on the preaching, worship, and experiential aspects of ministry. Such people often forget that the apostolic church of the book of Acts, in addition to enjoying fellowship with one another (Acts 2:38–42), also fed the hungry, clothed the naked, supported widows, healed the sick, and sent out missionaries. (See Acts 2:45; 6:1–5; 11:27–30; 13:1–4; 1 Timothy 5:16; James 1:27; 2:15–17.) But when the established church neglects any of the latter ministries, some person or group performs them independently; thus, the para-church agencies.

Sometimes the Pentecostal churches have excused themselves from doing humanitarian works by rationalizing, "We don't believe in the 'social' gospel." They forget, however, that the apostles, with their pattern of service, taught that the central "gospel" has social implications. Frankly, in making the statement that the para-church groups have sometimes slowed the growth of the denominations, the Pentecostal church must confess that the para-church groups have simply performed the established church's neglected service. Foursquare churches must seek to rediscover the pattern of a full-orbited ministry set by their founder.

Moderate but Consistent Growth

In recalling that the growth of The Foursquare Church slowed in the decade of the 1960s, at no time did the figures become negative; there was steady growth throughout. Also, the slowdown did not occur in all the individual churches; some areas and congregations experienced great growth and revival, even during that period of time.

A number of advances were accomplished that prepared the church for later renewal and numerical progress. Many churches acquired new properties and built new structures. Foursquare property valuation in the United States in 1962 reached $30,000,000. While fewer new missionary fields were penetrated in the 1960s, missionary offerings by the end of the ten-year period reached over one million dollars. The same year, the membership of the church, home and overseas, climbed to two hundred thousand people. In 1968 the number of converts in one year approached one hundred thousand.

At the 1962 convention, a bylaw revision was made that qualified offerings to service departments of the church with the IRS. A pension plan for retired ministers was initiated the same year. It was in the 1960s that the denomination's headquarters offices were moved from the cramped quarters of the L.I.F.E.

Bible College school building at Angelus Temple to the spacious second floor of the California Federal Savings building, on nearby Sunset Boulevard.

New Headquarters Personnel

During the decade, new personnel were added to the headquarters staff. Dr. Warren Koon retired from supervision of the Eastern District in 1961 and was appointed to a new office at headquarters to manage wills and endowments. Dr. Charles Duarte became the executive secretary of the denomination to assist Dr. Rolf McPherson with legal matters, the radio station, and to manage the finances of Angelus Temple.

Dr. Duarte had graduated from L.I.F.E. Bible College in 1943. He was ordained upon graduation, having been appointed to the Southern California District of Foursquare churches. He and his wife, Bettie, became pastors of the Hanford, California, Foursquare Church during 1943–1945. They then pastored in Compton, California (1945–1954); East Los Angeles, California (1954–1961); and Pomona, California (1961–1966).

While pastoring in Hanford, California, Dr. Duarte served as the superintendent of the San Joaquin Division, where he was instrumental in pioneering five new Foursquare churches: Tulare, Visalia, Lindsay, Exeter, and Coalinga—all in California. He later served as the superintendent of the Rio Hondo and Orange Belt Divisions.

As a member of the Cedar Crest Camp board from 1948–1966, he was involved in constructing many of the buildings of the camp. He also taught the Holy Spirit class and the science and the Bible class at camp for those years.

In April of 1966 he became the corporate executive secretary of the International Church of the Foursquare Gospel. In this capacity he served as the assistant to the president, general manager of the radio stations, and was instrumental in the acquisition of the Park-Sunset Building and the renovation of Angelus Temple. Dr. Duarte served as the legal liaison with the corporate attorneys concerning the major corporate legal matters. During the period of 1983–1988 he served as the corporate treasurer. From 1983–1991 he was a member of the missionary cabinet.

Prior to his retirement on May 30, 1991, Dr. Duarte worked closely with Dr. McPherson in a number of projects, including the Heritage and Founder's Ministries. He has continued to act in an advisory capacity and as a director on the board of Decatur Foursquare Broadcasting, the parent of the television station operated by the Decatur, Illinois, Foursquare Church.

In 1974, the personnel structure of the board of directors was changed to give laymen and pastors, who were to be elected by the convention body, representation at the top level of leadership. The first lay representative was Karl Williams, and the first pastor's representative was Charles Baldwin, then pastor of the Burbank, California, Foursquare Church.

Pastors who then served on the board of directors are: Guy Duffield, Robert Maynard, Paul E. Jones, Paul Risser (for two terms), Glenn Metzler, Harold Helms, James Ritch, and Loren Edwards. Succeeding laymen have been Curtis Correll, George Corsello, Dan Crotty, Dan Boone, and Douglas Slaybaugh. Similarly elected pastoral representatives served on the missionary cabinet. With grassroots representation at every level of leadership, greater enthusiasm for growth and participation has been generated.

Finally, during the decade of the 1960s, The Foursquare Church was being strengthened within. The foundation was being deepened to undergird greater height. The trunk of the vine was adjusting to support many new branches and an abundance of fruit. The decades of the 1970s and 1980s would bring growth and renewal, at home and abroad. A period of reassessment, reorientation, and refurbishment was preparing the church for renewal and revival.

Chapter 11

THE VINE RECEIVES NEW NOURISHMENT

1970–1990

THE ROOTS OF the vine often reach a new layer of moisture or richer soil springing into new life and growth. The psalmist, speaking of the man of God whose delight was in the Word of the Lord and who meditated on the Word day and night, penned:

> He shall be like a tree Planted by the rivers of water, That brings forth its fruit in its season, Whose leaf also shall not wither; And whatsoever he does shall prosper.
>
> —PSALM 1:3, NKJV

Chapter 10 identified the decade of the 1960s as being a period of reduced growth. Reasons for the slowdown were conjectured to be seasonal readjustment, cultural change, negative reaction to extremism, and some diminution of spiritual fervor. The reasons for renewal are a bit more complex. However, it seems clear that God has yet a new mission for renewed vessels.

In the first years of the 1970s, certain events and trends in the International Church of the Foursquare Gospel pointed toward renewal. The 1971 international Foursquare convention was named "Foursquare Congress on Evangelism."

Writing afterward about the convention, Dr. Rolf K. McPherson noted, "An unusual and special anointing of the Holy Spirit characterized the conclave and eternal results have been established." An outcome of the congress was the publication of a manual on evangelism that was made available to all pastors and workers.

In 1972 there was no international convention, but tri-district conferences were held in different areas of the United States. In each of these, God's power was manifest.[1]

A half century of Foursquare history was celebrated at the 1973 Golden Jubilee Convention. That historic gathering claimed the largest registration of any convention held until that time. Each of the evening convention services at Angelus Temple was filled to capacity. An overflow crowd watched by closed-circuit television from Angelus Auditorium. Ninety delegates from overseas and sixty missionaries were registered.

On Sunday morning of that convention, Southwest District Supervisor Harold W. Jefferies delivered the keynote message entitled, "It Hasn't Happened Yet." He challenged the denomination to a renewed dedication for the second fifty years. The last day of the Golden Jubilee Convention was designed as a day of renewal.[2]

By 1974 several pastors were beginning to set patterns of explosive growth and spiritual renewal. These would powerfully challenge the entire Foursquare movement. They included Jack Hayford in Van Nuys, California; Roy Hicks Jr. in Eugene, Oregon; Jerry Cook in Gresham, Oregon; Ron Mehl in Beaverton, Oregon; and John Holland in Vancouver, British Columbia. These and others were experiencing remarkable numerical growth and spiritual awakening.

The Church On The Way—Van Nuys, California

At The Church On The Way, the First Foursquare Church of Van Nuys, California, Jack Hayford was not only experiencing rapid growth in his congregation, but he was also influencing many other churches. Jack began to speak at ICFG conferences, strongly encouraging cooperation with the district tithe program. Positive response to Pastor Hayford's messages on church tithing made possible, for the first time, a reasonably adequate income for church planting.

In addition, a new annual event—the Fall Pastor's Conference sponsored by The Church On The Way—soon became known around the world. Capacity crowds filled the church each year to hear speakers who were experiencing growth and a fresh move of the Holy Spirit in their midst.

While attendees at these conferences included pastors from all Pentecostal and charismatic groups, many Foursquare pastors, hungry for renewal and guidance, were in attendance. The teaching helped many of them find a more effective ministry. Others discovered that imitation of other men of God does not always bring a formula of instant success. Many of the latter, however, were motivated to seek God for the approach that would bring growth to their congregations in their own communities.

Jack Hayford began to be invited to speak throughout the nation and in many foreign countries. Contact with Pentecostal and charismatic leaders who represented the whole spectrum of renewal ministry gave Jack a keen understanding of the Spirit's moving in the modern world. Jack Hayford's "formula" (if the author may presume to suggest it) is prayer and praise; taking authority over Satan's inroads into the church; worshipful music; faith to launch out; wise selection of capable

Spirit-guided helpers; sensitivity to the Spirit's moving; and strong Bible preaching. A keen sense of humor should also not be excluded from the list.

Jack Hayford graduated from L.I.F.E. Bible College in January 1956, in a class in which he had been student body president and valedictorian. He and his wonderful wife, Anna, pastored in Fort Wayne, Indiana, for five years, after which he was appointed to headquarters as national youth representative. In 1965 Jack accepted the position as dean of students at L.I.F.E. Bible College, an office in which he served until 1969, when he assumed the pastorate of the Van Nuys, California, Church. While continuing to pastor the church, Jack would also serve the college as president from 1977–1982.

By the time Dr. Hayford assumed the pastorate of the Van Nuys, California, Foursquare Church, the congregation had declined to only a handful of people. Yet, then district supervisor N. M. Van Cleave believed that a church in the midst of the rapidly growing San Fernando Valley, under Jack's leadership, would have an unlimited potential. He was not mistaken.

In his book *The Twentieth-Century Pentecostal Explosion*, church historian Vinson Synan has the following to say about Jack Hayford and The Church On The Way:

> A great impetus in this development (ICFG renewal) has been the ministry of Jack Hayford, whose Church On The Way in Van Nuys, California, has grown to be the largest Foursquare congregation in the United States. With over 6,000 members, his church is a modern-day counterpart to Angelus Temple. Hayford's influence goes far beyond the bounds of his denomination, however, since he is a popular speaker for many charismatic conferences.[3]

It should be noted that since Dr. Synan wrote the above, The Church On The Way grew to over eight thousand members. And the numbers continue to rise.

Accelerated Growth Nationally

Tremendous growth and renewal in the Foursquare Church has taken place in many other churches as well, especially in the Northwestern sector. During the 1970s and 1980s, the Northwest District grew from 60 to 190 churches. The increase in constituents was over 400 percent. Foursquare churches in the United States increased from 775 in 1970 to over 1,400 in 1989. In other lands, perhaps the greatest revival is taking place in Brazil and Argentina.

Referring to the Northwest churches, Synan observes:

> The greatest growth for the church (ICFG) in recent years has taken place in the Northwestern states where Roy Hicks Jr. has led in planting many churches in Oregon and Washington. Other significant growth has taken place in California and the East. By 1986 some of the largest Foursquare churches in America included... Ron Mehl's Foursquare congregation in Beaverton, Oregon, and the Faith Center church in Eugene, Oregon, pastored by Roy Hicks Jr. At least two Foursquare churches own television stations. These are operated by the Foursquare churches in Decatur, Illinois, and Roanoke, Virginia.[4]

Three things have contributed to the outstanding growth over the past two decades: (1) a genuine outpouring of the Holy Spirit; (2) leadership sensitive to the Spirit's guidance; and (3) a turning to God of the counter-culture youth of the post-Vietnam War period. Converts among the so-called "hippie" youth were known as the "Jesus people." The antiestablishment youth first turned to drugs, sex, and hard rock music. A number of able workers, such as David Wilkerson in New York, Chuck Smith in Costa Mesa, and Linda Meissner in Seattle, ministered among these young people.[5]

The "Jesus people" movement received nationwide publicity through television and magazine coverage of activities of Calvary Chapel, especially of Chuck Smith's baptism services on the beach of Corona Del Mar, California. In one evening, as many as seven hundred young people were baptized in the Pacific Ocean by Chuck and his staff. Smith's ministry continued to attract youth until he was preaching to as many as ten thousand in Sunday services. From Smith's Calvary Chapel in Costa Mesa, California, other congregations sprang up throughout California and across the United States.

Chuck Smith was the son of Foursquare parents and is a graduate of L.I.F.E. Bible College. He developed his ministry pastoring Foursquare churches in Arizona and Southern California. At this writing, Calvary Chapels in West Covina, Downey, Brea, Riverside, and San Diego are beginning to rival the "mother" church in attendance. All remain friendly to the International Church of the Foursquare Gospel, often inviting Foursquare teachers to minister at their services, which still attract a high percentage of youth.[6]

Many Foursquare churches in the Northwest likewise appealed to the younger generation. Faith Center in Eugene, Oregon, pastored by Roy Hicks Jr., ministered to a very large number of young people. The First Foursquare Church in Portland, Oregon, where Greg and Cindy Romine served as youth ministers under Pastor Allan Hamilton, soon filled several front rows with newly converted youth, many of whom were former "street people." The Beaverton, Oregon, congregation, pastored by Ron and Joyce Mehl, has attracted hundreds of young men and women. These are only a few of numerous similar examples.

Ron Mehl, a former star athlete, was youth director of the Great Lakes District before moving to Beaverton, Oregon. Having a natural appeal to youth, he was surrounded with young families and numbers of youth who were disillusioned with the soon-empty and mocking attractions of sin. In Pastor Ron they found a sympathetic and loving leader. They are only an example of others, betrayed by Satan's deceptions, who will find a way to those churches that are alive with the dynamic presence of God's blessed Holy Spirit.

It must be noted that all those churches in Foursquaredom that have experienced great growth over those two decades had a strong appeal to young people. One excellent example is the Foursquare church in Hermosa Beach, California, called "Hope Chapel."

In 1970 Ralph Moore, then youth pastor of the Granada Hills, California, Foursquare Church, approached Nathaniel Van Cleave, his Southern California District supervisor, with the request to be appointed pastor of a small congregation in Hermosa Beach. Located in a "beach" community, the church was at the point of being closed for complete lack of success.

Ralph's request was granted, together with a promise of support by the district for six months to a year. Ralph, who had been student body president at L.I.F.E. Bible College, persuaded a group of students to assist him with beach evangelism. Soon the one-on-one evangelism harvested a number of converts, who became Ralph's congregation in the formerly empty chapel. After only three months Ralph informed the district supervisor that he no longer needed the district support.

It was not long until the chapel was full at multiple Sunday services. Later, the teeming congregation, most of whom were converted beach people, purchased a bowling alley that had been closed. The "lanes" were converted into sanctuary seating one thousand people. When this large church was filled, Ralph left the Hermosa Beach Hope Chapel in the hands of his capable associate pastor, Zachary Nazarian, and moved to Hawaii to pioneer. In Hawaii at this writing there are twenty-three Foursquare churches, overflowing with young people. In the first eight years of its existence, Hope Chapel Kaneohe pioneered twenty-one churches in the United States, Japan, Canada, and Australia. Ralph and his wife, Ruby, pastored in Windward, Oahu.

From those humble beginnings, there have at this writing been more than seventy churches pioneered as a first, second, or third generation effort of Hope Chapel, Hermosa Beach.

Accelerated Growth Internationally

According to the Book of Acts, chapter 1, when there is an empowering of the Holy Spirit in the life of Christ's church, the natural result will be greater witness to the far corners of the world. And as the Foursquare Church was beginning to enter a period of renewal "at home" in the United States, there was a stirring of the church's missionary vision and expansion.

In 1974, under the auspices of the Billy Graham Evangelistic Association, the "International Congress on World Evangelization" was called in Lausanne, Switzerland. At that conference Dr. Ralph Winter revealed to the 3,200 conferees, including representatives from Foursquare Missions International, that one-half of the world's 2.4 billion people had little or no knowledge of God's redemptive plan. Ardent missiologists had calculated that there still remained 17,000 unreached or hidden "people groups." The church was called upon to expand their proclamation of the gospel into these new frontiers.

Foursquare Missions personnel, under the leadership of Dr. Leland Edwards, carefully evaluated their commitment. A unanimous decision was reached that "by faith, Foursquare Missions International would reach 100 hidden and unreached people groups with the Gospel by 1990." Over the months that followed, the vision began to take on substance.

In 1982 a fivefold plan, "Advancing Through the Eighties," was published and presented to the entire Foursquare Church in North America. Through cooperative effort with missionary and national leadership around the world, the International Church of the Foursquare Gospel would seek to: (1) reach at least 100 unreached people groups around the world; (2) advance the ministry of the Foursquare Church into eighteen additional countries, thereby increasing the number from thirty-seven to fifty-five; (3) increase the number of Foursquare missionaries from 100 to 185; (4) multiply the number of Foursquare members and adherents from 740,326 to over 1,500,000; and (5) seek to raise missionary giving from $2.8 million to an annual goal of $10 million. A target was set for December 31, 1990.[7]

However, in May 1982, leaders and representatives from Foursquare churches in thirty-six countries gathered for the First Global Leadership Conference and raised the above figures far beyond one's wildest expectations. In May 1988 the Second Global Leadership Conference was convened, under the chairmanship of Rev. Phil Starr, to continue the bonding of national leadership from Foursquare churches, which had by that time skyrocketed to sixty-two countries of the world. The original vision was expanded to consider a strategy of manpower and networking within Foursquare Missions through the year 2000.

In retrospect, many of the goals envisioned in 1982 were met.

By the end of 1990, there were Foursquare churches ministering in more than seventy countries of the world; the number of hidden people groups reached far exceeded the original vision. The goal of 1.5 million Foursquare members was surpassed. However, God had a different plan as to how The Foursquare Church would expand, for much of that increase would not be through the sending of North American missionaries but through the raising up of national workers whom He would lead to assume leadership and still others who would affiliate with the International Church of the Foursquare Gospel.

One outstanding example and testimony is that of Ram Sharan Nepal (whose Christian name is Simon Peter), whom God has raised up in the nation of Nepal. For centuries this predominantly Hindu and Buddhist nation had been closed to the gospel of Jesus Christ. Yet, 1974, Simon Peter came to know the Lord through a European building contractor who was working on the high school where the lad was attending. In 1975 he was baptized in water, completed high school, and moved away from his home to the city to pursue God's will for his life. At risk to his life, he immediately began to spread the message of Jesus Christ.

In 1982, while Simon Peter was on Christmas break from a Bible college in India, he was approached by a woman who had come to share a prophecy from the Lord. Her words were, "You will have a long table with many children, and the Lord will provide." In the years to follow, that prophecy would come true for Simon and his wife, Meena.

Having sovereignly been led to meet with representatives from Foursquare Missions International, Simon and Meena joined their hearts and hands with the International Church of the Foursquare Gospel. As of this writing he serves as the general supervisor of the Church of the Foursquare Gospel in

Nepal. Under his leadership the Lord established fifty churches, claiming three thousand baptized, committed believers and two thousand adherents. He has also taken on the responsibility of giving life and love to more than 125 children, whom Simon and Meena have legally adopted in addition to their two natural children. Simon and Meena pastor a local church and operate a school and Bible institute, and most recently, a vocation training school for the children. Foursquare churches in North America are assisting in the establishment of a headquarters property and building, as well as in the intensive training of ministers.[8]

In 1991 the government of Nepal underwent major changes. One of the results was that the preaching of the gospel is now legally permitted by civil authorities. Having been imprisoned on many occasions for their boldness in sharing the message of the Foursquare Gospel, Simon and the Foursquare pastors who serve with him are rejoicing in their newfound freedom. They are also taking every advantage in seeing that the 20 million inhabitants of that nation hear the message of hope and redemption.

A similar story could be told about the Foursquare Church in Trinidad and Tobago. Before his birth, Peter Hosein had been dedicated to Allah, the Muslim god. His father had promised that should he be given another son, the boy would become a priest in that religion. As a lad, Peter was trained in the forms, rituals, and ceremonies of the Muslim priesthood. At the age of ten, he even started to officiate priestly duties under the guidance of his uncle.

Finding a Bible on the shelf of a grocery store owned by his brother, Peter came to a saving knowledge of the Lord Jesus. He returned home and, in spite of great persecution, began to preach the gospel. He was also healed of a serious speech impediment, an undeniable miracle that led many of his family to accept Christ. He was miraculously baptized with the Holy Spirit, simply by reading the Scriptures. He began to preach, and through the blessings of God, many churches were established in Trinidad/Tobago.

In 1956 he came in contact with a magazine that contained an article about the vision of Aimee Semple McPherson and the Foursquare Church. God witnessed to his spirit that he should contact the denomination, but there was no address on the article.

Six years later, a missionary from the Foursquare Church passed through Trinidad on a visit and met Peter. In 1986, a member of a Foursquare church in the United States visited the home of Peter and his wife, Esther. Peter wrote a letter expressing his vision and asked the young lady to deliver it to Dr. Leland Edwards. Following much prayer and discussion among Peter, his church leadership, and Foursquare Missions International, the churches officially voted to unite with the Foursquare Church Family.[9]

Under the leadership of Peter Hosein, the Foursquare churches in Trinidad and Tobago continue to grow in size and in maturity. In addition, this anointed man of God has assisted in the formation of congregations in the islands of Grenada and St. Vincent.

Another major development during the decade was the establishment of regional councils in various parts of the world, where missionary and national leaders from a particular sector of the world could gather to consider cooperative strategy, financial support, and even the mutual sending of personnel to emerging opportunities in their respective regions.

In Asia the Eastern Council of Foursquare Churches now provides a forum for fourteen nations where the Foursquare

Church is ministering. Through the sending of personnel, cooperative financial support, and spiritual unity, missionaries from the Philippines have been sent to minister in Papua New Guinea and Australia and among Filipinos in Hong Kong. The Foursquare Bible schools in the Philippines are providing training for leaders from many of the Asian nations. Australian Foursquare believers continue to send and support missionaries to Papua New Guinea, and there is a Foursquare minister from Papua New Guinea who has started a Foursquare church among the Aborigines of Australia. New fields such as Myanmar (Burma), Pakistan, and Thailand continue to grow.

With the fall of Communism in Eastern Europe, new opportunities await the Foursquare churches in Europe. Through Foursquare Europe, believers from that continent and the United States are combining giftedness and resources to reach those who are now looking for new meaning in life. A Mid-America Council has been formed among the Foursquare churches in Central America, providing increased understanding and unity. A similar regional forum brings The Foursquare Church throughout South America together.

The renewing of vision, the maturing of national leadership, the receiving of God-sent national leaders into the Foursquare family, and the mutual sharing of resources marked the decade of the 1980s as one of the most exciting and accelerating period of missionary growth for the Foursquare Church. And that pace of growth continues with an overwhelming rapidity, as the Foursquare Church enters the 1990s. At this writing, Foursquare believers are ministering in more than seventy countries of the world, compared with thirty-seven in 1982. In 1991 someone in the world found Christ every one hundred seconds, and there were ten new churches started each day of the year.

It must also be noted that through the leadership of professors such as Dr. John Amstutz, Dr. Paul Watney, Dr. John Louwerse, and others, a thorough cross-cultural track of studies was developed at L.I.F.E. Bible College, resulting in renewed missions orientation and vision for future Foursquare ministers. New programs for preparing Foursquare members and future leaders to live and work on the mission field continue to be enhanced and evaluated.

Renewed Interest in Foursquare Heritage

During the 1960s there appeared in the younger ministers an attitude of disinterest in the roots and early history of the Foursquare denomination. When referring to the founder and the early revival in which the Foursquare Church was birthed, speakers met a reaction that voiced the sentiment, "Let's not live in the past."

As the Foursquare churches entered the reawakening period of the middle 1970s, a new interest in the church's history was rebirthed. Older ministers and teachers who remembered the founding revival were frequently invited to the churches to recount those beginnings. Mrs. McPherson's autobiography, *This Is That*, which had been in small demand, now required republication. Apparently, the better one understands the past, the better one is equipped to face the future.

Academic Advancement of Foursquare Bible Colleges

With the postwar prosperity and cultural changes, Foursquare Bible colleges tended to be academically upgraded. Accrediting associations for Bible colleges began to function. When parents and students began to be concerned about the "transferability" of Bible college credits to accredited colleges and universities, the Pentecostal schools awoke to the dilemma and openly faced the question, "Can any Bible college endure in the modern world without accreditation?"

In their beginnings, Pentecostal Bible institutes and colleges existed primarily to train pastors, evangelists, missionaries, and workers of like doctrine. Subject matter was personal experience, the Bible, soul-winning, and ministry methods. Prerequisites for faculty were ministry experience and little more than a high school diploma.

After the war, when students enrolled in the Bible colleges already possessing college degrees, the faculty members were forced to upgrade their qualifications by studying part-time in universities and seminaries. Later, only men and women who had earned master's and doctor's degrees were in demand for "chairs" in even the Pentecostal Bible colleges.

In spite of numerous warnings that academic advancement would undermine Pentecostal foundations, in the early 1960s L.I.F.E. Bible College began to prepare for accreditation. Faculty began to take evaluation tests and submit their courses to student evaluation. Other requirements of the Accrediting Association of Bible Colleges (AABC) were an upgraded library, the educational level of the faculty being an average of a master's degree, a standard curriculum, a board of regents, a budget and accounting system independent of the church corporation, and a limit on the size of classes.

Dr. Clarence Hall, dean of L.I.F.E, initiated the quest for accreditation, and in 1974 his successor, Dr. Donald McGregor, appointed an accreditation committee that approved application to the AABC for applicant status. Active in the quest with these were William Cochrane, Dorothy Jean Furlong, Herman Rosenberger, Sam Middlebrook, and Steve Cauble.

In 1967 the library of L.I.F.E. Bible College moved to a larger space on the second floor of the college building, with the L.I.F.E Alumni Association supplying the needed resources. This crucial addition made advancement possible with the accrediting agency. In 1976 the newly appointed president of L.I.F.E., Dr. N. M. Van Cleave, together with the academic dean William Cochrane, traveled to Chicago, Illinois. It was there, at the annual meeting of the AABC, that L.I.F.E. Bible College was granted "candidate" status, the essential step paving the way to earned accreditation. The final goal of full accreditation was realized in 1980, during the presidency of Dr. Jack Hayford.

Some people still predict that maintaining accreditation standards will be too costly, both in finances and spiritual blessing. However, since the charismatic outpouring of the Holy Spirit upon traditional denominations, many see in advanced scholarship no hindrance to Pentecostal anointing.

In 1976 a new board of regents was selected to oversee the development of L.I.F.E. Bible College. The board, consisting of Rolf McPherson, Howard P. Courtney Sr., N. M. Van Cleave, Merrill Nicholls, Richard Schmidt, Paul E. Jones, Sidney Westbrook, Jack Hayford, Allan Hamilton, Alvin Heimbuch, Leland Simonson, Gerald Canning, Andrew Sawchuck, Malcolm McGregor, and Jack Saffell, met annually and later semi-annually to study and expedite the school's advancement.

In later years the following regents replaced the original board: college president Jack Hamilton, Fred Wymore, Barney Northcote, Andrew Sawchuck, Carl Cadonau, Bob Richards, Paul Chambers, Dennis Easter, Paul Hackett, Cliff Hanes, Eugene Kurtz, Roger Mattison, Ron Mehl, John Watson, Roger Whitlow, and at this writing, chairman Bernard Porter.

In 1982 Jack Hayford's five-year season as president (simultaneous with his pastorate) was followed by that of Jack Hamilton. Born in Rock Island, Illinois, on May 1, 1939, Jack began attending, at an early age, the Moline Gospel Temple, pastored by Charles and Ruth Hollis.

While serving in the U.S. Army, stationed at Fort Bliss in El Paso, Texas, he attended the Foursquare church pastored by Paul and Christine McEachern. There he accepted Christ as Savior and soon afterward began a correspondence course from L.I.F.E. Bible College. In 1961, through the influence of the McEacherns and the Hollises, Jack enrolled for residence study at the college, graduating in 1965 with a Bachelor of Theology degree. It was while Jack was a L.I.F.E. student that he met Carole Chambers, who worked at the college and Angelus Temple as a secretary. Their romance budded while they sang together in the Angelus Temple choir, and they were married in 1963.

The Hamiltons began their ministry in the newly formed Western Canada District as the district youth directors. They later served on the pastoral staff at the Kingsway Foursquare Church in Vancouver, British Columbia, and pastored the Hastings Foursquare Church in the same city.

In 1970 Jack and Carole were appointed as pastors to the Santa Maria, California, Foursquare Church, where their flowering ministry came into full bloom. When they assumed pastorate of that congregation, the annual missionary offerings totaled $1,000. In 1981, their last full year in Santa Maria, the missionary offerings were in excess of $25,000. The board of directors, ICFG, honored Jack with the degree of doctor of divinity in 1985, and Dr. Hamilton received his master's degree from Azusa Pacific College in 1987.

Special mention must be made of L.I.F.E.'s faculty members, a number of whom have now retired from classroom teaching. They not only offered years but decades to the work of preparing aspiring preachers.

Who will ever forget Charles Walkem, who never passed the

fourth grade in formal education, yet was a masterful musician who arranged most of Mrs. McPherson's oratorios. He taught Greek and Hebrew, as well as wrote many books on Bible subjects. Unforgettable also is the faithful teaching of Christopher Gabie, who knew his Bible from the Garden of Eden to the New Jerusalem. He had such a sense of humor that he would tell his jokes twice unless the class responded.

William Cochrane, the mathematical genius who was L.I.F.E's academic dean during the latter years of his tenure, served the college for decades. A great contribution to L.I.F.E. was made by Charles Tate, who taught hundreds the skill of public speaking and who, by example as well as by word, exemplified as much about Christian living. Hundreds of Foursquare pastors will have their theology more correct because of Guy P. Duffield, coauthor with Nathaniel Van Cleave of *Foundations of Pentecostal Theology* and who, for seventeen years, was the pastor of Angelus Temple. One could not count the number of students who entered the fullness of the Holy Spirit and an understanding of "Him" as a person under the faithful tutoring of Ralph Hammon. He and Dorothy modeled the fruit of the Spirit as well as His variety of giftings. And of course, no list of L.I.F.E.'s beloved teachers would be complete without the inclusion of "Mr. Romans," Leslie Eno, who in retirement was still in demand for Bible conferences.

One of the most faithful, versatile, and resourceful of L.I.F.E.'s faculty members if Dr. Dorothy Jean Furlong. Dorothy Jean grew up under the ministry of Harold and Ione Jefferies, who inspired her to ministry. She enrolled in L.I.F.E. in 1942, graduating in 1945. Together with Rev. Juanita Conger, a very capable associate, she pastored churches in Canada, Oregon, and Idaho. In 1955 she became the director of Christian education and choir leader of the Pomona, California, Foursquare

Church. There she and Juanita served for five years, between 1955 and 1960. Dorothy Jean joined the faculty of L.I.F.E. part-time in 1957 and full-time in 1960. Dorothy Jean and Juanita were an important part of the college for thirty years before retiring in 1988.

For a number of the latter years, Dorothy Jean Furlong was L.I.F.E's academic dean. In 1989 she was invited by Sterling Brackett, president of L.I.F.E. Bible College East, to serve the eastern college as academic dean. Dr. Furlong has held the positions of pastor, CE director, youth director, director of Christian service, college professor, and in two colleges, academic dean. Rev. Conger has capably shared in most of these ministries, and in a number of capacities related to her own unique talents.

L.I.F.E. has been capably directed by several deans, executive directors, and presidents; a number of very talented teachers have come and gone, but few have matched the highly resourceful hand of Dr. Dorothy Jean Furlong, keeping the college operating on the day-to-day level with little fanfare. She has been to L.I.F.E. Bible College what Henrietta Mears was to the Hollywood Presbyterian Church and to the Forest Home Conference program.

Since the early 1970s L.I.F.E. Bible College had contemplated relocation. A gift of five million dollars marked for new property and facilities made this a real possibility. After serious consideration of at least five different campus locations, the regents and denomination's board of directors finally settled upon a former drive-in church property in San Dimas, California. The new site for the campus was purchased in May 1985. A fund-raising drive was launched; to make the move possible, at least three million dollars more would be needed for the first stage of construction. A historic groundbreaking service was conducted in March 1987.

Construction was begun in February 1989 and completed in time for the 1990 fall semester. Occupancy of the facilities began in September 1990. On October 7, 1990, hundreds of friends, faculty, fellow ministers, and denominational leaders filled the chapel for the dedication of the new campus and facilities.

Mount Vernon Bible College (MVBC), Foursquaredom's Bible college east of the Mississippi River and located in Mt. Vernon, Ohio, experienced circumstances similar to those of L.I.F.E., except that until now the eastern college has not attained accreditation. (Serious thought is at this writing being given to the process.)

In the mid-1970s MVBC suffered a decline in enrollment, as did a number of other Bible colleges and institutes across America. Additionally, the area became financially depressed with only low-paying jobs available for students. On several occasions thought was given to the closing of MVBC; however, the pressing need for a Bible college on the eastern seaboard kept it open.

A quest for a more suitable campus site for MVBC began in 1987. An excellent sixty-five-acre piece of property was located in Christiansburg, Virginia, near the strong church and television station in Roanoke, Virginia, pastored by Rev. and Mrs. Ken Wright. The property contained a complex of nearly completed buildings originally being erected as a Muslim college. However, the project had failed and was now being sold by the bank for $2,700,000, or about three-fifths of its value.

The board of regents for MVBC, including the supervisors of the districts east of the Mississippi River, explored the area and the property and recommended its acquisition. At the time it was believed that a buyer had been found to purchase the old Mount Vernon campus. There were also several large gifts and promises of assistance in making the Christiansburg property ready for occupancy. One donor offered to furnish trucks and men to move the school equipment form Mount Vernon, Ohio. Another would do the extensive landscaping.

Following considerable discussion on the part of the international board in Los Angeles, the purchase was approved and made. MVBC, headed by President Mark Ballard, moved to Christiansburg, Virginia, in 1988. The school's name was changed to L.I.F.E. Bible College East. Most of the gifts, however, were needed for the "start up" costs of the college at the new location. Meeting the mortgage was another thing.

The counted-on sale of the Ohio property fell through, and the drive for money, though appreciated, would have only equaled the first month's interest. The international board had no choice but to refinance, with money being borrowed from various headquarters department reserves. A six-year program (barring the sale of the Mt. Vernon property and with interest being waived) was set up to replace the borrowed funds by curtailing other organizational and district programs. The new campus has been very costly but is believed to be well worthy of the effort and sacrifices.

When President Ballard resigned in 1989, Rev. Sterling Brackett was named to fill the responsibility of president of L.I.F.E. Bible College East. President Brackett instituted a stable budgetary operation, installed new staff and faculty, and at the same time greatly improved the property. He also enlisted the assistance of Dorothy Jean Furlong, who had served at L.I.F.E. Bible College for nearly thirty years to serve as academic dean of the school. Dorothy Jean, aided by Juanita Conger, has assisted in the development of a curriculum and the selection of a faculty. At this writing needs are now being met, and new students are enrolling, providing a brighter future for L.I.F.E. East.

Another positive factor during the 1980s has been the growth of the Eastern and Southeast districts, under Dewey Morrow and Glenn Burris Sr., respectively. Expansion and development in these districts have been among the most rapid among the U.S. Foursquare Church.

Increased Church Extension Tithe

During this renew era, with the churches giving almost 100 percent cooperation in the church extension tithe program, not only has the International Church of the Foursquare Gospel experienced notable growth, but also substantial funds have been placed in reserve. Occasional criticisms in the past had been aimed at the denomination's leadership over the matter of reserve funds. Certain persons contended that such conservative budgeting exhibited a lack of faith. However, when three large church ventures failed during the 1980s (including the Mount Vernon Bible College relocation), help was required from headquarters for their survival, and a much greater appreciation for the previous fiscal conservatism prevailed. Today, the reserves are carefully preserved to meet the minimum required to secure the corporate credit for its nearly $60 million in church loans.

Influx of Pastors from Local Church Institutes or Other Denominations

For years, a diploma from one of the Foursquare Bible colleges was almost the only door leading to Foursquare ministry. And, over the years, the Bible college courses were extended from two to four years. Graduates who may well have added to their preparation for ministry by taking several more years of graduate studies were reluctant to pioneer new churches. Many hoped to be appointed to an established pastorate or as a member of the pastoral staff of a larger church. Workers able and willing to start new Foursquare churches in outlying areas became scarce.

On the other hand, pastors of the large renewal centers, such as Faith Center in Eugene, Oregon, found that a number of their converts were eager to "pioneer churches." Most of these convents already held diplomas from secular colleges and needed only six months to a year of study in Bible, doctrine, and church polity to prepare them for church planting.

To fill such a need, local institutes such as those in Eugene, Oregon; Portland, Oregon; Escondido, California; Ventura, California; Artesia, California; and Easton, Massachusetts, were established. With a church planting program helped by "graduates" from one of these institutes, one of the districts grew from almost one of the smallest conclaves of Foursquare churches to become the largest.

The local institute, however, created another challenge. Institutes did not lead to ordination. When the new churches started by young couples from the institutes grew larger than many of the established churches, a way had to be found to recognize their pastoral status.

An answer was found in the establishment of a credential created to enable temporary lay pastors of local churches to perform pastoral duties until a permanent pastor could be appointed. A "district license" requiring renewal each year was developed for use by the district supervisor. Later, an avenue was opened for one with a district license to upgrade, in time, to an international license and to full ordination.

Two institutes that merit special mention are those that focus special attention on students of Hispanic origin, or those people contemplating ministry to Spanish-speaking locations. Facultad de Teologia, headed by Dr. Enrique Zone, is located in Montebello, California. Angelus Bible Institute is conducted at

Angelus Temple by Pastor Harold Helms and Rev. Raymundo Diaz, pastor of that historic church's Hispanic congregation. Both of these excellent schools are supplying trained works for the rapidly expanding Hispanic population of our nation.

For many years, only a few independent ministers or ministers from other organized movements gained credentials with the International Church of the Foursquare Gospel. It was not that they were unwelcome; the Foursquare Church simply seemed to be experiencing sufficient growth by graduates from its own denominationally supported schools. Other pastors and churches were not solicited.

In recent years, a number of pastors and churches sought fellowship in the ICFG. Some have been attracted because of Foursquare's form of church government, which does not submit the pastor to periodic election by the congregation. Others have been impressed by the Foursquare Church's openness and family spirit. Still others have been drawn to one another because of well-known Foursquare leaders.

Interdenominational Relationships

Years ago, cooperation or friendly dialogue with Roman Catholics seemed extremely unlikely. That Roman Catholics would seek dialogue with Pentecostals seemed equally unlikely. When Catholic believers began to seek the baptism with the Holy Spirit and to experience charismatic renewal, however, the picture changed. Soon charismatic conferences were held in which Roman Catholics participated.

One such gathering was the Conference on Charismatic Renewal held in 1977 in the NFL football stadium in Kansas City, Missouri. Approximately 45,000 people attended, a majority of whom were charismatic Catholics. One of the speakers at that conference was ICFG General Supervisor Howard P. Courtney

Sr. Chairman of the conference was Fr. Kevan Ranaghan, who was prominent in the early outpouring of the Holy Spirit at Notre Dame University. Kevan and Dorothy Ranaghan were guests at the 1969 International Foursquare Convention held in Decatur, Illinois. Kevan was one of the convention speakers.

Another interchurch conclave was the Congress on the Holy Spirit and World Evangelization, which convened at the New Orleans, Louisiana, Superdome in 1987. Thirty-five thousand people attended, and again, the majority of attendees were Roman Catholic believers. Assisting Chairman Vinson Synan, historian from the Pentecostal Holiness Church, were members of the organizing committee, Jack Hayford and Harold Helms. It was during the same conference that the Missionary Cabinet for the International Church of the Foursquare Gospel met to select a new president for the denomination, the person being John Holland.

Fellowship with Spirit-filled Roman Catholics has also found expression in an activity called "The Pentecostal-Catholic Dialogue," the purpose of which is to explore the area of possible understanding of matters of doctrine and fellowship. Only minimal progress has been made, except in the area of mutual appreciation. Among Foursquare delegates to the dialogue have been Dan Crotty, member of the board of directors; John Amstutz, professor at L.I.F.E. Bible College;[10] Allan Hamilton, pastor of the Portland, Oregon, Foursquare Church; and Coleman Phillips, pastor of the Escondido, California, Foursquare Church.

Transition of Leadership

During 1970s and 1980s a number of changes took place in the leadership of the denomination. In 1974 Dr. and Mrs. Howard P. Courtney Sr. retired after thirty years of outstanding service in the capacity of general supervisor. The Courtneys were succeeded by Dr. and Mrs. Merrill Nichols.

Merrill Nichols graduated from L.I.F.E. Bible College in the early 1930s. From 1937 to 1959 he and his wife, Vinita, pastored churches in Torrance, California; La Habra, California; and the Goodyear Foursquare Church (Florence Avenue Foursquare Church), which they relocated to Santa Fe Springs, California. In 1959 the Nicholls were appointed to the position of supervisors of the Great Lakes District, where they served until 1974. Dr. Nicholls occupied the office of general supervisor with distinction until his sudden death in 1981.

The position of general supervisor was temporarily held by Dr. Nathaniel Van Cleave until the beginning of 1982, when Dr. Roy Hicks Sr. was installed into the office. Roy and Margaret Hicks were ordained to the ministry in 1944. They pioneered the Foursquare churches in Coshocton, Ohio (1944–1946), and Columbus, Ohio (1950–1955), and Omaha, Nebraska (1958–1964). From 1964 to 1969 Dr. and Mrs. Hicks served as supervisors of the Western Canada District, and from 1969–1982, supervised the Northwest District. It was under their tenure that the number of churches in the Northwest District climbed from sixty to about 225 congregations.

Dr. Hicks continued in the office until his semi-retirement in 1986. After another several months of provisional leadership by Nathaniel Van Cleave, Dr. J. Eugene Kurtz was appointed as general supervisor, a position that together with his wife, Donna, he holds at this writing.

Eugene Kurtz graduated from L.I.F.E. Bible College in 1950; his first church was in Oxford, Pennsylvania (1950–1951). In his early years Eugene was a successful evangelist and district youth leader. Other pastorates have been in Harrisburg, Pennsylvania (1951–1954); Muir, Pennsylvania (1954–1961), where he was also the division superintendent; Amherst, Ohio (1961–1978), during which time he was elected to the Missionary Cabinet; and Gettysburg, Pennsylvania (1978–1981). In addition to pastoring established churches, the Kurtzes also pioneered Foursquare churches in Mt. Carmel, Pennsylvania, and Norwalk, Ohio.

In 1981 Rev. and Mrs. Kurtz were appointed as Eastern District supervisors, making their home in Mt. Vernon, Ohio. They succeeded Dr. and Mrs. Howard Clark, who retired. During the less than five years of the Kurtzes' leadership of that district, a number of new churches were added.

Any story recounting the activities of those two decades must include the ministry of Dr. and Mrs. Ronald D. Williams. Ron Williams graduated from L.I.F.E. Bible College in 1965, where he met his wife, Carole. Prior to going as a missionary to Hong Kong in 1969, Ron and Carole pioneered the Sunshine Hills Foursquare Church in Delta, British Columbia; served with district youth; and taught at L.I.F.E. Bible College of Canada. Ron distinguished himself as an outstanding missionary and linguist during sixteen years of yeoman service in Hong Kong, the gateway to China.

Upon return to the United States in June 1985, Ron was appointed as managing editor of the *Foursquare World Advance* magazine. By general agreement across the entire denomination, his improvement of an already presentable periodical has been extraordinary. Besides editing the magazine, Ron is a member of the denomination's board of directors, a faculty member of L.I.F.E. Bible College, as well as responsible for other writing/publishing assignments at Foursquare headquarters.

Preceding managing editors of the *Advance* have been Raymond Becker, Jenny Acuff, Margaret Gomez, Pam Duarte, Janice Pedersen, and Tim Peterson.

It is only natural that the last chapters in this history of The

Foursquare Church be about the first new president of the denomination in forty-four years—the first president not of the McPherson family, and the first president selected by popular consensus, as well as the new leaders God has raised up to guide our church in the exciting yet challenging days ahead.

However, before relating that exciting part of our history, we must survey some of those programs on which the International Church of the Foursquare Gospel has put special emphasis.

Chapter 12

VARIOUS EMPHASES IN THE VINE'S DEVELOPMENT

1923–1991

IN THE DEVELOPMENT of a vine, various climates, methods of cultivation, and types of plant food receive special attention. While all the above-mentioned factors are important throughout the whole development of the vine, at various seasons each receives its own special emphasis. The same holds true in the life of a church.

Which have been the emphases of the International Church of the Foursquare Gospel? When have they occurred? Who participated in their application?

REVIVAL

When the many large doors of Angelus Temple opened in January 1923, the irrepressible expectation born of earnest intercession was that Holy Ghost revival would come to Los Angeles. God answered prayer and fulfilled those expectations. For many years, waves of heaven-sent revival resounded throughout Southern California. Many forms of activity and outreach were conceived in the creative mind of Aimee Semple McPherson and implemented by the willing hands of those who worked with her. Yet, revival was always the prevailing atmosphere.

Sunday school, organized youth programs, Bible institute training, and a twenty-four-hour prayer tower were in operation from the beginning. Shortly afterward, radio broadcasting and the sprouting of branches followed. But initially, maintaining the manifestation of God's presence and power was the chief concern.

The around-the-clock prayer tower, the daily 500 Room prayer meetings, and the altar calls topped the priority scale. Every activity was measured in value by its instrumentality of getting people saved, healed, and filled with the Spirit. Frequent articles in the *Bridal Call* magazine appear with statistics showing that the primitive revival power was undiminished. It is not surprising, then, that during the 1920s the principal problem was "finding a seat."

Heaven-sent revival power in manifestation during the 1920s far exceeded anything derived from the founder's innumerable talents, human attractiveness, and charming personality. Many evangelists such as Paul Rader, Watson Argue, Hardy Mitchell, Roxy Alford, Smith Wigglesworth, Billy Black, and A. G. Garr occupied Angelus Temple's pulpit, but the mercury of the spiritual thermometer remained above the revival arrow.

To what can the continuance of revival be attributed? Man cannot discern the mystery of God's wisdom and sovereignty, but during the early years of the Foursquare movement, by far the greatest emphasis was REVIVAL.

Evangelism

Evangelism is not necessarily a separate emphasis from revival. While there can be evangelism without revival, properly applied evangelism is a vehicle of revival. Jesus' commission to the church was, "Preach the gospel to every creature!"

"Preach the gospel" is merely a synonym of "evangelize" or better, a translation of the word. The Greek words translated "gospel" and "preach the gospel," verb and noun, occur almost one hundred times in the New Testament. Mrs. McPherson was by calling and experience an evangelist. Carved indelibly in Angelus Temple's cornerstone one finds the expression of Foursquaredom's goal, world evangelization.

Church history reveals that revival often accompanied evangelism. Certainly, every sincere, knowledgeable evangelist prays fervently that God will pour out the power of the Holy Spirit upon their preaching of the gospel and that the community would be moved Godward. Jesus, quoting Isaiah, defined the evangelism that brings revival:

> The Spirit of the Lord is on me, because he has anointed me to preach good news to the poor. He has sent me to proclaim freedom for the prisoners and recovery of sight for the blind, to release the oppressed, to proclaim the year of the Lord's favor.
>
> —Luke 4:18–19, niv

One Pentecostal writer defines evangelism as:

> ...the good news of deliverance over against the bad news that humanity is dead and bound in the oppression of sin. Pentecostal evangelism therefore calls for a confrontation; it is the conveyance of truth as encounter. The Pentecostal witness preaches for a verdict and expects results.[1]

Revival rarely comes unless someone, in obedience to the Great Commission, proclaims the gospel in some form with the anointing of the Holy Spirit.

One of the first departments of Angelus Temple was a Bible institute where evangelists could be trained. If the Foursquare Gospel was to be proclaimed around the world, many evangelists and missionaries would be needed. The response was phenomenal! Before the 1920s ended, the institute that later became L.I.F.E. Bible College counted nearly one thousand students.

The spirit of evangelism could be seen in the fact that the early students all aimed to be missionaries or evangelists. It was difficult to find anyone among the early students who would admit to being called to any kind of service but evangelism in some form. If one's evangelism led to a permanent congregation, like Angelus Temple, one could be the pastor-evangelist.

When Mrs. McPherson conducted campaigns or meetings away from Angelus Temple, she would bring in prominent evangelists. During those times groups of students could be found gathered in a circle mildly protesting the need to import evangelists, since they were well able to substitute. In fact, by the end of the 1920s, there were branches of Angelus Temple all over Southern California and beyond. Pastors-evangelists of the branches, such as Harold and Ione Jefferies of Portland, Oregon; Jack and Louise Richey of Des Moines, Iowa; and Anna D. Britton of Vancouver, British Columbia, produced revival centers with branch institutes included.

There were Foursquare evangelists who pioneered new churches, like Sidney and Helen Correll Ralph Correll, Floyd Brock, Paul Krebs, Fred Beard, Louise Webster, Evelyn Taylor, Malcolm and Isabelle Hall, Mrs. A. A. Carpenter, Bert and Bessie Bruffet, etc. These often would remain as pastors for a period; many later settled into pastoral work.

Another category of evangelist gave full-time to minister from church to church. Depending on their callings, some preached primarily to win souls; others specialized in encouraging believers to seek and receive the fullness of the Spirit.

A third type of evangelist sought the general edification of believers and the increase of church attendance. Some of this latter category include Judy Chavez, Lloyd E. and Mary Johnson (who were credited with leading Dr. Charles Blair of the large Calvary Temple in Denver, Colorado, to Christ), Henry Marty, Harry Miller, Walter Wentworth, Dick Mills, C. E. Swanson, Ethyl Heidner, Arleta Keck, Fred and Coleen Morrow, and Wayne and Mary Westberg.

During and immediately following World War II, church attendance at multiple midweek services declined. When attendance at "revival" meetings became so low that such began to be impractical, those who ministered from church to church became scarce.

In 1976 there was an attempt to encourage "evangelists" by the creation of a Department of Evangelism whose mission was to develop a list of successful evangelists available to the churches. The department was also to make available to the evangelists churches seeking special ministries. Dr. Don McGregor was appointed overseer of the new ministry.

After Don assumed responsibility, the name was changed to Department of Evangelism and Church Growth. Since church growth held greater appeal than the old-style evangelism, the clearinghouse for evangelists failed to materialize. When church growth seemed to naturally accompany the renewal of the 1980s, the department vanished. Don McGregor, former missionary supervisor of the Philippines, had already become so urgently in demand overseas that ministry to the missionaries and leaders fully consumed Don and his wife, Sally's time. Don and Sally then served in the Department of Foreign Missions as field representatives.

As of this writing special ministries seem to be returning as weekend conferences or events.

Crusader Youth

Along with the prayer tower and 500 Room was raised a young people's department called the "Foursquare Crusaders." As one of the first departments of Angelus Temple, the Crusaders gathered on Friday evenings, one thousand strong. They conducted their weekly service, chose officers, signed their covenant of dedication pledging themselves to unreservedly serve the Lord, held street meetings, and witnessed at home, at school, and at work. Their early presidents were John Gleason, Clarence Hall, Bert Teaford, Hubert Mitchell, and Harold Chalfant. Of these, one became a pastor, two became deans at L.I.F.E. Bible College, one became a missionary, another a Youth for Christ leader and world-renowned prayer warrior, and the last-mentioned came to be Foursquare's international director of youth and Christian education.

Ministry to youth has always been an important concern for The Foursquare Church. The strongest years of youth emphasis, however, were 1935–1954, under the leadership of Harold Chalfant. On the strength of his unusual leadership ability, he was immediately named national crusader president. In his first year (1935) he visited all the districts, including forty-eight local churches.

That same year, patterned after Chalfant's week at Camp Seely in Southern California, youth camps were conducted in several districts. In 1936 there were seven camps projected, including the first at Camp Radford. From that year on, Crusader camps became a Foursquare institution. At first, camping facilities were rented. At this writing every Foursquare district except one owns a summer camp property.

The Chalfant-style Crusader camps were primarily spiritual rather than recreational. The leaders of the camps were deeply involved in revival. Mornings were devoted to Bible teaching, with the last class usually given to seeking the fullness of the Spirit. Evening services were evangelistic, aimed at decisions for Christ. The afternoons were given to sports, games, crafts, and hiking. Such sports as baseball, volleyball, and swimming were highly competitive; on occasion umpires drew heavily upon Christian ethics to resolve disputes. But the poet was right when he wrote, "All's well that ends well."

Highlight of the entire week at camp focused on the "victory circle." Chalfant, however, had a theory that a midweek fun break relaxed the campers, making the finale more effective. Wednesday nights were known as "skit night" when a number of church groups would prepare short skits, usually humorous. Some were skilled; others were ridiculous.

Perhaps the best remembered acts were those performed by leaders like Ulphin Davis, Tom Matthew, and Don Stauffer. No camp was complete with the "cake baking" act. There were always a few who criticized the sports and skit night as being unspiritual, but as Billy Sunday used to say, "Even God has a sense of humor, or He never would have created monkeys, parrots, and some of us."

Statistics revealed that after sports and skits, the devotional atmosphere would intensify. A special speaker would be brought to camp to address the victory circle around the bonfire. When the youth entered the setting, they were given a pine cone, which represented their heart's total consecration to Christ for the months and years ahead. At the invitation, each youth was invited to cast their cone into the fire, avowing, "I'll do what You want me to do; I'll go where You want me to go."

Was it a superficial act? For some, perhaps; but thousands

testify to making their dedication at camp's victory circle to ministry as pastors, evangelists, and missionaries. Many high school seniors who went to camp enrolled the next fall at L.I.F.E. Bible College. Some young pastors who attended camp volunteered for missionary service.

Camps were not the only Crusader activity. Each church scheduled a weekly Crusader service. Each month a divisional Crusader rally would be conducted with two hundred to six hundred in attendance. Twice each year a mass rally would be conducted with two thousand to four thousand young men and women in attendance. In 1940 Rev. Chalfant traveled sixty thousand miles, speaking 312 times in rallies and local churches. Two train rallies were held when entire trains were filled with Crusader Youth, one traveling to Ventura and the other to San Diego.

In 1941 the Crusaders gave over $40,000 to missions; in 1943, $56,000. One successful fund-raising aid was small barrel-shaped banks, known as "boom barrels," distributed to the churches. There were Crusader commanders in each district. In 1943 these commanders were: Great Lakes—Everett Dennison; Midwest—Evelyn McGowan; Gulf States—Roy Bell; Northwest—Emma Davis. Karl Williams was missionary secretary. Later commanders were Orville Broker, Norman Smith, Lester Vollmer, Curtis Correll, Jerry Jensen, Max Siesser, Ulphin Davis, Paul Talbot, and Arthur Larson.

At the 1954 international convention in Moline, Illinois, leadership made a decision to discontinue the office of district Crusader commander, as supported by headquarters. This left the selection and support of a district youth leader to the local district office. Reason for the difficulty was that some felt that the centrally supported commanders had become unduly independent of the local district's direction. Of course, the commanders told a different story.

When many of the districts employed a youth leader, youth activity continued, especially the camps. But in the local churches and on a divisional level, there was a noticeable decline in enthusiasm.

With the discontinuance of the Crusader commander officer, some of the unemployed former commanders accepted churches, some were employed by a district to direct youth activities, and others went into Youth for Christ work. Lester and Hope Vollmer were promoted to headquarters as national youth directors, assisting Harold Chalfant. When Harold Chalfant resigned in 1960 because of ill health, Vincent Bird was assigned the position. Lester Vollmer moved into the missions department as executive secretary until his retirement.

Christian Education

Already, in the 1950s, Christian education was beginning to receive heavy emphasis. Pentecostal churches were beginning to discover the Sunday school, a discovery already made by many evangelical churches. Large churches employed directors of Christian education. Sunday school contests captured the front pages of denominational magazines, especially in the months leading up to Easter. Top ten Sunday schools received wide publicity; winners won coveted prizes. The Sunday school bus seemed indispensable.

So intense became the urging to boost attendance and win contests, that some of the methods became suspect. For some, numbers became more important than the quality of teaching. Of course, attendance was important; a church without Christian education is only half a church. The church with a strong Sunday school will be a strong church tomorrow.

In 1947 Isabelle Hall was appointed to the office of youth and Christian education to assist Harold Chalfant as secretary of Christian education. Having taken college courses in Christian education in Minneapolis where she had pastored, Isabelle was well equipped to modernize ICFG's Christian education department. Already a member of the Evangelical Teachers' Training Association (ETTA), Isabelle was prepared to introduce the course into L.I.F.E. Bible College, where teachers like Dorothy Jean Furlong and Juanita Conger perpetuated the ETTA course as a part of the college's curriculum.

Representing the International Church of the Foursquare Gospel, Rev. Hall participated in national and local Sunday school associations. Through these she was able to make solid contact with publishers of Sunday school literature, such as Gospel Light Press. Isabelle was able to use these publishers to develop a full line of Foursquare Sunday school quarterlies and materials, including teaching for adults written by Foursquare authors (Duffield, Meier, and Van Cleave). Some of these materials are still available in another format. Teacher training materials and vacation Bible school literature were developed. From these solid beginnings, a department of Foursquare Publications was formed.

In 1960 Isabelle Hall/Helmle retired, and Dr. Vincent Bird replaced Harold Chalfant as director of youth and Christian education. Edith Campbell, a friend and protégé of Isabelle, was invited to direct Sunday schools. Robert Inglis was invited to oversee the Cadet program, and Jack Hayford came to serve as national youth director. For a decade the Sunday school had been ICFG's emphasis.

Foreign Missions

Recalling what has been written above, one notes that the 1920s focused on revival, followed by evangelism in the 1930s, youth in the 1940s, Sunday school in the 1950s, organization and structure in the 1950s and 1960s, church growth in the 1970s, and renewal in the 1980s. Obviously there was wide overlapping, with periods when the Foursquare Church was capable of several emphases simultaneously or intermittently.

Certainly foreign missions has, from the beginning, been a top concern for the Foursquare Church. Its founder was a missionary at heart. Consequently, sharing the Foursquare Gospel was inbred. However, if one gauges emphasis by activity and results, the decade of the 1950s has to be the peak of missionary fulfillment.

At the 1951 international Foursquare convention, it was resolved to send a number of gospel teams to the foreign fields. These teams would be composed of the denomination's most effective leaders, evangelists, and newly called missionaries.[2] The teams far exceeded all expectations.

In 1953 Dr. Mitzner reported that the previous year was the greatest ever in Foursquare missions, with record totals in giving and in converts.[3] In 1952 twenty-three new appointees were set apart and sent to the mission fields.[4] In the 1954 yearbook Dr. McPherson wrote, "More missionaries were thrust forth into foreign fields than in any preceding year."[5]

The 1954 convention set new goals for Foursquare missions: four million dollars in missionary income by 1960, an ambitious goal indeed. Increased funds would be needed to match the dedications to foreign service.[6]

Additional figures will show that the decade of the 1950s was, indeed, the "Decade of Missions" for the International Church of the Foursquare Gospel. In 1950 fifty-one missionaries were serving in twelve countries other than the United States and Canada; by 1960 the figures had doubled: there were one hundred three missionaries in twenty-seven countries.

In 1955 twenty-three more missionary candidates, with eighteen children, were approved for service on the mission field.[7] The slogan adopted by the 1955 convention body was, "Enlarge at Home to Expand Abroad." Missions giving goals were set at four million dollars by the year 1960, with one thousand Foursquare churches and Sunday schools.[8]

It would be 1967 before the annual missionary income would reach one million dollars and 1981 before the number of Foursquare churches would count one thousand churches. Missions giving did not reach four million dollars until 1988. Maintaining the above-mentioned goals in 1955 was unrealistic, but it did demonstrate the abiding fever pitch of concern for going around the world with the Foursquare Gospel.

What is the present status of the International Church of the Foursquare Gospel as of this writing? What will be the central emphasis of the new leadership? What is the vision of President John Holland for the decade of the 1990s? What dreams of progress occupy the thoughts of missions director Roy Hicks Jr.? What plans are being drawn by the board of directors for the last decade of the century? The answers to these questions and others will be our quest in the final chapter of this book.

Chapter 13

THE VINE AND THE NEW HUSBANDMAN

1988–

THE THEME OF this history is taken from the analogy of the vineyard. With the title *The Vine and Its Branches*, the key verse is John 15:1, "I am the true vine, and my Father is the husbandman."

Scripture is rich in the vocabulary of husbandry (gardening). The genuine vine is Jesus Himself. However, we, His church, are the branches that bear the fruit: "I am the vine, ye are the branches" (John 15:5). God the Father is the "husbandman" who owns the garden, tills the soil, and provides the seed. Without the vine, the branches *cannot* bear fruit; without the branches, the vine *will not* produce fruit; without the husbandman, there *would be neither* vine nor branches (John 15:4–8).

According to the English dictionary, the word *husbandman* is defined as "one that plows and cultivates land."[1] The Greek word is also translated in various versions as: *farmer, gardener, tiller of the soil*, and *vine-dresser*. Divided into two components, the word is *ge*, meaning "earth," and *ergo*, "to work. The name *George* comes from the same origin.[2]

While Jesus is the vine, He prayed that the church might be

one with Him and with the Father. Therefore, in a figurative sense, the church in Christ may be represented by the vine; the local churches as well as individual believers may be represented as the branches. As to the metaphor *husbandman*, Paul uses the idea in 1 Corinthians, applying it to the workers over the church:

> Now he who plants and he who waters are one, and each one will receive his own reward according to his own labor. For we are God's fellow workers; you are God's field [husbandry].
>
> —1 CORINTHIANS 3:8–9, NKJV

Husbandry is the management of soil under cultivation; the husbandman is the manager of the garden.

The very first garden provides an excellent illustration. God, the Husbandman, planted a beautiful garden eastward in Eden, and:

> ...there He put the man whom He had formed. Then the LORD God took the man and put him into the garden of Eden to tend and keep it.
>
> —GENESIS 2:8, 15, NKJV

Likewise, today the Lord has many gardens where the seed of the gospel is being planted and cultivated. While in reality they are all one garden, this modern, complex world of many nations, languages, and cultures seems better reached by a variety of approaches, as long as the same seed is planted and reaped.

Aimee Semple McPherson, as the first husbandman of the Foursquare vineyard, was given the right to name her successor. After more than twenty years of labors (as leader of the ICFG), God took her to her reward. It was her choice that her son should become the president of the Foursquare work, and for the following forty-four years the vineyard was well managed and cultivated by the founder's son, Rolf K. McPherson. During his stewardship the vineyard was extended many times over, at home and around the globe.

In accordance with the church's bylaws, Rolf K. McPherson was given a unique prerogative while occupying the office of president:

> The office of president shall be held by Rolf K. McPherson during his lifetime unless or until he should desire to resign or retire.[3]

Only complete physical or mental incapacity would void such a provision. Dr. McPherson always maintained physical health, mental soundness, and a fondness for his work. Moreover, there had been no major groundswell of opposition to his leadership. Under such circumstances of guaranteed, lifetime tenure, it is rare that any religious leader would voluntarily relinquish their office.

As early as 1985, Dr. McPherson began to talk of retirement from the presidency, relinquishing the helm of the ship to a younger person. At the 1986 International Foursquare Convention in Glorietta, New Mexico, Dr. McPherson obtained from the convention a list of persons who seemed best suited to fill such an important position of leadership. It became clear that Dr. McPherson was seriously seeking a successor.

The Selection of a President

At the 1987 International Foursquare Convention in San Diego, California, Dr. McPherson publicly announced his retirement, to become effective after the 1988 convention. With that announcement, a business meeting of the delegates was scheduled, in which ten nominations would be received. From those nominations, three candidates would be chosen. Among those prominently mentioned were: Jack Hayford, Paul Risser, John Holland, Ron Mehl, Roy Hicks Jr., Harold Helms, Allan Hamilton, Eugene Kurtz, and Dorothy Jean Furlong, the only woman included in the top ten nominations.

The three candidates selected were Jack Hayford, senior pastor of the First Foursquare Church in Van Nuys, California; Paul Risser, senior pastor of the Florence Avenue Foursquare Church in Santa Fe Springs, California; and John Holland, supervisor of the Southwest District.

It was determined that the missionary cabinet, composed of the board of directors, the district supervisors, the president of L.I.F.E. Bible College, the executive secretary, and five elected members, would convene in Los Angeles in May of that year to interview the candidates. The cabinet would meet again in July, in New Orleans, to select a new president of the International Church of the Foursquare Gospel.

Reason for the choice of New Orleans in July 1987 was two-fold. First, it would give the cabinet members time to think and pray over the choice of the new president, the first such choice in the history of the Foursquare Church. Second, it would give the denomination's leadership an opportunity to attend the North American Congress on the Holy Spirit and World Evangelization, scheduled for July 22–26, 1987. Since the Congress was to be a meeting of charismatics of all denominations, the atmosphere would be ideal for prayer and the guidance of the Holy Spirit.

In New Orleans, the missionary cabinet selected Dr. John R. Holland to the office of president of the International Church of the Foursquare Gospel, to become effective after the 1988 International Convention. In order to provide a transition period, Dr. Holland was invited to work closely with Dr. McPherson in the time remaining before inauguration. As well as familiarizing himself with the many executive duties of the denomination's presidency, Dr. Holland was able to share in decisions affecting the future.

The 1988 convention, held at Angelus Temple in Los Angeles, gave opportunity to The Foursquare Church to express gratitude and pay tribute to Dr. and Mrs. Rolf K. McPherson for their many years of untiring service to their church. During his tenure Dr. McPherson worked long hours and seldom took a vacation. And though the term "retirement" referred only to the presidency, as president emeritus Dr. McPherson continued to manage a newly formed office called "Founder's Ministries" and perform other delegated activities as well as retain a five-year position as a member of the board of directors.

On May 31, 1988, Dr. John R. Holland was installed as the third president of the International Church of the Foursquare Gospel.

John R. Holland

President John R. Holland was born on June 3, 1933, to John R. and Josephine Holland. The family lived on a cattle ranch in Fisher County, Texas, located ten miles from the city of Hamlin. John was the last of six children, three brothers and two sisters. In Hamlin, where he attended school, John was the president of the high school student body and co-captain of the football team. He played on the baseball team and was a member of the track team. The Holland family were Methodist, but the maternal grandmother was a devout Nazarene.

When he was nine years of age, John had a spiritual experience in which he perceived God speaking to him and calling him into the ministry. During the growing-up years he struggled with that calling because he desperately wanted to become a professional athlete.

His first association with the Foursquare Church came when his mother's sister moved from Monterey Park, California (where she had become acquainted with Sister McPherson's ministry), to Fisher County, Texas. Because she did not drive, it was necessary for John to take her into Hamlin to attend the Foursquare church. It was under the ministry of Rev. Alice Harrell that he (accompanied by the Sunday school teacher of the high school class) surrendered to the calling of God. From the age of nine he had battled that calling; now the Lord gave peace and great love for the ministry.

It was by the counsel of Pastor Harrell that John came to L.I.F.E. Bible College after graduating from high school. She had to dislodge the notion that Jesus' soon return would not allow enough time for pastoral training. The urgency of the Word of the Lord made him think he must begin ministry immediately.

With the new understanding that "occupying until the Lord came" was fulfilling his call, John enrolled in Bible college. He was barely seventeen years old.

In 1951 John invited a lovely young lady named Doris Jean Hines to accompany him to a school banquet. A courtship followed, which blossomed fully in a romantic marriage on January 1, 1953. The marriage vows were exchanged at the Chapel of Roses at the conclusion of the Tournament of Roses Parade.

Doris came from a very dedicated Christian family, active in an independent Pentecostal church in Issaquah, Washington, a suburb of Seattle. She had accepted Christ as Savior at the age of sixteen, followed by full commitment to Christian service. Dr. and Mrs. Holland have two sons and two daughters: Bradley, Johnnea, Barton, and Jodi.

John Holland graduated from L.I.F.E. Bible College in 1953, receiving ordination at the same time. He and Doris have pastored churches in Caldwell, Idaho (1955); Bremerton,

Washington (1956); Hamlin, Texas—his home church (1957–1958); and Woodburn, Oregon (1959–1964), where the excellence of their ministry was observed by Supervisor Roy Mourer, who promoted them to the pastorate of the Kingsway Foursquare Church in Vancouver, British Columbia (1964–1974). In 1970 John followed Roy Hicks Sr. as supervisor of the Western Canada District (1970–1974).

Their ministry in Canada came to the notice of Dr. Rolf K. McPherson. They were asked to assume the pastorate of Foursquaredom's "mother" church, Angelus Temple (1974–1977). In 1977 John and Doris succeeded Nathaniel and Lois Van Cleave in the supervision of the Southwest District, where they ministered for eleven years and until elected to the office of president of the International Church of the Foursquare Gospel.[4]

The 1989 International Foursquare Convention met in Dallas, Texas, with Dr. John Holland, the new president, in full leadership. The president's philosophy of leadership had been described in the theme of the convention, "Servanthood—Our Highest Calling."

Tone of the convention and keynote for the future was well expressed in the president's message, which introduced the 1989 yearbook:

> The International Church of the Foursquare Gospel has just passed a most challenging moment in its history. The transition of leadership from one generation brings into sharp focus the challenge of our historic calling and the clarification of our corporate vision. Wherever one travels and to whomever one speaks, there is a growing sense of dynamic expectation.
>
> In such a time as this, there could be no more appropriate reminder than the theme of our Convention,

> "Servanthood—Our Highest Calling." Jesus said, "Whosoever will be great among you, let him be your minister, and whosoever will be chief among you, let him be your servant" (Matthew 20:26,27). If we are to fulfill God's calling in this time and in His way, there can be no substitute for taking up the towel of the servant, the water of the Holy Spirit, and the pitcher of loving care and concern for everyone around us.
>
> We praise the Lord for His honoring of our ministry as a corporate family during the year 1988. We recorded 261,506 persons who accepted Christ as their personal savior, 64,021 who were baptized in water, 73,504 who received the baptism with the Holy Spirit, and there are now 19,309 Foursquare churches and meeting places in 59 countries of the world. Each day of 1988, 192 new members joined our Foursquare family, giving us a world total of 1,216,284.
>
> I am convinced that this is only a small token of what the Lord wants to accomplish through this fellowship of Foursquare believers. We were born into the Kingdom for such a time as this, and the only two things which could prevent our fulfillment of destiny would be, our failure to discern the times or to take pride in our accomplishments. I pray that the Lord of the Harvest will reveal the first and keep us from the pitfall of the second.

The financial figures for the transition year of 1988 were also encouraging. Twelve hundred ninety churches in the United States provided $7,128,863 in district extension tithe and $4,083,396 for world missions. In 1989 the tithe increased to $7,879,579; the missionary giving climbed to $4,502,603. The ICFG property valuation was computed to be $475 million. In 1989 the total membership rose to 1,409,674, with the number of U.S. churches increasing by 44 congregations to reach a total of 1,404.

In 1990 there were 116 Foursquare missionaries and 17,766

national workers ministering in 66 different mission fields, not including Canada and the United States. In the United States, in 1990, there were 1,451 Foursquare churches, giving a total of $8,845,238 in district tithe and $5,015,548 to Foursquare missions. During the year 311,936 persons found Jesus Christ as Savior worldwide, and there were 1,553,968 members worshiping God in 25,608 churches and meeting places.

Foursquare's new, younger leadership has been willed a solid heritage in material and spiritual values. The leaders appear to be prepared in the Lord's assured strength to lead the Foursquare Church to unprecedented attainments. At the 1989 convention in Dallas, Texas, President Holland demonstrated a firm grasp of the issues, innovative methods of communication, and a clear vision of the goals. No one left doubting that God had guided the Foursquare Church in the choice of a successor to their retiring but esteemed helmsman, Dr. Rolf K. McPherson.

Naomi Shivers

If, at any time, President Holland needed a review of Foursquare history, his personal secretary, Naomi Shivers, could provide such from her family records. Her grandfather, Thomas Johnson, provided ministry in music from the very beginning of Angelus Temple. His rich baritone voice thrilled the audiences for many years. He sang the parts of the leading male characters in Mrs. McPherson's oratorios.

On her mother, Almita's, side of the family, Naomi's aunt, Marie Johnson, was for many years a missionary to Brazil, teaching in the Bible college of Sao Paulo and leading the Sunday school work throughout the nation. Five members of Naomi's family are graduates of L.I.F.E. Bible College; her sister Deborah, along with her husband and daughter, ministered in child evangelism; her sister Rachel a member of L.I.F.E.'s faculty, teaching Hebrew; her sister Lois involved with child evangelism and ministers in singing on mission impact teams in Central and South America as well as locally. Naomi's brother David and their father (until his passing) have been engaged in a Christian video business.

On her father's side, her aunt Juanita is married to Rev. Marvin Smith and, until their retirement, served as co-pastors of the West Adams Foursquare Church in Los Angeles. Prior to becoming President Holland's secretary, Naomi was employed by Home Savings of America as organizer and coordinator of recreational activities.

The board of Directors

President John Holland is at this writing assisted by a board of directors composed of: Rolf K. McPherson, who remains on the board as president emeritus; Roy Hicks Jr., vice president and director of foreign missions, former supervisor of the Northwest District, and pastor of Faith Center in Eugene, Oregon; J. Eugene Kurtz, general supervisor, formerly supervisor of the Eastern District; Howard P. Courtney Sr., former general supervisor and pastor of Angelus Temple; John W. Bowers, corporate secretary and assistant to the general supervisor; Harold E. Helms, senior pastor of Angelus Temple, former pastor at Decatur, Illinois, and dean of students, Mount Vernon Bible College; Ronald D. Williams, editor of the *Foursquare World Advance* magazine and former mission to Hong Kong; Loren Edwards, pastor of La Iglesia en Camino, the Hispanic congregation at The Church On The Way and former missionary to Venezuela and Panama (elected pastoral representative); and Douglas Slaybaugh, member of Christian Assembly Foursquare Church in Eagle Rock, California, and director of operations at the Charles E. Fuller Institute in Pasadena, California.

Serving very closely with the president are the director of foreign missions, Dr. Roy Hicks Jr.; the general supervisor, Dr. J. Eugene Kurtz; and Rev. Jim Rogers, executive assistant to the president.

Roy Hicks Jr.

Roy Hicks Jr. was born to Roy Sr. and Margaret Hicks while they were attending L.I.F.E. Bible College. Thus, he claims to have attended L.I.F.E. twice, once as an infant and the second time as a student. He must have made the most of his time in the halls and classrooms of his alma mater, because after graduation his development in ministry was rapid.

In the mid-1960s Roy was named youth director of the Northwest District, and his work was very fruitful. However, he soon became burdened for the city of Eugene, Oregon, which was the site of the University of Oregon. In 1969 Roy Jr. assumed the pastorate of the Foursquare church in that city, which had been a very small congregation and unable to keep a permanent pastor.

Roy and Kay Hicks' ministry began to attract new people, especially young men and women. Before long, the congregation was numbered by scores, then hundreds, then thousands, requiring a much larger building. In the early 1980s the Eugene church "gave away" two sizable congregations, one to Springfield, Oregon, and one to an area in North Eugene. As people were sent to these new works, there was no diminishing of the size of Faith Center.

In 1982, when Roy Hicks Sr. became general supervisor, the Northwest District pastors requested that Roy Jr. be appointed as district supervisor. He accepted the appointment without being required to relinquish the Eugene pastorate, a privilege no district supervisor had been given in years. In 1988, upon the retirement of Leland R. Edwards from leadership from Foursquare Mission International, Roy Hicks Jr. was appointed director of Foursquare Missions and to a seat on the board of directors. With a new, enlarged office staff, Roy reorganized the missions department and introduced a number of innovations.

J. Eugene Kurtz

The position of general supervisor was ably filled by Dr. J. Eugene Kurtz. In 1987, on the retirement of Dr. Roy Hicks Sr. from that office, Dr. Kurtz, who had very successfully served as supervisor of the Eastern District, was invited to move to headquarters as interim general supervisor. It was an invitation he declined until after much prayer and further urging prompted him to accept. The "interim" in his appointment was due to the other transitions of leadership then taking place.

When Dr. Holland was installed as ICFG president in 1988, it became clear that Eugene was admired and respected by all the district leaders. He was asked by the board of directors to serve as the general supervisor. The term "interim" was removed.

Eugene Kurtz had many years of experience as a youth leader, pioneer evangelist, and pastor of leading churches in the Eastern District. His persistence, friendliness, and positive attitude make him a strong arm to President Holland. Following the pattern of the Courtneys, Dr. and Mrs. (Donna) Kurtz work closely together. Donna, a faithful and capable companion, gave timely encouragement to her husband.

Jim Rogers

In August 1990 Jim Rogers, his wife, Carol, daughter, Amy, and son, Darren, moved from British Columbia to Los Angeles, to serve as executive assistant to the president. He was responsible to the president in thc priorities of legal and financial matters, headquarters properties, and the radio stations KFSG-FM and KHIS-AM/FM.

Following graduation from high school in Vancouver, British Columbia, Jim attended L.I.F.E. Bible College for two years and in 1963 entered the real estate profession. In 1969 he joined Wall and Redekop Realty as a branch manager. Under his leadership the branch soon became the most profitable in the company, and in 1974 he became the vice president and general manager, directing a staff of three hundred persons serving in twelve branch offices with over $200 million in annual sales.

Jim also served as director of business development for Realty World Canada, acting as consultant to more than 150 offices in Western Canada, as well as being responsible as Western Canada regional director of the commercial division.

While in Canada, Jim served in many local church responsibilities, such as council member of the Kingsway Foursquare Church in Vancouver, British Columbia; board member for Youth for Christ of Greater Vancouver; member of the president's advisor committee of Trinity Western University; and member of the board of directors and regents for L.I.F.E. Bible College of Canada. He was one of the founding directors and officers of the Foursquare Church of Canada and, from 1979–1990, was a member of the national board, serving at various times in several capacities.

Virginia Cravens

A headquarters department whose efficient operation is vital to the function of leadership is the accounting department. It was directed by the corporate treasurer, Virginia Cravens. She had overseen the department since 1962 and was appointed by the board to the office of corporate treasurer in 1987.

Virginia grew up in the San Diego, California, Foursquare Church, where she was active in Sunday school and Crusader ministries. She studied accounting and business management at San Diego State University, after which she was employed by the U.S. Navy as an accountant.

Later, while she was working in Army accounting at Pasadena, California, God spoke to her, directing her to relinquish her job. Almost immediately she was offered a job in the accounting department at Foursquare headquarters. Shortly thereafter she was appointed accounting supervisor. In addition to her corporate responsibilities, she served in the Sunday school and United Foursquare Women at Angelus Temple and taught periodically at the Angelus Bible Institute.[5]

District Supervisors

Very important to top leadership are midlevel leaders who are in close and discerning contact with the individual churches. At the same time, such leadership must be capable of mediating the focus and goals of a spiritually sensitive directive. A president and his board can communicate efficiently with churches near and far only through district supervisors and divisional superintendents who work close enough to feel the pulse of pastors who shepherd the flocks.

Dewey Morrow—Eastern District

Most remote in distance from the central offices is the Eastern District, which was supervised by Rev. Dewey Morrow. Dewey was born in 1933 to Christian parents, Carl and Mildred Morrow. Dewey shares that he always felt called to ministry but had a definite conversion experience at Camp McPherson when he was eighteen years old. The camp experience only strengthened his call, with the result that he enrolled, one year later, in L.I.F.E. Bible College.

While attending L.I.F.E., Dewey met Kathy, who was to become his devoted wife and coworker. Following graduation in 1956, they pastored several churches in Ohio, including Marion, Whitehall, Vermilion, Mt. Vernon, and Dover. It was while pastoring in Dover, one of the district's strongest churches, that Dewey was invited to succeed Eugene Kurtz as supervisor of the Eastern District. As of this writing, some of the leading churches in the Eastern District are those in Dover, Amherst, and Parma, Ohio; Gettysburg, Pennsylvania; Frederick, Maryland; Rockland, Massachusetts; and Collins Lake, New Jersey. The district also includes three strong Hispanic congregations.

Glenn Burris Sr.—Southeast District

The other district on the Atlantic Seaboard is the Southeast District, for many years supervised by Glenn and Garnette Burris. Born in 1927 to Dee and Hannah Burris, Glenn was converted at the altar of the Concord, North Carolina, Foursquare Church. The year was 1947. He soon received a call to the ministry.

Not only did Glenn find God in the Concord church, but he also found a splendid wife and companion in ministry, whom he married in 1948. In 1949 Glenn and Garnette Burris enrolled in L.I.F.E. Bible College, graduating in 1952.

The first pastorate of Rev. and Mrs. Burris was in Macon, Georgia. From 1957 to 1964 they pioneered churches in Rock Hill and Chester, South Carolina, as well as Ft. Lauderdale, Florida, and Alexander City, Alabama. They also served as district evangelists for one year.

The ministry of the Burrises was so outstanding they were invited to assume the pastorate of their home church in Concord,

North Carolina, where they ministered with distinction for ten years. On the retirement of A. B. Teffeteller, the district's first supervisor, they were appointed to the office of supervisor of the Southeast District.

In 1992, upon Dr. and Mrs. Burris' retirement, their son, Glenn Jr., and his wife, Debbie, were appointed as Southeast District supervisors.

Fred Parker—Great Lakes District

There are three districts east of the Mississippi River. The third district, more westward, is the Great Lakes District, overseen by Rev. and Mrs. Fred Parker. Fred was born in Kansas City, Missouri, in 1934 to Keith and Belle Parker. Following high school, he attended the University of California at Santa Barbara for three years.

In 1955 he gave his life to Christ at the altar of the El Monte, California, Foursquare Church under the ministry of Ben Griffith. Instead of returning to college in Santa Barbara, Fred enrolled in L.I.F.E. Bible College, where he met and married Shirley Resler of Akron, Colorado. He graduated in 1959, having been selected as class speaker and student body president.

Fred and his wife, Shirley, had their first pastoral experience as assistant pastors to Dr. Clyde Greisen in Kansas City, Fred's birthplace. Rev. Greisen, who served on the faculties of both L.I.F.E. Bible College and Mt. Vernon Bible College, was an excellent mentor.

In 1960 Fred and Shirley were appointed to the pastorate of the Grand Junction, Colorado, Foursquare Church, where they served for twenty-six and a half years. They then were appointed as supervisors of the Great Lakes District to succeed Rev. and Mrs. Lynn Charter.

Glenn Metzler—Midwest District

One of the oldest districts outside of California is the Midwest District, with its central offices in Colorado Springs, Colorado. The present supervisor is Glenn Metzler, born in Burlington, Kansas, in July 1928 to Christian parents, Glenn and Olive Metzler. Glenn was converted at the age of eight years, in a closet where he was overhearing a conversation between his mother and aunt relative to his mother's conversion experience.

Glenn relates that full dedication to ministry came with time and circumstances. Having musical talent, Glenn joined a group of youth who played and sang in the churches. Their ability was brought to the attention of a L.I.F.E. Bible College dean of students, who invited the group to travel in the interest of the college.

When the group was interviewed by the dean, Dr. W. B. Teaford, he agreed to use them, provided they enroll in the college. Glenn reluctantly agreed and enrolled upon his parents' strong urging. As a student, he continued with his music, visiting churches and playing in student radio programs over Radio KFSG, having little thought of ever becoming a minister. But in his second year of study, during a strong dedication service at Camp Radford, a full commitment to the ministry was made.

Immediately following graduation, Rev. Metzler entered evangelistic work. It was during an evangelistic meeting in Greeley, Colorado, that he met his wife, Norma, who was the church's pianist. Glenn and Norma were married in 1951. Their first pastoral assignment was to the Foursquare church of South Denver, Colorado, and their most prominent pastorates were Colorado Springs, Colorado, and Burbank, California, where Glenn also served on the denomination's board of directors.

After the sudden death of Midwest supervisor Don Ballinger

in 1979, Glenn and Norma were appointed to that vacant office, where they still serve as of this writing.

Sidney Westbrook—South Central District

For many years the state of Texas vied with Ohio for leadership in the number of Foursquare churches outside of California. However, Texas has been surpassed by Oregon and Washington, each of which has about ninety churches at this writing. However, Texas, a part of the South Central District, remains strong.

Supervisors of the South Central District are Sidney and Fran Westbrook, whose offices are located in Cedar Hill, a suburb of Dallas, Texas. Sidney was born in Stamford, Texas, on October 24, 1931, to Sidney B. and Gladys A. Westbrook, both Foursquare ministers. At eight years of age Sidney had a born-again experience when he responded to an invitation to accept Christ at an altar of the Lubbock, Texas, Foursquare Church, pastored by Fred Dawson Sr. At the age of twelve years Sidney felt a clear call to the ministry.

By the time Sidney enrolled in L.I.F.E. Bible College in 1950, he had fallen in love with Fran, who was the youth leader of the Lubbock church. They were married in 1951.

Following Sidney's graduation from Bible college in 1953, the Westbrooks were appointed to their first church in Abernathy, Texas. In 1955 the Westbrooks returned to Lubbock to pastor the Second Foursquare Church in that city. Later pastorates were in Texarkana and Dallas. In each of the latter churches, Sidney and Fran served for ten-year periods.

Upon the resignation in 1974 of Rev. and Mrs. Craig Bigg, the Westbrooks were appointed supervisors of the South Central District. In Under their leadership, the district experienced accelerated growth, from 74 to 123 churches.

Cliff Hanes—Northwest District

The district that experienced the greatest growth in the 1970s to the early '90s is the Northwest District. In just two years, 1990 and 1991, Supervisor Cliff Hanes and his staff began 70 pioneer churches in the eight states of this district. Not only did it expand in the number of churches (65 in 1972 to 309 in 1991), but also in the size of churches. As of this writing thirteen congregations number over one thousand (Beaverton, Oregon; Bend, Oregon; Billings, Montana; Eugene, Oregon; Everett, Washington; Gresham, Oregon; Hilo, Hawaii; Kirkland Eastside, Washington; Olympia, Washington; Portland, Oregon; Spokane, Washington; Sunnyside, Oregon; Windward Hope Chapel, Hawaii). Others that enjoyed steady growth are Springfield, Klamath Falls, Roseburg, Salem East, and Milwaukee, Oregon; Federal Way, Yakima, Seattle, Oak Harbor, Marysville, Snohomish, Redmond, Tacoma, and Bellevue Messianic, Centralia and Vancouver, Washington; Great Falls and Missoula, Montana; and Bismarck, North Dakota.[6]

The supervisors of the Northwest District, Cliff and Mari Hanes, began their term in 1986, and succeeded Dr. and Mrs. Roy Hicks Jr.

Cliff was born July 1, 1952, in Vancouver, Washington, and was raised in The Foursquare Church. In 1970 he enrolled in L.I.F.E. Bible College, from which he graduated in 1975. Cliff met Mari at Camp Crestview when both were sixteen years of age. It was a genuine romance on which the Lord's blessing rested, for it led to a happy marriage and ministry partnership.

His first assignments were on the pastoral staffs of the Van Nuys, California, Foursquare Church under Dr. Jack Hayford and the Beaverton, Oregon, Foursquare Church under Dr. Ron Mehl. Before assuming their supervisor responsibilities, they then pastored in Olympia, Washington, for five years and Bend,

Oregon, for four years. During each of these pastorates the congregation grew rapidly from a small number of believers to more than one thousand members.

Cliff has also had active ministry in many areas, including serving on the personal staff for Dr. Billy Graham in the massive Amsterdam 1986 crusades. Mari has authored several books, including three for Tyndale House and one for Bantam/Doubleday.

Fred Wymore—Western District

The Western District, comprised of Central and Northern California, Northern Nevada, and Utah, was created in 1946 by a division of the California District. The southern portion was retained by Dr. Earl Dorrance, who had directed the entire state since 1943. Dr. Frank Cummings, who had pioneered the Midwest District in the 1930s, was this district's first supervisor. In 1957 Rev. and Mrs. Olin Duncan assumed the district's leadership until their retirement in 1971.

Fred and Betty Wymore were appointed supervisors of the Western District in 1971 and have served the longest tenure in the supervisory capacity of any district supervisors, as of this writing (twenty-two years).

Fred Wymore was born in 1922 in Ontario, California, to Fred and Jesse Wymore, prosperous farmers who were charter members of the Ontario, California, Foursquare Church. Fred intended to study at the University of California at Davis with the hope of becoming a teacher of agriculture. However, at a youth rally he received a call of God to preach the gospel. He enrolled in L.I.F.E. Bible College in 1940, at only eighteen years of age. He graduated in 1943. His first church was in Santa Rosa, followed by churches in Woodland and Fresno, where he served for fifteen years.

It was his home church in Ontario, California, that Fred met and fell in love with his wife, Betty. They were married during his last year in Bible college. Their most effective ministry was in El Monte, California (eight years), from which, in 1971, they were selected to supervise the Western District.

As of this writing, over the past ten years the Western District experienced the largest percentage gain in number of churches (101 Percent) of any of the nine districts. Growth happened also in the size of a number of congregations, such as Danville, California, pioneered by Jim and Betsy Hayford and at this writing pastored by Rev. and Mrs. Jim Tolle; and Aptos, California, pioneered and pastored by Dr. Daniel Brown. The Valley Christian Center Foursquare church in Fresno, California, has experienced phenomenal growth. Its pastor, Roger Whitlow, served also on the Missionary Cabinet and the board of regents of L.I.F.E. Bible College.

John Watson—Southwest District

Another districted that resulted from the "division" of the original California District is the Southwest District, created in 1954. Bounded on the west by Lakewood/Rosemead Blvd., on the north by Barstow/Las Vegas, on the south by the Mexican border, and on the east by the Arizona/New Mexico line, the district was first supervised by Nathaniel and Lois Van Cleave (1954–1960; 1972–1976). Later supervisors were Harold and Ione Jefferies (1960–1972) and John and Doris Holland (1976–1988). As of this writing he present supervisors are John and Bonnie Watson.

John Watson was born on May 7, 1934. He grew up in a Foursquare family that contributed several members to Foursquare ministry. From a very early age he attended Angelus Temple. He and Bonnie, whom he married in 1953, attended L.I.F.E. Bible

College. John had also done graduate work at San Diego State College, George Fox College, San Diego Bible College, and the University of Southern California. He has served on the faculties of L.I.F.E. Bible College of Canada and Berean Bible College of San Diego, California. They have pastored in Pendleton, Oregon; Vancouver (Rupert), British Columbia; Woodburn, Oregon (1967–1978); and San Diego, California (1978–1988).

After long and successful pastorates in the Northwest and Southwest districts, the Watsons were appointed, in 1988, to the officer of supervisors of the Southwest District to succeed John and Doris Holland. As of this writing, some of the leading churches of the Southwest District are Florence Avenue (Paul and Marilee Risser) in Santa Fe Springs, California; El Monte, California (William and Beverly Brafford); Arlington, California (Ronald and Anita Williams); Escondido, California (Coleman and Mary Phillips); Artesia, California (William and Carol Burnett); Las Vegas, Nevada (Fred and Carol Dawson); Las Vegas Grapevine, Nevada (Bud and Agnes Higgenbotham); Glendale, Arizona (Robby and Bonita Booth); Flagstaff, Arizona (Jack and Jane Lankhorst); Tucson Grace Chapel in Arizona (John and Marguerite Casteel); Orange, California (Jim and Melinda Scott); La Puente, California (Jack and Polly Watkins); Riverside, California New Jerusalem (Jerry and Phalia Louder); Hesperia, California (Ron and Marty Long); Palm Springs, California (Fred and Marsha Donaldson); El Cajon, California (Michael and Kathy Marcy); and San Diego, California (John and Lois Schmidt).

Don Long—Southern California District

The Southern California District, although reduced in size by two divisions that created Western (1946) and Southwest (1954) districts, is still the second largest district in the United States with its 208 churches. Being the original and oldest district in the Foursquare Church, its leaders have been many including William Black, Giles Knight, Myron Sackett, Earl and Edythe Dorrance, Nathaniel and Lois Van Cleave, and Paul and Joy Jones, followed by supervisors Don and Luann Long.

Don Long was born on March 19, 1950, to Sam and Rogean Long. He grew up in Western Colorado and accepted Christ as Savior in the Assembly of God church in Grand Junction, Colorado. While attending the Midwest District youth camp in Beulah, Colorado, like numbers of other young men and women at Foursquare summer camps, he dedicated his life to gospel ministry. He attended Fort Lewis Bible College in Durango, Colorado, and then entered L.I.F.E. Bible College in 1970, graduating in 1973. He met his wife-to-be, Luann Hannay, on an occasion when she, a student at Southern California College, was visiting girlfriends at L.I.F.E. Bible College. One year later they were married.

Don's first ministry experience was as youth minister of the Burbank, California, Foursquare Church. Don and Luann became senior pastors at El Segundo, California; Ventura, California; and Santa Maria, California. Under their ministry the Santa Maria congregation continued the spiritual and numerical growth that had also been experienced under previous pastors, Jack and Carole Hamilton. Multiple services were required, and combined giving to missions and extension tithe was exceeded in the district only by The Church On The Way and Hermosa Beach Hope Chapel. In 1987 Don and Luann Long were appointed to the office of supervisors of the historic Southern California District.

Pastoral Leaders

Four strong pastoral leaders, while not holding offices at Foursquare headquarters, are very useful to President Holland and the denomination. They are Jack Hayford, Paul Risser, Roger Whitlow, and Ron Mehl. While these have been suggested and approached on various occasions for top leadership offices, they prefer to serve as local pastors of their large churches, available to leadership for counsel and assistance.

In chapter 11 a biographical summary of Jack Hayford has been provided. However, one additional note might be the fact of his conversion as a ten-year-old boy in the Oakland, California, Foursquare Church under the preaching ministry of Maurice Tolle. His parents had earlier, during his infancy, received Christ in the Long Beach, California, Foursquare Church as the Word of God was preached by Watson B. Teaford. His wife, Anna, was raised in the Foursquare church of North Platte, Nebraska, from which she traveled to Bible college, where they met in 1952. At that time Allan and Dorothy Hamilton were the pastors. The influence of earlier leaders upon current leaders is worthy of note. This effect is repeated many times over in the Foursquare movement.

Paul Risser

Dr. Paul Risser was born in Dayton, Tennessee, in 1937 to Otto and Martha Risser, founders and pastors of the Foursquare church in that city. In addition, the Risser family served in Muncie, Indiana, and Battle Creek, Michigan, in which places Paul's father, Otto, was also state superintendent. This gave Paul an early and wide knowledge of Foursquare ministry.

While his parents were in Battle Creek, Paul enrolled in L.I.F.E. Bible College and graduated in 1959. Before entering Bible college, Paul had known Marilee Bigg, daughter of South

Central District supervisor Craig and Clarice Bigg. However, it was not until they were fellow students in L.I.F.E. Bible College that romance bloomed, and just prior to graduation in 1958, they were married.

The Rissers' first ministry was as youth ministers under Paul's brother-in-law, Warren Twyford, in the Lynwood, California, Foursquare Church. Paul often relates that he had no intention of becoming a pastor and preacher; however, God's providence ruled and the Rissers accepted a pastorate in Brownfield, Texas. According to Paul, there were frequent moments of decision to quit the ministry, but God and Marilee helped him to reconsider. In 1972 the strong Florence Avenue Foursquare Church in Santa Fe Springs, California, hearing of their success, welcomed Paul and Marilee as their pastors.

Over the past twenty years of ministry in Santa Fe Springs, the church experienced steady growth. This made it necessary to erect a new multimillion-dollar twelve-hundred-seat sanctuary, dedicated in September 1990. However, the new physical improvement did not significantly diminish the church's missionary activity or its giving to needy projects around the world. While continuing to pastor, Paul has served the Foursquare denomination on the board of directors, the Missionary Cabinet, L.I.F.E. board of Trustees, the Executive Council, and in other capacities.

Roger Whitlow

Readers will want to know more about Roger Whitlow, born on the last day of 1940 to Frank and Gladys Whitlow in Cleveland, Ohio. Frank was an elder in the Cleveland, Ohio, Foursquare Church during the greatly anointed healing ministry of Rev. Howard Clark (1948–1952), whom he assisted. Thus it is not surprising that Roger was converted when he was only five years old while viewing the film *Missing Christians*.

Roger's father, desiring to attend L.I.F.E. Bible College, moved the family to California. He graduated in 1952, after which he pastored churches in Rochester, New York; Columbus, Ohio; Kearney, Nebraska; and McPherson, Kansas. It was while the Whitlow family was in Kansas that Roger decided to attend Kansas State Teachers College. But at a youth rally led by Pastor Phil Hyde, he was challenged to send in an application to L.I.F.E. Bible College. As soon as he obeyed, the Holy Spirit gave clear witness that he was doing God's will.

It was in 1961 that Roger enrolled in L.I.F.E., where he met Donna, and they were married in March 1963. Following graduation in 1965, the Whitlows' first pastorate was in Powell River, British Columbia, and the second in Rupert (Vancouver), British Columbia.

In 1970 Roger and Donna accepted the pastorate of the Foursquare church in Fresno, California, where they still minister as of this writing. The congregation numbers more than two thousand people worshiping on Sundays in multiple services. Roger is highly respected in Fresno for his citywide cooperative efforts. Valley Christian Center cosponsors, together with seven other churches, a Christian school with more than seven hundred students enrolled—a school that compares favorably with the public schools academically, socially, athletically, and culturally.

Ronald Mehl

At this writing Dr. Ronald Mehl pastors the Beaverton, Oregon, Foursquare Church. Graduating from L.I.F.E. Bible College in 1966, Ron and his lovely wife, Joyce, were invited by Dr. Paul E. Jones to serve on the staff of the Portland, Oregon, Foursquare Church. In 1969 Great Lakes District supervisor Merrill Nicholls needed a youth director for that district. He knew that

Ron had grown up in the Great Lakes District and that he possessed leadership ability. He invited the Mehls to serve in that capacity, and under their ministry the district's youth missionary giving and summer camping programs reached unprecedented proportions.

In 1973 the small Beaverton, Oregon, church was without a pastor. Friends urged Ron and Joyce to take the pastorate, and sensing the Lord's will, they accepted. Before long, the Beaverton church building was too small, and the first solution was multiple services. When no additional service could be scheduled to handle the crowds, it became evident that enlargement was needed. Even with a new nineteen-hundred-seat sanctuary, three Sunday morning services were necessary. The growing Sunday school required a separate Christian education building and the purchase of an adjacent vacant church building. In addition to strong Bible preaching, an evident presence of the Holy Spirit gives the Beaverton church a powerful attractiveness.

All three of the above men respond to the call of duty to serve God's work around the world. These pastors are typical of the many Foursquare pastors whose contributions equally merit recounting. Unfortunately, space does not permit. Fortunately, God's records are not limited.[7]

With scores of ministers possessing such experience, responsibility, and the fullness of the Holy Spirit giving ability to oversee the people of God, the affairs of the International Church of the Foursquare Gospel are in good hands.

Chapter 14

THE FOURSQUARE VINE OF TOMORROW

SEVENTY YEARS AGO this coming January of 1993, the doors of Angelus Temple opened, inviting native sons as well as newcomers to Southern California to experience Holy Spirit–sent revival. Multitudes responded, resulting in a continuous revival that endured unabated for at least a decade. For another decade great Pentecostal meetings continued to draw capacity crowds into Angelus Temple while Foursquare "branches" of the original vine were springing up from the Pacific to the Atlantic and across both oceans.

The growth that began seven decades ago has, at the last reckoning, amounted to more than twenty-three thousand churches ministering in more than seventy-four countries of the world. And although nearly seven decades have passed, there is no indication that any of the "four corners" of the Foursquare Gospel that brought the revival has been severed, or that any major truth in the *Declaration of Faith* has been compromised. Any anxieties expressed by Aimee Semple McPherson that after her day the church or the colleges might blunt the corners of the Foursquare gospel were for nought. If she were present today, she no doubt would be as proud of the younger leaders and pastors of the twentieth century's last decade as she was of those of her era.

What can be said about the unique vision of the founder? Around what ideals was the Church of the Foursquare Gospel formed? What has made the Foursquare Church unique? What complex of biblical truths, forms of worship, and practical goals justified the founding of a separate movement? Has the International Church of the Foursquare Gospel been faithful to the original vision? Are the original goals still incorporated in the church's future focus?

The founder's vision is stated in Hebrews 13:8, "JESUS CHRIST IS THE SAME, YESTERDAY AND TODAY AND FOREVER" (NKJV). In his commencement address at the June 1990 graduation of L.I.F.E. Bible College, Dr. Ralph Hammon reminded those gathered in Angelus Temple that the truth of this verse is the very heart of the Foursquare Gospel. It was and is intended that every Foursquare church prominently display Hebrews 13:8 somewhere in the sanctuary. While some denominations have departed from fundamental truths based on an inerrant Bible, most evangelicals are in agreement with the Foursquare stance about Jesus as the Savior and soon-coming King, and some share with us Pentecostalism's faith in Jesus as the healer of physical sickness. But the Foursquare Gospel Church and an increasing number of others go further in preaching Jesus as the Baptizer with the Holy Spirit, understood as an experience of empowerment, subsequent to conversion and distinct from regeneration.

Preeminence of the unchanging Christ is a unique Bible truth. Many propound a doctrine of faith in an inerrant Scripture, in Christ's atoning work on the cross, and in a coming kingdom of peace and righteousness. But at the same time, they contend that all miracles and apostolic experiences ceased with the completion of the New Testament. Bookstores are filled with volumes authored by prestigious writers who do not accept the Book of Acts as a pattern for today's church. But the heart of the Foursquare Gospel is a summons to heed the promise of Christ: "He who believes in me, the works that I do he will do also; and greater works than these he will do, because I go to my Father" (John 14:12, NKJV).

The world will respond to the preaching of a changeless Christ with signs following. The International Church of the Foursquare Gospel has not in any way compromised this preaching. However, this is not to say, "Nothing has changed." Many fresh insights regarding modes of worship, methods of approach, avenues of evangelism, vehicles of communication, and attitudes toward cultural change have emerged. But the substance of the Foursquare Gospel and the interpretation of major biblical doctrines remain unaltered. The same creedal statement appears in every successive "bylaws."

Another unique gleam of light in the founder's vision is captioned in the *Declaration of Faith*: "Moderation." The interpretive paragraph reads:

> We believe that the moderation of the believer should be known of all men (Phil. 4:5); that his experience and daily walk should never lead him into extremes (Eph. 4:14,15), fanaticisms, unseemly manifestation (1 Cor. 13:5), backbitings, murmurings, but that his sober, thoughtful, balanced, mellow, forgiving, and zealous Christian experience should be one of steadfastness, equilibrium, humility, self-sacrifice, and Christ-likeness.

While Mrs. McPherson often cautioned against "worldliness," she interpreted "Godliness" not only as what believers *should not* do, but more positively as what they *should* do.

The founder frequently emphasized the fact that the

Foursquare "way" in worship was a path that ran between the wildfire of fanaticism and the iceberg of formality. On several occasions she published a sermon entitled, "The Middle of the Road," with which there appeared a cartoon of her crossing between flames of fire and arctic ice floes. In the early days of the Pentecostal movement there were those who carried the blessing of the Spirit's power to fanatical extremes, giving the movement a questionable reputation. Such also happened in the Wesleyan movement. It appears that when Satan cannot prevent revival, he tries to lead the undiscerning into unbiblical extremes. The apostle Paul warns of this in 1 Corinthians 14.

Beginnings of the Pentecostal movement are attributed to the outpouring of the Spirit at Charles Parham's Bible school in Topeka, Kansas, and in the Azusa Street Mission in Los Angeles. The two are related, for Elder Seymour of Azusa Street was a pupil of Parham. Spiritually hungry leaders from across the land and around the world traveled to Los Angeles to receive the baptism in the Holy Spirit. However, the Azusa Street revival was not long-lasting, for the meetings finally drifted into fanaticism. When Charles Parham visited those meetings, he immediately objected to the extremes. Still, when the leaders returned, they rejected Parham's counsel, and many who were immersed in the extreme manifestation dubbed Parham a "power fighter."[1]

The Foursquare Church's dedication to moderation is seen in the expressed goal of interdenominational and worldwide evangelism, chiseled in granite on Angelus Temple's cornerstone. Principal speakers at the first Foursquare conventions were denominational pastors who had been filled with the Spirit under the ministry of Mrs. McPherson. Great figures such as Dr. K. Towner (Baptist), Dr. Charles Price (Congregational), Dr. C. Shreve (Methodist), and William Jennings Bryan (Methodist and presidential candidate) would not have been attracted to an extremist minister or ministry.

Today's leading Foursquare pastors and churches count among their number leaders in business, science, academics, and entertainment, as well as those form every walk of life. The Foursquare Gospel appeals to a wide spectrum of society. The same may be said of the leaders of all classical Pentecostal denominations; however, Mrs. McPherson's moderate and broad societal appeal was unique for her day. Today, Dr. Jack Hayford, pastor of The Church On The Way and Foursquaredom's most widely known figure, believes that the International Church of the Foursquare Gospel can be instrumental in bringing about a closer fellowship and common goal of ministry among all Pentecostals and charismatics.

Lessons Learned From History

What has the Foursquare Church learned from its seventy years of history? The answers seem to be very clear.

First, the Foursquare Gospel, with its emphasis on an unchanging Christ, can be as powerful and effective at the end of the twentieth century as it was in the second and third decades. No change in the message has been necessary in order to win souls and raise up healthy churches. God will pour out great blessing upon His church whenever there is prayer, faith, and spiritual renewal.

Next, the Foursquare Gospel message, with the preaching of a Savior who is ever the same, is capable and effective in reaching all the nations of the world. Great revival in Brazil, Argentina, the Philippine Islands, Africa, Sri Lanka, and in other fields demonstrates that biblical truth, as exemplified by the Book of Acts, is readily embraced by people of all races and languages. As long as the Foursquare Church is faithful to New Testament truth preached in faith and power, the world will be waiting for its message and its messengers.

The International Church of the Foursquare Gospel has discovered that it can maintain through the decades its founding message and fundamental faith without being bypassed by a scientifically sophisticated society. Since the 1920s, scientific progress has produced television, passenger airlines, atomic energy, space travel, transistors, computers, facsimile machines, and much besides. However, nothing has been discovered or devised that outmoded the gospel of Jesus Christ as presented in Pentecostal power as a means of delivering sin-sick mankind from the power of darkness into the kingdom of light.

When the apostle Paul arrived in Ephesus, a city steeped in sin and paganism, he immediately saw to it that the small group of believers experienced Pentecostal power. His preaching, witnessed to by signs and wonders, brought a great citywide revival. The church grew to such proportions that when he returned to the area, a delegation of one hundred elders met with him in Miletus. In Paul's address to those elders he reminded them that he had declared to them "all the counsel of God" (Acts 20:27). He charged them to be faithful in preaching and teaching the truths that had liberated them. The gospel had pervaded the entire surrounding area.

Today, that same gospel has produced similar results in many great communities across North America and around the world. The church has certainly learned that the gospel does not have to be changed to keep up with a rapidly changing society.

Is the International Church of the Foursquare Gospel satisfied with its progress? The answer would have to be "Yes!" and "No!" The church is, indeed, thankful for the progress and extension that have been made. Yet, leadership, contemplating the church in retrospect, confesses to seeing avenues of progress and doors of opportunity that were unnoticed or neglected. Careful appraisal of the past reveals periods of spiritual decline, relaxed enthusiasm, diminished self-sacrifice, and brief detours from the highway of obedient servitude. Statistics will also show that progress was steady and that losses of "first love" and primitive enthusiasm were recovered by spiritual renewal. Leaders affirm that lessons learned will make the church more effective for the century that is not far around time's corner.

Future Goals for the International Church of the Foursquare Gospel

Where does The Foursquare Church go from here? Several goals revealed by President Holland to the board of directors are already in place. One of these is the *integration of all headquarters departments*, with the formation of the departmental leaders into a team striving together for the realization of selected aims. Activities scheduled with such a purpose to expedite the common ends are interdepartmental planning sessions, prayer meetings, and social gatherings. Centralized direction will benefit all areas of the church and give direction to each department's functions.

Benefit of such integration and coordination will be *improved communication*. The entire church must be kept informed of corporate goals and the means for their achievement. Through the media of the *Foursquare World Advance* magazine, the "Minister's Update," specialized publications, and other media, information on goals and projects will pass from the president and board through the already established organizational structure to local churches and preaching places. Local church and district victories and discoveries in turn will be communicated to headquarters for the benefit of all.

Another improvement in efficiency will be implemented by

an *operations policy manual* already published for all employees at Foursquare headquarters. The manual clearly defines the philosophy and common goals and policies for those working in our headquarters offices, and shows the inter-relationship of the departments. Improved working conditions and mutual trust among leaders and employees will bring holistic attitudes instead of departmentalized specialization.

Much thought and planning have already gone into a *program of personal and pastoral enrichment* through various forms of "continuing education." A committee consisting of John Holland (chairman), Don McGregor, John Amstutz, Eugene Kurtz, Roy Hicks Jr., and Jack Hamilton has been selected to develop the enrichment program. With the help of the colleges, it is hoped that study courses and materials may be provided for both home and residence studies.

Questionnaires have been sent to pastors asking for areas of need and choices of study subjects. In a recent "Minister's Update," the results revealed some graphic answers. In the area of personal development, the perceive needs were in devotional life—marriage and the family; regarding biblical knowledge, preferences were for theology—doctrine and study methods; as to ministry skills, the pastors expressed need for preaching—pastoral care and leadership; and in the arena of ethics, the most desired subjects were on the matters of abortion and the poor and homeless. As the program is developed, pilot courses and conferences will give the committee greater understanding as to how to implement such a desired, yet demanding program of enriching those who shepherd Foursquare flocks.

A *national program of Foursquare Church expansion* across the United States, entitled "2,000 Before 2000," is still going forward. The plan is to plant churches with the financial help and encouragement of the districts. Leadership believes, however, that the pastoral enrichment program will greatly improve church expansion, on the premise that pastors and workers with greater educational and spiritual capacities will possess more capacities for church growth and church planting.

Goals of Foursquare Missions International have been partly expressed by Director Roy Hicks Jr. While continuing with the long-time activities of sending missionaries, planting new fields and churches, and nurturing existing fields and stations, the Foursquare Missions department is working for *further transition from a paternal to a fraternal missionary/national church relationship.* In other words, the national churches are to be considered not as children, but as brothers.

Progress has been already achieved in the development of "indigenous missions." Many of the Foursquare fields around the world have established national leaders and locally incorporated structures. Almost all the fields have reached a stage of maturity where they can be self-governing, self-supporting, and self-sustaining. Meetings have been planned and held in which leaders of various Foursquare fields can sit together as equals and together plan the evangelization of the world. Many national boards are sending missionaries to adjacent countries and to areas that correspond with their missionary vision. Enrichment programs are being made available to national leaders and pastors. The goal is for many centers of missionary outreach to work together on an equal basis.

At home, one department deserving special mention is the Foursquare Youth Ministries, directed by National Youth Minister Gregg Johnson. Over the past five years, the department has been revitalized, and tremendous strides are being made to *unite the youth of Foursquare churches throughout North America, and across the globe, in an effort to preach the gospel to every creature.* District youth leaders have worked together with Gregg to develop materials and to plan conclaves in various areas of the country with the aim of youth involvement in the ministry of the Foursquare Church. Two special "Summit" conferences have been held. The first Summit drew nearly 3,000 young men and women to Denver, Colorado, in 1988 to consider God's call to commitment. In January 1991, more than 6,100 Foursquare youth "invaded" Ft. Worth, Texas, to consider the "last call of all," a life commitment to missions giving, living, and going. It is believed that The Foursquare Church is seeing a "new day" in the role of young men and women in the ministry of the denomination.

The Department of Christian Education, directed by Rick Wulfestieg, has appointed a new coordinator of Christian education ministries, Mary Lou Canata. Mary Lou is experienced in child evangelism and in the work of the Christian education department, having served for several years under Dr. Vincent Bird. The immediate goal is to *restore Sunday school enthusiasm* with more measured goals than those of the 1950s and 1960s.

In Conclusion

In the troubled times in which this history is being written, The Foursquare Church will need the wisest leadership, the deepest dedication to the task, and the fullest measure of spiritual power. As The Foursquare Church grows, so does the opposition of the enemy. As the church presses for the achievement of higher goals, it may expect fiercer trials launched by the adversary. Walking hand in hand with the Lord, who promised, "I will never leave you or forsake you," the Foursquare Church may experience tribulations. But the presence of God Himself will be in every crisis, lifting the church above the circumstances, and He will teach great lessons from every experience.

Aimee Semple McPherson, having been subjected to one of the most severe trials of her life, wrote:

> My former life in the work had been like that of a vine which twined about the stalwart oak, but when that stronghold to which I clung had been taken away and transplanted into the heavenly garden—when my clutch had been loosened and let go, there was nothing left of the vine that had reached so high but a pitiful, broken, crumbled little heap which lay in tumbled confusion on the earth. But now I had found one to cling to, and fastening my hold upon, who was the Cedar of Lebanon, who would endure forever, from whom I could not be removed—the One who would never die or leave me. Oh, it was Jesus! Thank God for the hard places—for the very blasts of winter's storms. 'Twas there I learned for the first time a little of what it meant to be rooted and grounded and settled, to die out and go through a valley of Crucifixion that led to resurrection power and glory.[2]

The Foursquare Church has been likened to a vine planted in revival soil that has sprouted branches that have climbed across the nation and around the world. Winter blasts and summer heat may test the resiliency of the vine, but no scourge will wilt the vine unless the waters of God's Spirit are wanting. But instead of drought, every weather report is for showers of blessing. A new emphasis on prayer and yielding to the Spirit indicates a continuance of renewal around the world.

Robert & Aimee Semple, 1908.

Aimee Semple McPherson honors Foursquare chaplain Howard Rusthoi upon return from World War II.

THE GOSPEL CAR IN WHICH AIMEE SEMPLE McPHERSON MADE HER FAMOUS TRANSCONTINENTAL TOUR — NEW YORK CITY TO LOS ANGELES

The famous Gospel Touring Car and evangelistic team.

Groundbreaking of Angelus Temple, February 1921.

Dedication of Angelus Temple, January 1, 1923.

Groundbreaking of Angelus Temple, February, 1921.

The Angelus Temple "Silver Band," 1924.

Cornerstone laying of Bible Institute, April 1925.

Crusade in Wichita, Kansas, May, 1922.

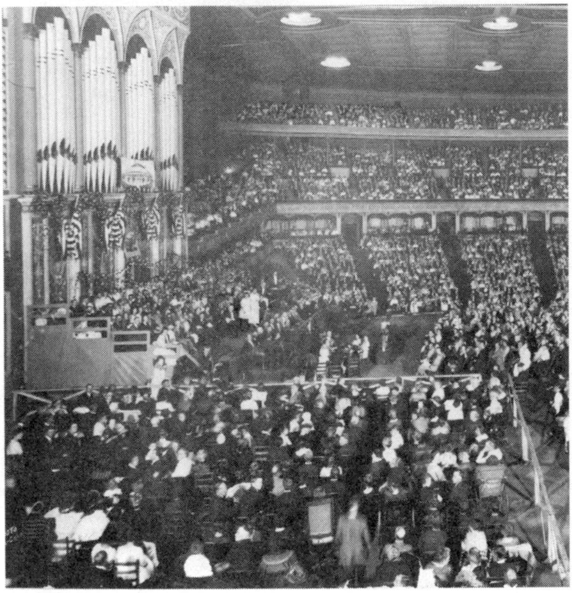

Denver, Colorado Crusade, 1921.

Angelus Temple's "City Sisters," forerunners of United Foursquare Women.

Aimee Semple McPherson with daughter-Roberta, son-Rolf, and mother-Minnie Kennedy in Los Angeles.

Dr. & Mrs. Rolf K. McPherson, new appointed President and First Lady of the International Church of the Foursquare Gospel, Fall 1944.

Crusada in Wichita, Kansas, May 1922.

Rolf & Lorna De McPherson, with daughters Marleen and Kay, 1942.

Rev. & Mrs. (Dr.) Arthur Thompson

L.I.F.E. Bible College Administration: Watson B. Teaford (Dean), Rolf K. McPherson (President), Durward Myers (Assistant Dean).

Rev. & Mrs. Vincent DeFante

Harold McPherson holding son, Rolf; Aimee on right with mother, Minnie Kennedy, and daughter, Roberta.

Aimee Semple McPherson, the evangelist.

Aimee Semple McPherson at Great Lakes District Convention, 1933: from left: Charles Rosenthal, Myron Sacket, Helen Correll, Billy Black, Amiee Semple McPherson, R. J. Turner, Sidney Correll, Ellsworth Johnson.

Divine Healing Service in Denver, Colorado.

Re. & Mrs. Claude Updike

Rev. & Mrs. Frank Ziegler

Dr. & Mrs. Arthur Edwards

Dedication of Angelus Temple, January 1, 1923.

Aimee Semple McPherson, the first woman religious broadcaster in America.

Dr. & Mrs. Joseph Knapp

Kall FourSquare Gospel, second religious broadcasting station in North America, 1924-present.

NOTES

Introduction
A History of the International Church of the Foursquare Gospel

1. Aimee Semple McPherson, *This Is That* (Los Angeles: Echo Park Evangelistic Association, 1923).
2. Genesis 49:22.
3. Ezekiel 17:8.
4. Song of Solomon 7:12. This verse is quoted by Mrs. McPherson to begin chapter 7 of *This Is That*, the story of her ministry.
5. John 15:5, NKJV.
6. Andrew Murray, *The True Vine* (N.p.: N.d.), 9.
7. *Bridal Call*, July 1925, 16.
8. *Bridal Call*, March 1934, 14.

Chapter 1
Roots in Revival

1. Matthew 13:3; Mark 4:3; Luke 8:5.
2. Harold W. Jefferies, "Rooted in Revival," *Foursquare World Advance*, January/February 1988, 3.
3. Vinson Synan, *The Twentieth-Century Pentecostal Explosion* (Lake Mary, FL: Creation House, 1987), 100.
4. Raymond Cox, *Aimee* (Los Angeles: Foursquare Publications, 1979), 112.
5. McPherson, *This Is That*, 12.
6. Aimee Semple McPherson, "A Continuous Revival," *Bridal Call*, September 1925, 6.
7. Greg Rothwell, *Oxford Sentinel Review*, February 11, 1989.
8. "A Man Who Is Never Tired," *Bridal Call*, December/January 1924, 21.
9. *Bridal Call*, May 1923, 11.
10. Acts 1:15; 1 Corinthians 15:6.
11. Ada W. Wischusen, *Bridal Call*, July 1925, 11.
12. *Bridal Call*, March 1928, 15.
13. "The Foursquare Beehive," *Bridal Call*, January 1929, 5–7.
14. *Bridal Call*, February 1924; February 1925.
15. William W. Menzies, *Anointed to Serve* (Springfield, MO: Gospel Publishing House, 1970), 65, 170.

16. Aimee Semple McPherson, *The Foursquare Declaration of Faith* (Los Angeles: International Church of the Foursquare Gospel), 73.
17. J. Gilchrist Lawson, *Deeper Experiences of Famous Christians* (1911; repr., Anderson, IN: Warner Press, 1972), 160–161.
18. McPherson, *The Foursquare Declaration of Faith*.

Chapter 2
The First Branches of the Vine

1. William Black, "The Vine and the Branches," *Bridal Call*, July 1925, 16.
2. *Bridal Call*, May 1923, 11; July 1928, 7.
3. R. Bryant Mitchell, *Heritage and Horizons* (Des Moines, IA: Open Bible, 1982), 116–128.
4. Bylaws of Local Foursquare Gospel Lighthouses, 1928. (These are the original bylaws pertaining to the local church.)
5. Ibid., 5.
6. Ibid., 7.
7. 1931 *Yearbook of the International Church of the Foursquare Gospel*, 13.
8. Ibid., 4.
9. 1933 *Convention Yearbook of the International Church of the Foursquare Gospel*, 4.
10. Joel 2:28–29; Exodus 15:20; Judges 4:4; 2 Kings 22:14; Isaiah 8:3; Luke 2:36; Acts 18:1–2; 21:9; Romans 16:1–3.
11. Mitchell, *Heritage and Horizons*, 115–116.
12. Synan, *The Twentieth-Century Pentecostal Explosion*, 107.
13. William H. Gentz, *The Dictionary of Bible and Religion* (Nashville: Abington, 1986), 923.
14. "Role of Women" in Stanley Burgess, Gary McGee, Peter Alexander, *Dictionary of Pentecostal and Charismatic Movements* (Grand Rapids: Zondervan, 1988), 893.
15. Harold Helms, *Foursquare Bylaws*, 1988.
16. *Foursquare World Advance*, May/June 1988, 2.
17. "Lutherans Vow Action on Harassment of Women," *Tribune/News* (Whittier, CA), August 27, 1989.

Chapter 3
The Bible Colleges

1. *Carry On*, 1927 Yearbook of the International Institute of Foursquare Evangelism, 15.
2. Aimee Semple McPherson, *Bridal Call*, September 1923, 12.
3. Mari Hanes, *L.I.F.E. Yearbook* supplement, 1975.
4. *L.I.F.E. Bible College Yearbooks*, 1925–1980.
5. *Bridal Call*, February 1924, 15.
6. Interview with Dr. Roy Hicks Jr.

Chapter 4
The Tender Shoots of the Vine

1. See Genesis 12:1–3; 22:15–18; 28:3–4; Acts 21:4–5; Romans 16:3, 5, 10–11; 2 Timothy 1:5; 3:14–15.
2. *Bridal Call*, January 1925, 25.
3. Ibid.
4. 1951 *Foursquare Convention Yearbook*, 35.
5. 1953 *Foursquare Convention Yearbook*, 40.
6. Interview with Mrs. Helmle, October 1989.
7. Convention yearbooks 1937–1977. Personal interview with Dr. Vincent Bird, October 1989.
8. Convention yearbooks 1970–1980. Personal interview with Dr. John Bowers, October 1989.
9. *Bridal Call*, Foursquare, January 1932, 11.
10. Crusader Covenant, *Bridal Call*, Foursquare, January 1932, 11.
11. See Paul A. Keinel, *The Philosophy of Christian School Education* (Whittier, CA: ACSI Publications, 1978). Interviews with Christian school leaders, October 1989.

Chapter 5
The Vine Grows

1. Psalm 80:8–11, NKJV.
2. Black, "The Vine and the Branches."
3. *Bridal Call*, July 1928, 16–17.
4. *Bridal Call*, August 1929, 4–5.
5. *Bridal Call*, May 1932; May 1934.
6. See John 17:17, 19; Romans 15:16; 2 Thessalonians 2:13; 1 Timothy 4:5; Hebrews 10:29.
7. Aimee Semple McPherson, Creedal Statements, found at http://www.foursquare.org/images/assets/Creedal_Statements.pdf (accessed September 16, 2013).

8. Stella Correll, Good Years (N.p.: Stella Correll, 1940).
9. William Black, *Bridal Call*, July 1925, 16.

Chapter 6
Transplants of the Vine

1. Menzies, *Anointed to Serve*, 86.
2. Burgess, McGee, and Alexander, *Dictionary of Pentecostal and Charismatic Movements*.
3. Menzies, *Anointed to Serve*, 84.
4. Foursquare Convention Yearbooks, 1930–1989.
5. Yeol Soo Eim, "The Worldwide Expansion of the Foursquare Church" (doctoral thesis, Fuller Theological Seminary, 1986), 208. Chart by John Amstutz.
6. "Foursquare Gospel World-Wide Missions," *Bridal Call*, October 1927, 15.
7. "The Sun Never Sets on the Foursquare Gospel," *Bridal Call*, January 1929, 4.
8. "The Convention Supreme," *Bridal Call*, February 1928, 17.
9. *Bridal Call*, February 1928, 25.
10. Eim, "The Worldwide Expansion of the Foursquare Church."
11. Interview with Dr. Leland Edwards, January 1990; *Bridal Call*, 1928.
12. Interview with Dr. Leland Edwards, January 1990.
13. Eim, "The Worldwide Expansion of the Foursquare Church."
14. 1951 *Foursquare Convention Yearbook*, 22.
15. Eim, "The Worldwide Expansion of the Foursquare Church," 112–117.
16. Menzies, *Anointed to Serve*, 321–325; Edith L. Blumhofer, *The Assemblies of God* (Springfield, MO: Gospel Publishing House, 1989), 57–67.
17. 1956 *Foursquare Convention Yearbook*, 28.
18. "Cover Story," *Foursquare World Advance*, September, 33.
19. Dr. Eim, Heritage Department Records.
20. "Foreign Missions," *Foursquare Magazine*, May, 27.
21. Peter Wagner, *What Are We Missing?* (Carol Stream, IL: Creation House, 1973).
22. *Foursquare World Advance*, September/October 1989, 5.
23. "A Brief History of the Foursquare Church in Papua New

Guinea," unpublished.
24. Virgene Hughes and Ronda Wolf, "Brief Unpublished History of the Foursquare Gospel Church in PNG," 1981.
25. Ibid.41.
26. Eim, "The Worldwide Expansion of the Foursquare Church."
27. Eloise Clarno, "Networking With Asia and the South Pacific," *Foursquare World Advance*, September/October 1989, 8.
28. *Foursquare World Advance*, April 1985, 20–21.
29. *Foursquare World Advance*, September/October 1988, 21.

Chapter 7
The Separated Branches of the Vine

1. Acts 15:36–41.
2. Mitchell, *Heritage and Horizons*, 147. Actual text of the newspaper read: "'Thirty-two ministers, representing the Iowa and Minnesota Division, have voted to withdraw from the International Church of the Foursquare Gospel and all affiliations with Aimee Semple McPherson Hutton,' the Rev. John R. Richey, Divisional Officer, announced Wednesday. 'Certain widespread publicity' and policies of the International Church's leadership were given by the Rev. Mr. Richey as reasons for the withdrawal. The Rev. Mr. Richey, in behalf of the ministers, expressed appreciation of Mrs. Hutton's past ministry and influence upon their individual lives."
3. Ibid., 148.
4. Read Aimee Semple McPherson, *Aimee* (Los Angeles: Foursquare Publications, 1979), 138–139.
5. Ibid.
6. Mitchell, *Heritage and Horizons*, 148.
7. *Foursquare Convention Yearbooks*, 1931–1940.
8. *Bridal Call*, January 1934, 6–8.
9. International Church of the Foursquare Gospel.

Chapter 8
The Vine Adapts to Stress

1. *Funk and Wagnalls Standard Reference Encyclopedia*, vol. 25 (1959), 9312.
2. *Foursquare Magazine*, August 1942, 3.

3. *Foursquare Magazine*, July 1942, 13.
4. 1943 *Foursquare Convention Yearbook*, 2.
5. *Foursquare Magazine*, May 1945, 15.
6. Ibid.
7. *Foursquare Magazine*, September 1945, 22.
8. *Foursquare Magazine*, May 1945, 15.
9. Ibid.
10. *Foursquare Magazine*, 1945.
11. C. M. Robeck Jr. in Burgess, McGee, and Alexander, *Dictionary of Pentecostal and Charismatic Movements*, 571.
12. Information derived from a personal interview and from the author's acquaintance with the subject.
13. *Foursquare Magazine*, August 1945, 2.
14. Burgess, McGee, and Alexander, *Dictionary of Pentecostal and Charismatic Movements*, 103, 107; see also Ibid., Courtney, Howard Perry, 227.

Chapter 9
The Vine Bears More Fruit

1. Harold Chalfant, "Jubilee Convention Briefs," 1948 *Foursquare Convention Yearbook*, 1.
2. Rolf K. McPherson, "Awake," 1952 *Foursquare Convention Yearbook*, 3.
3. 1952 *Foursquare Convention Yearbook*, 5.
4. "President's Report," 1957 *Foursquare Convention Yearbook*, 3.
5. 1956 *Foursquare Convention Yearbook*, 29.

Chapter 10
The Vine Grows More Slowly

1. Blumhofer, *The Assemblies of God*, 130; Menzies, *Anointed to Serve*, 344.
2. Burgess, McGee, and Alexander, *Dictionary of Pentecostal and Charismatic Movements*, 97, 785–786.
3. Ibid. See also, Synan, *The Twentieth-Century Pentecostal Explosion*, 40.
4. Synan, *The Twentieth-Century Pentecostal Explosion*, 106.

Chapter 11
The Vine Receives New Nourishment

1. 1971 *Foursquare Convention Yearbook*, 2.
2. 1973 *Foursquare Convention Yearbook*, 2.
3. Synan, *The Twentieth-Century Pentecostal Explosion*, 106.
4. Ibid.
5. Burgess, McGee, and Alexander, *Dictionary of Pentecostal and Charismatic Movements*, 492.
6. Ibid., 792.
7. *Foursquare World Advance*, September/October 1986, 4–5.
8. *Foursquare World Advance*, March/April 1991, 10–14.
9. *Foursquare World Advance*, September/October 1988, 14–15.
10. Burgess, McGee, and Alexander, *Dictionary of Pentecostal and Charismatic Movements*, 110–117.

Chapter 12
Various Emphases in the Vine's Development

1. L. G. McClung, "Evangelism," in Burgess, McGee, and Alexander, *Dictionary of Pentecostal and Charismatic Movements*, 285.
2. 1951 *Foursquare Convention Yearbook*, 7.
3. 1953 *Foursquare Convention Yearbook*, 25.
4. Ibid., 30.
5. 1954 *Foursquare Convention Yearbook*, 3.
6. Ibid., 28.
7. 1955 *Foursquare Convention Yearbook*, 6.
8. Ibid., back page.

Chapter 13
The Vine and the New Husbandman

1. Merriam-Webster, *Webster's Ninth New Collegiate Dictionary*, s.v. "husbandman."
2. Joseph H. Thayer, *Thayer's Greek-English Lexicon of the New Testament* (Grand Rapids: Baker, 1977); William Arndt and F. Wilbur Gingrich, *Greek English Lexicon of the New Testament* (Chicago: University of Chicago, 1973); W. E. Vine, *Expository Dictionary of Biblical Words* (Nashville: Nelson, 1985), 315.
3. Articles of Incorporation and Bylaws of the International

Church of the Foursquare Gospel, Article XI, sec. a, subsec. 2, par. (a), 1986 ed., 20.

4. Data verified by *Foursquare Convention Yearbooks* 1955–1989.
5. Information derived from a personal interview, July 11, 1990.
6. Ibid.
7. All biographical sketches given above were taken from the *Foursquare Convention Yearbooks* and from personal interviews with the subjects during 1990.

Chapter 14
The Foursquare Vine of Tomorrow

1. Blumhofer, *The Assemblies of God*; Frank Bartleman, *How Pentecost Came to Los Angeles* (Los Angeles.: 1925), 54. This book was republished in 1980 by Bridge Publishing, under the title *Azusa Street*, in which the same quote is found on page 63.
2. McPherson, *This Is That*.